Stand Right There

A Pictorial Celebration of Riverdale

by Gillian Austin

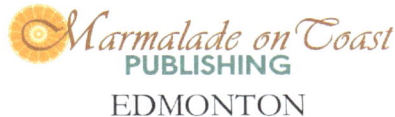

Marmalade on Toast
PUBLISHING

EDMONTON

Cataloguing data available from Library and Archives Canada

ISBN 0-9937430-1-3
ISBN 978-0-9937430-1-6

Austin, Gillian, 1960-
Canada

Marmalade on Toast Publishing
#10 Sundance NW
Edmonton, AB T5H 4B4

Matted images included in this book are available for purchase. Please contact Gillian Austin at marmaladeontoast@shaw.ca for details.

It's not what you look at that matters, it's what you see.

—*Henry David Thoreau*

For Willow

I consider myself extremely fortunate to be living in the community of Riverdale. I moved to Riverdale 15 years ago with my five-year old daughter, Willow, and was pleasantly surprised, and somewhat nervous, to be almost immediately drawn into Riverdale's infectious community spirit. I didn't make a conscious decision to live in the community. A series of events occurred and this is where I ended up. From talking to neighbors, over the years, this seems to be a common thread among many Riverdalians; that an almost esoteric guidance led them to making Riverdale their home.

~

Riverdale is one of Edmonton's most picturesque communities. It is a diverse river valley neighbourhood located just east of Edmonton's downtown center. The community is bordered by the North Saskatchewan River and surrounded by the cliffs of the river valley. Because of this location Riverdale remains distinct and retains its identity as a separate and unified community. Riverdale has been able to maintain much of its original charm and small town feel; where community pride and spirit run strong.

Riverdale's proximity to Fort Edmonton encouraged the fur traders of the late 1700s to take up residence. They were followed by pioneers who began panning for gold along the river. In the

1880s settlers arrived and developed Riverdale into one of Edmonton's first industrial districts. These newcomers to Canada were instrumental in establishing Edmonton's growing economy by founding lumber yards, brick yards and coal mines on the large flat area which was then becoming known as Fraser Flats. Sharing a common cause, these entrepreneurs and tradesmen worked together to build a strong community with traditions that last to this day.

~

Beginning in 2013 I began a personal visual arts project. At the time I had no plan of sharing my project, but as I became more immersed I considered celebrating Riverdale's character and distinctiveness with others. I had no idea what the end result would be.

No matter where you stand in Riverdale there is always something intriguing to discover. With this in mind I compiled my paintings into this book which is a pictorial celebration of Riverdale. I have used minimal text throughout because I wanted the reader to enjoy the paintings without direction. They are simple paintings that speak clearly on their own. Using the different seasons as a backdrop, I have created a collection that I believe represents the community's character. I feel that this is my opportunity to share Riverdale's uniqueness and illustrate her charm.

Spring

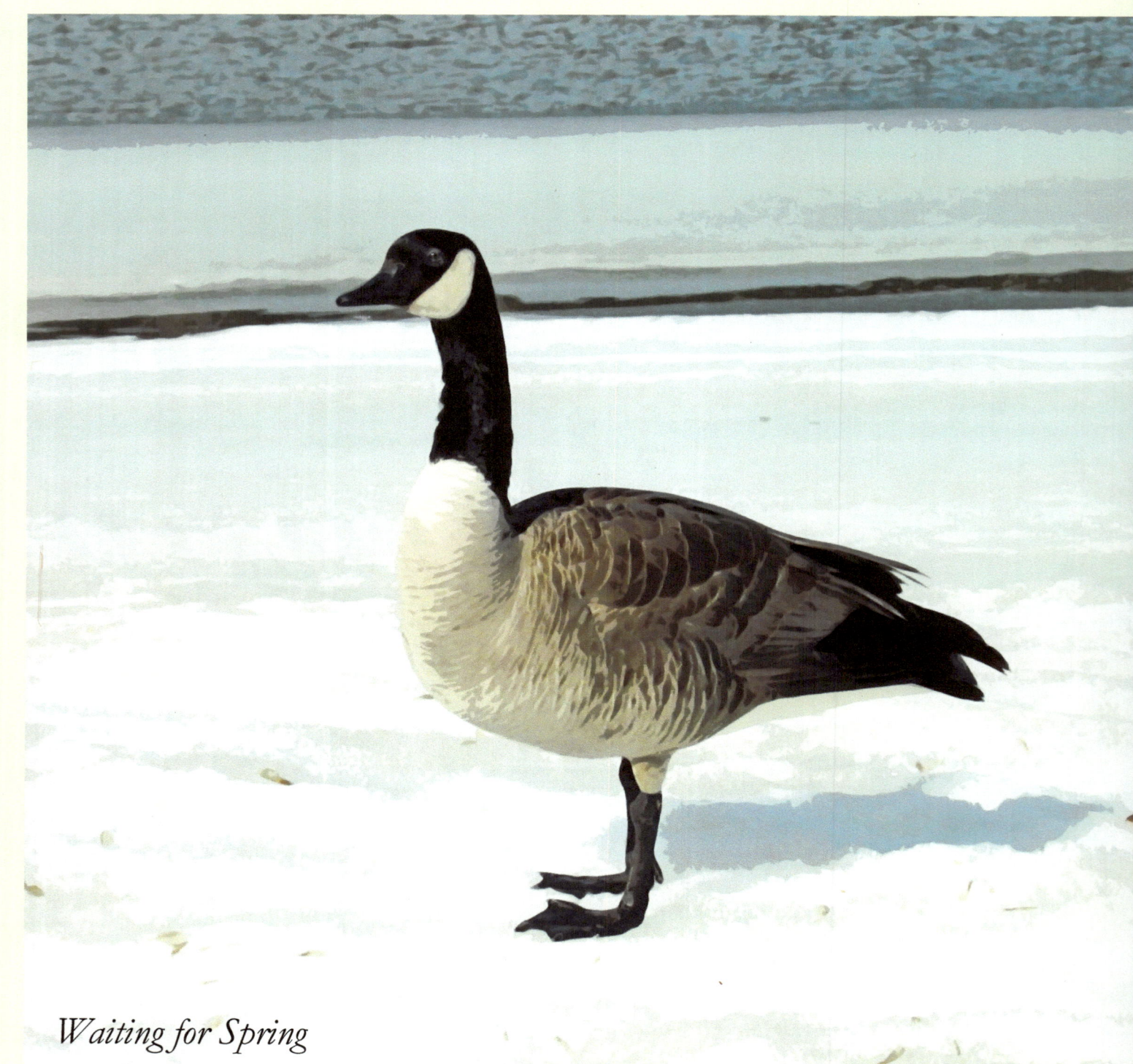

Waiting for Spring

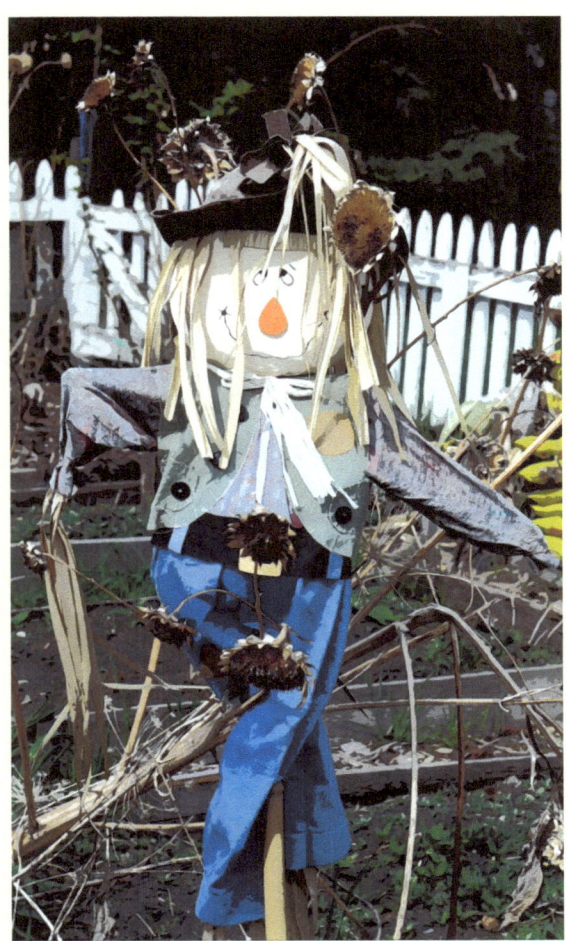

Scaring the Crows

Peacock Gate

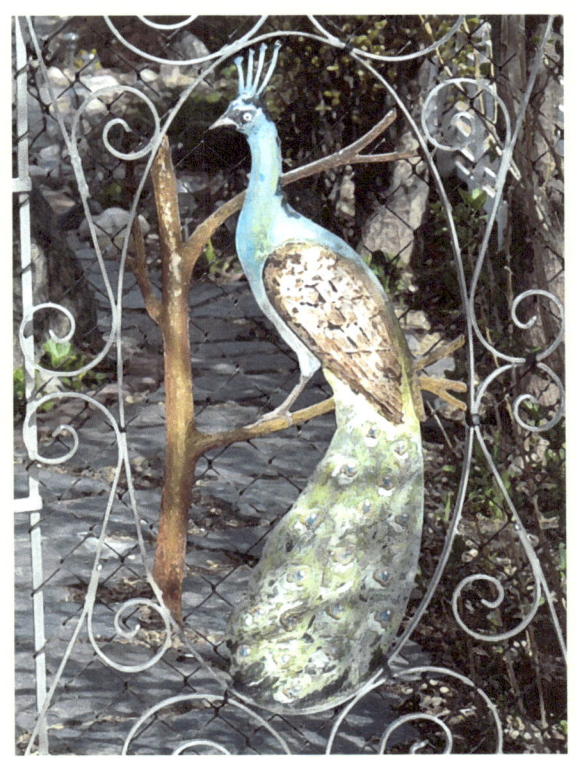

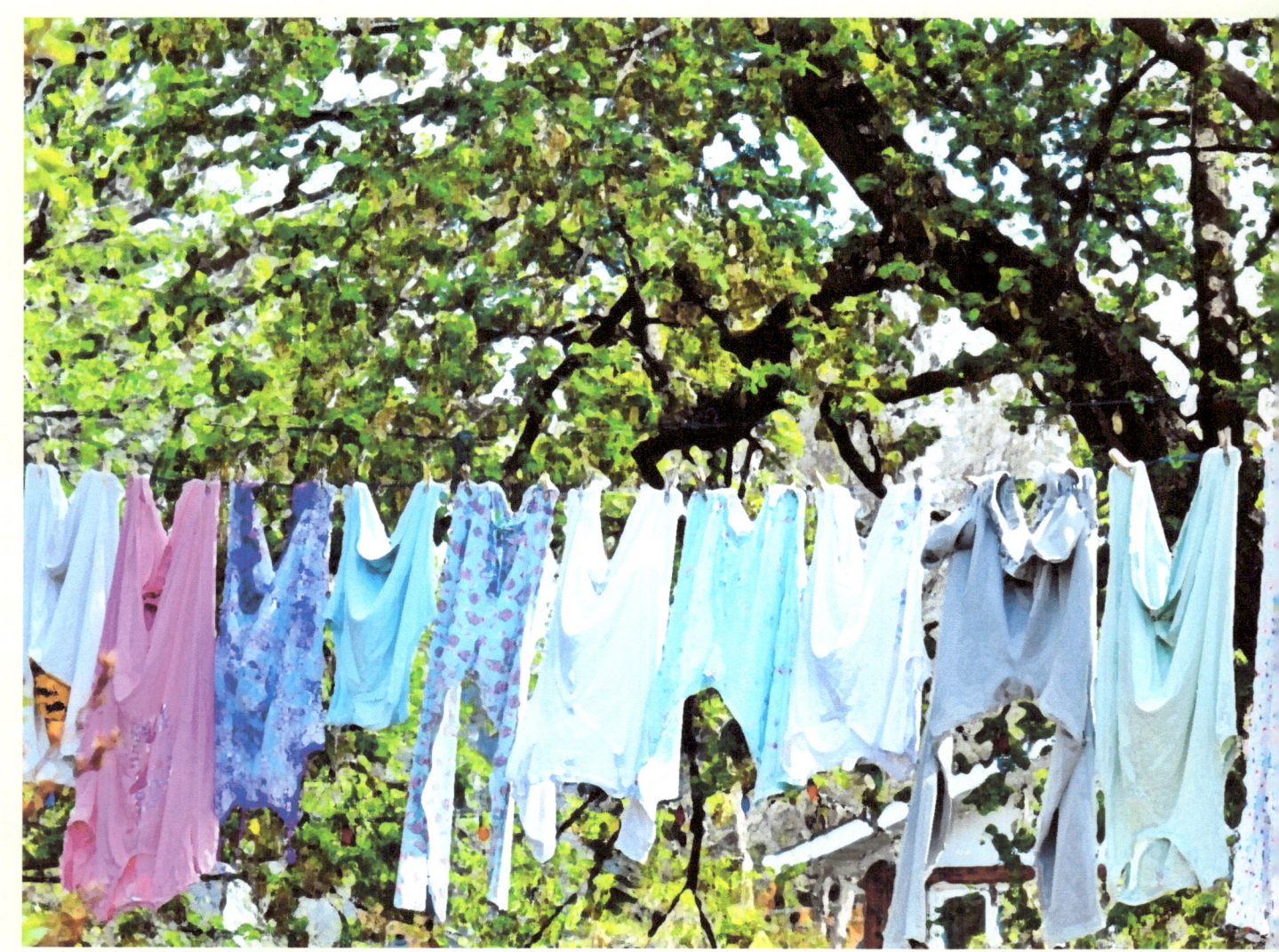

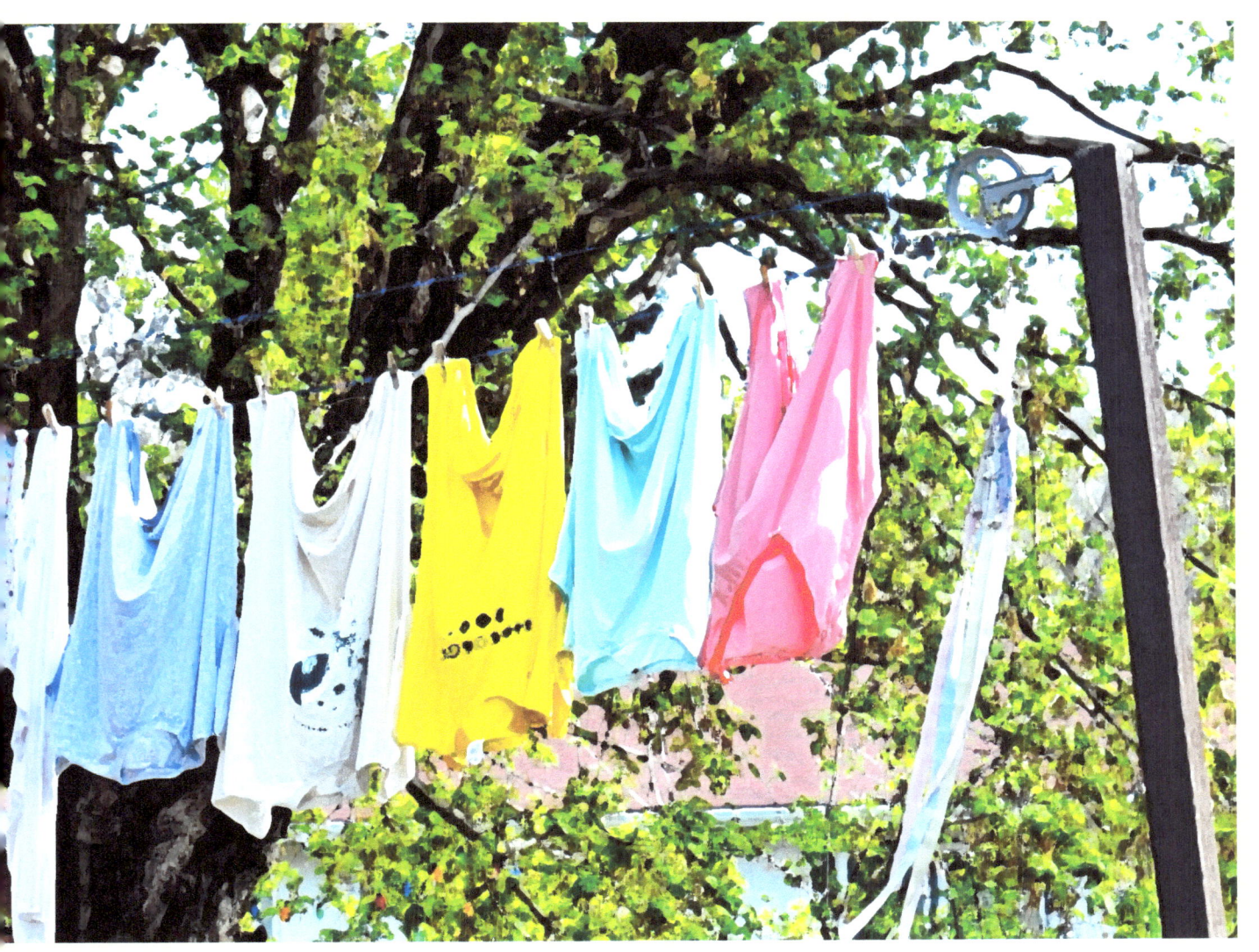

Hanging Out

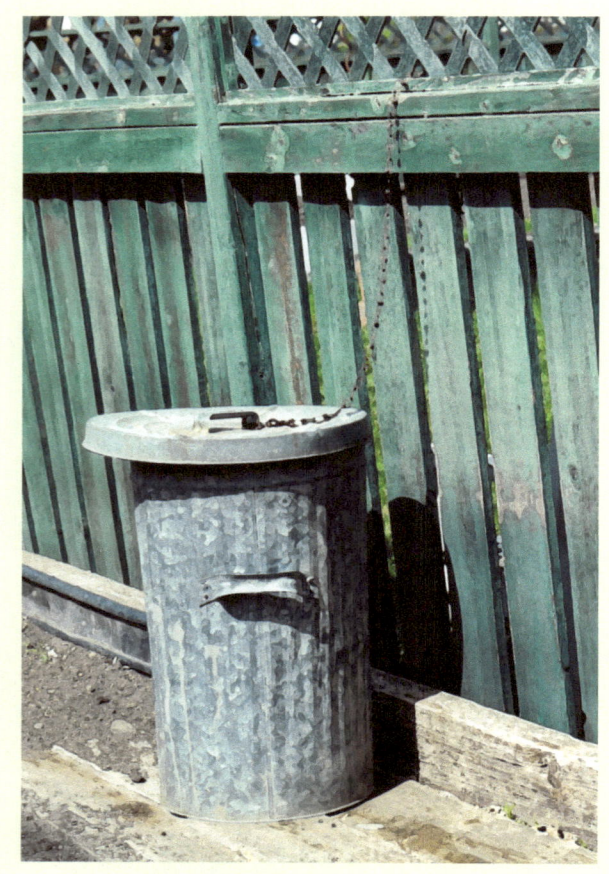

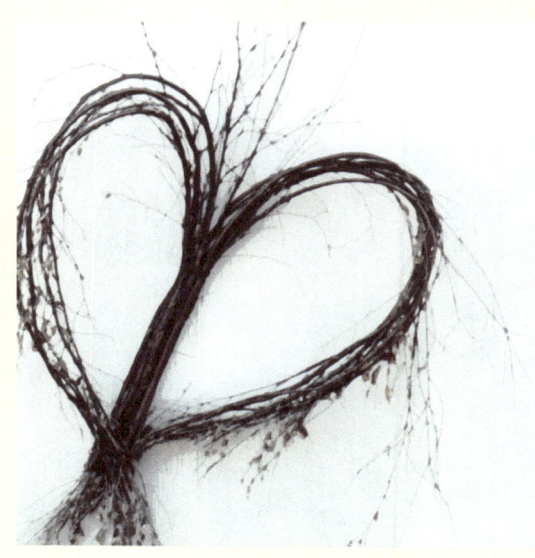

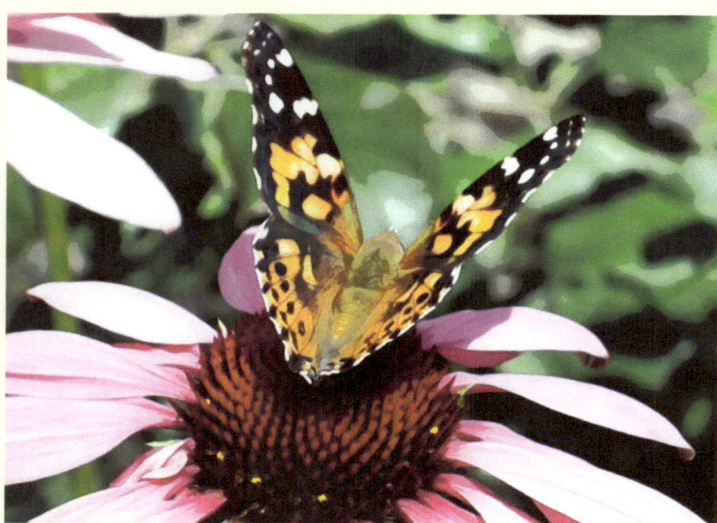

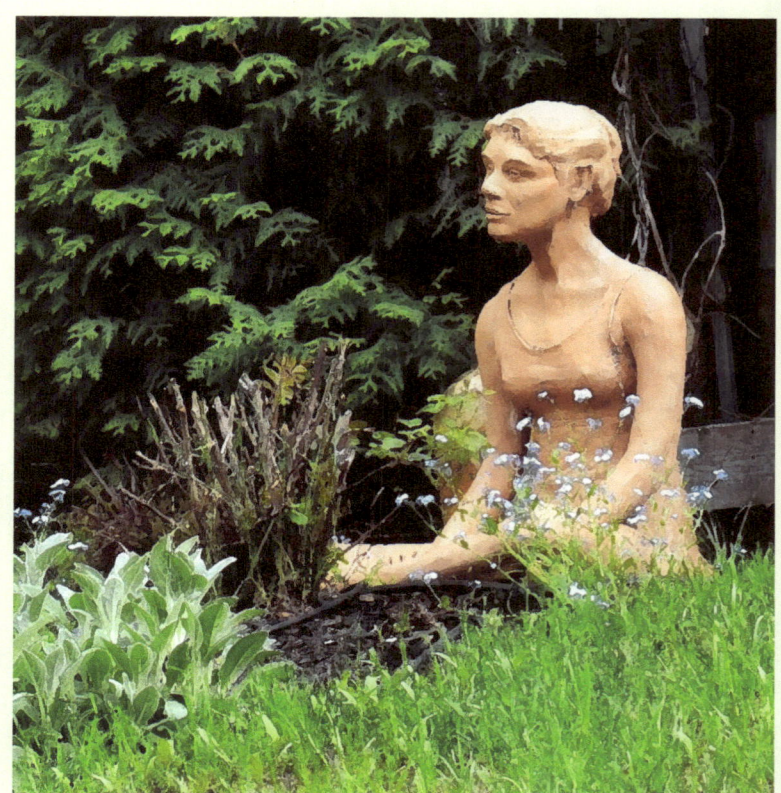

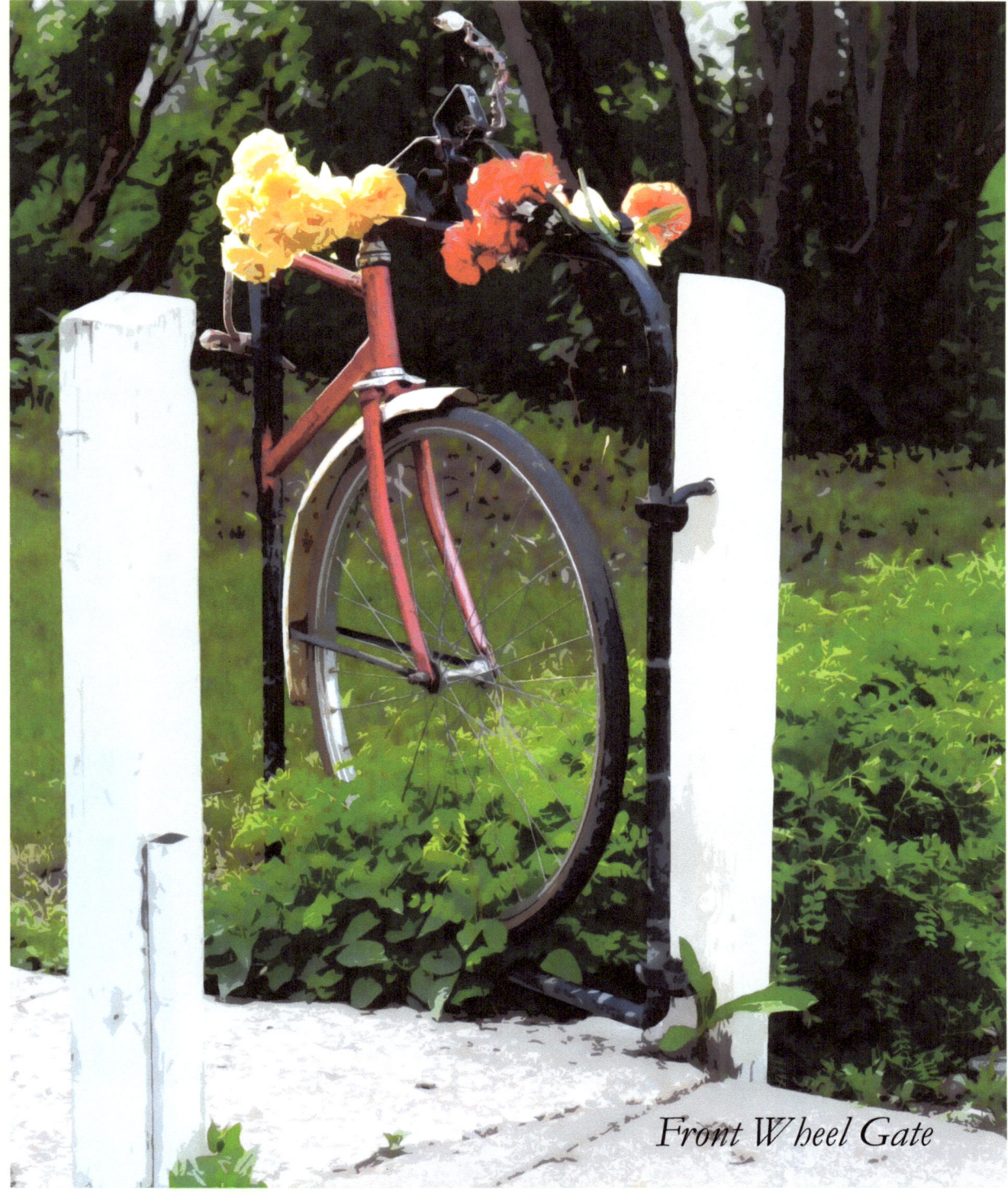

Front Wheel Gate

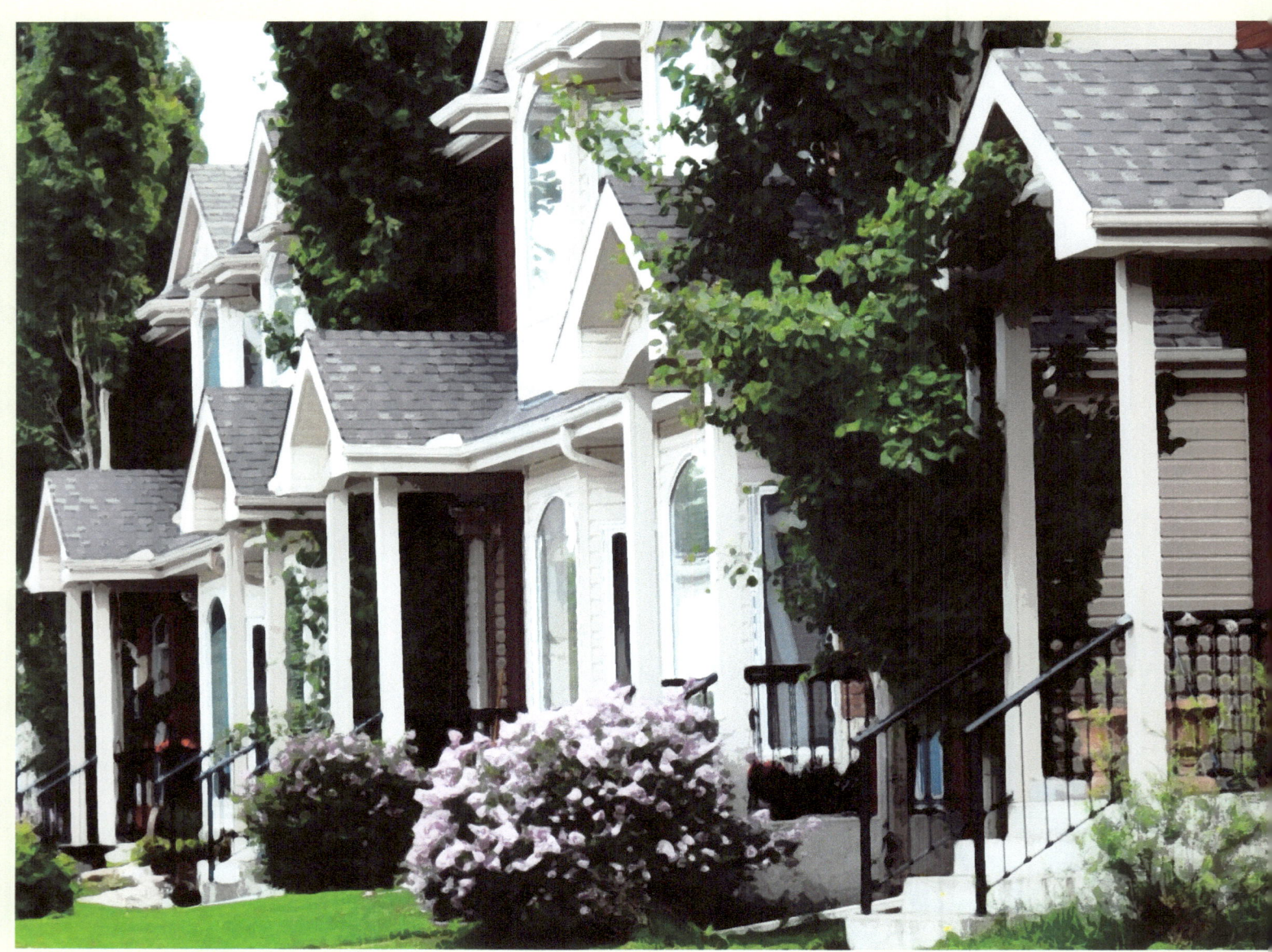

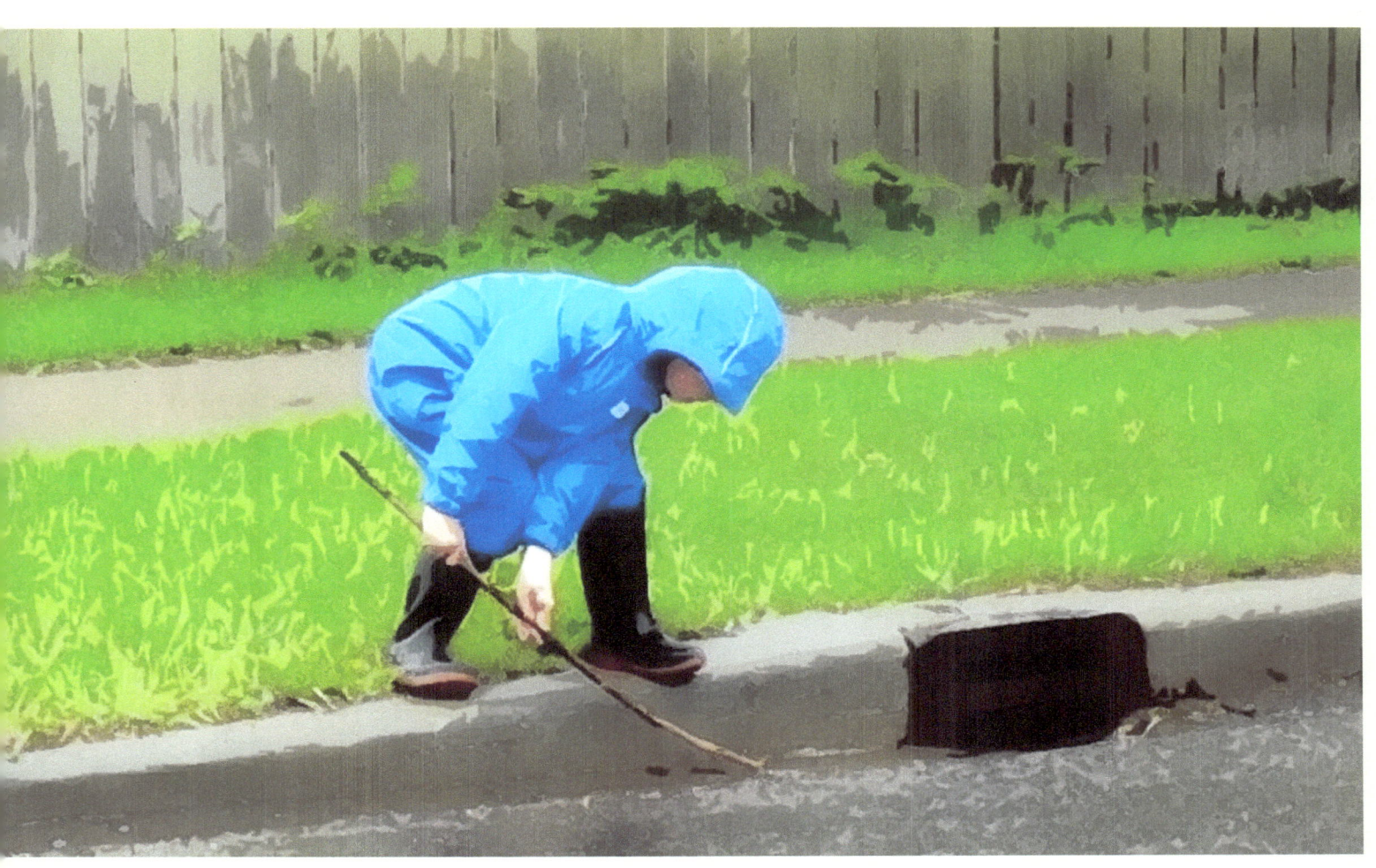

Rainy Day Fun

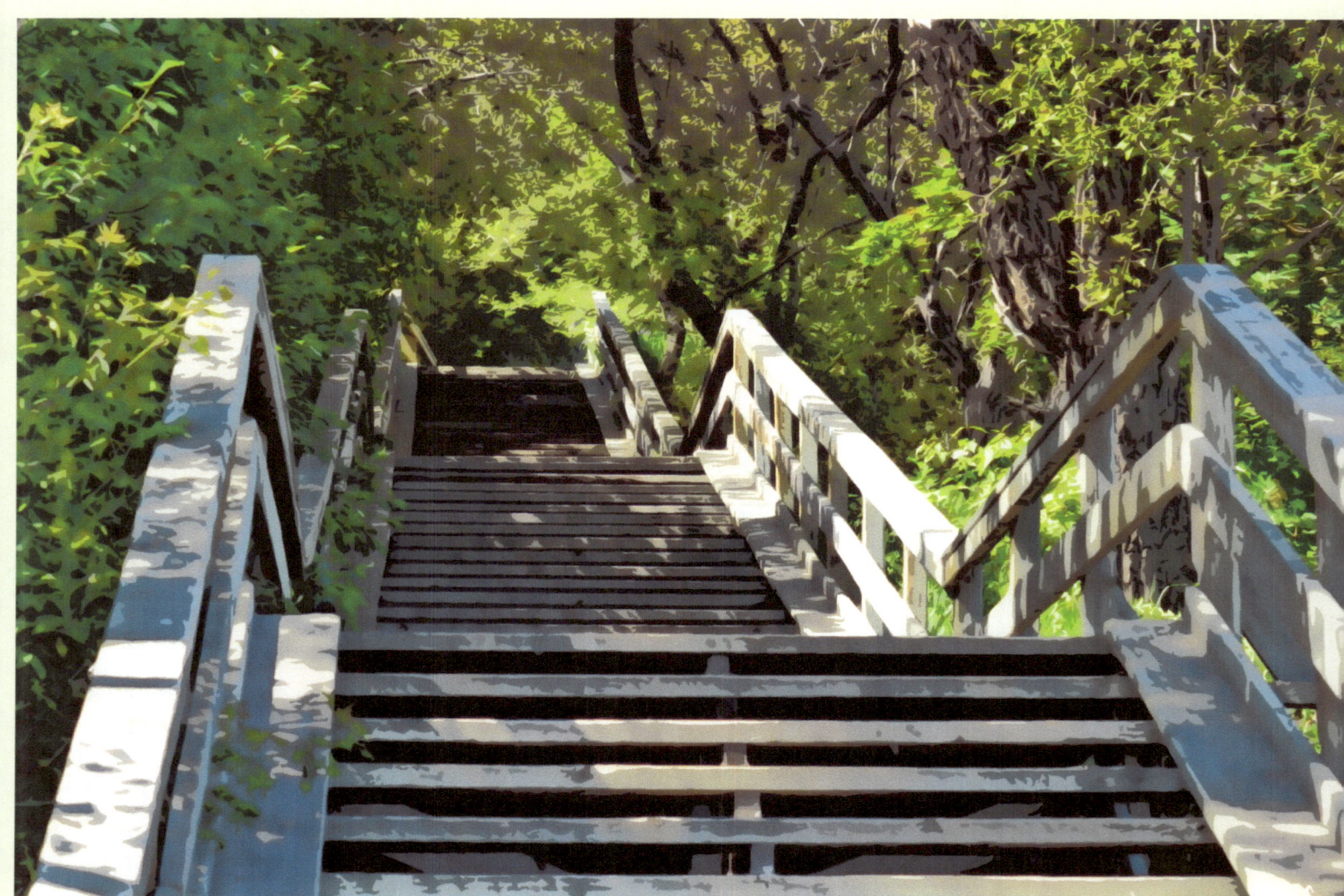

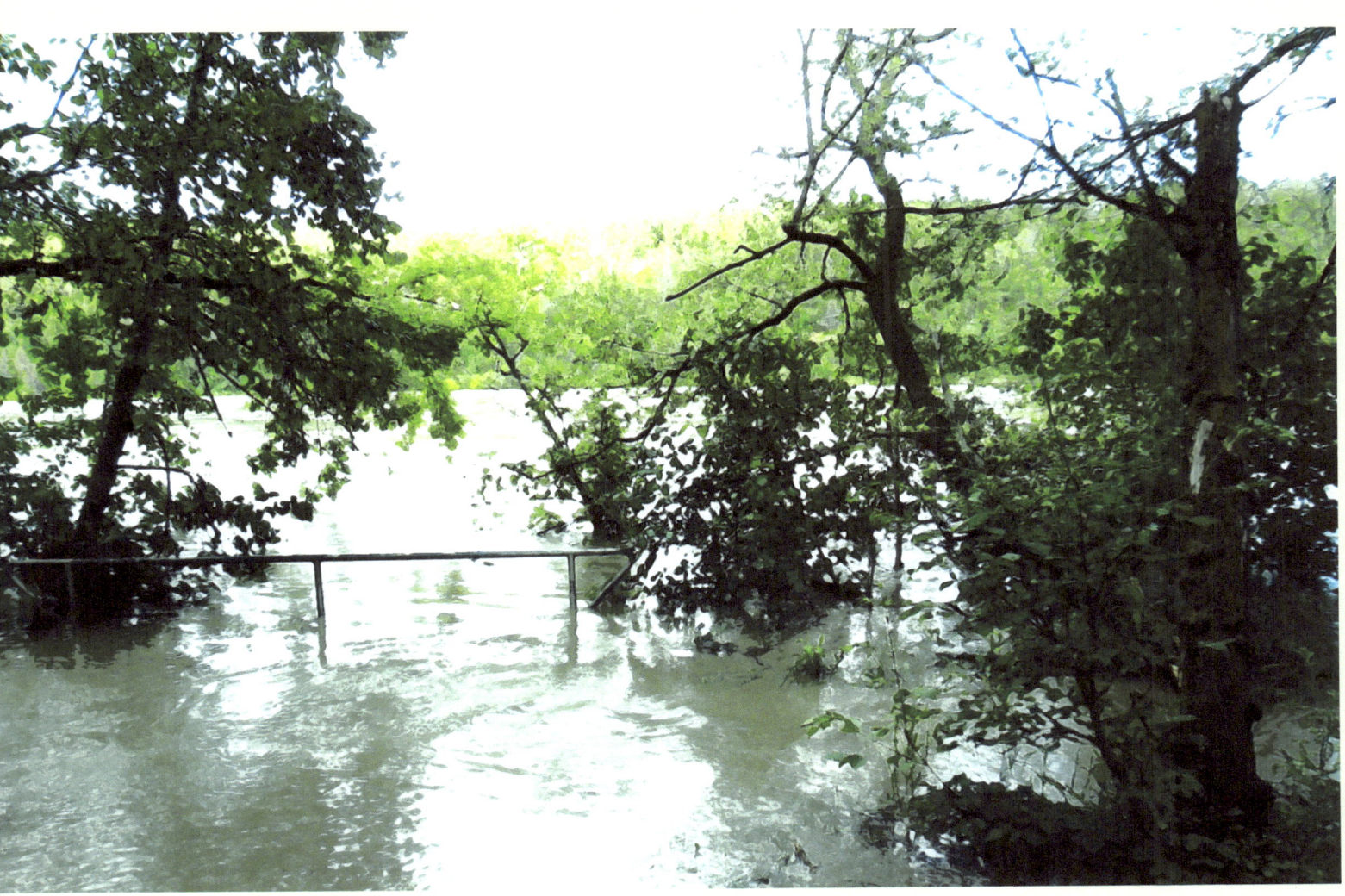

Spring Flood

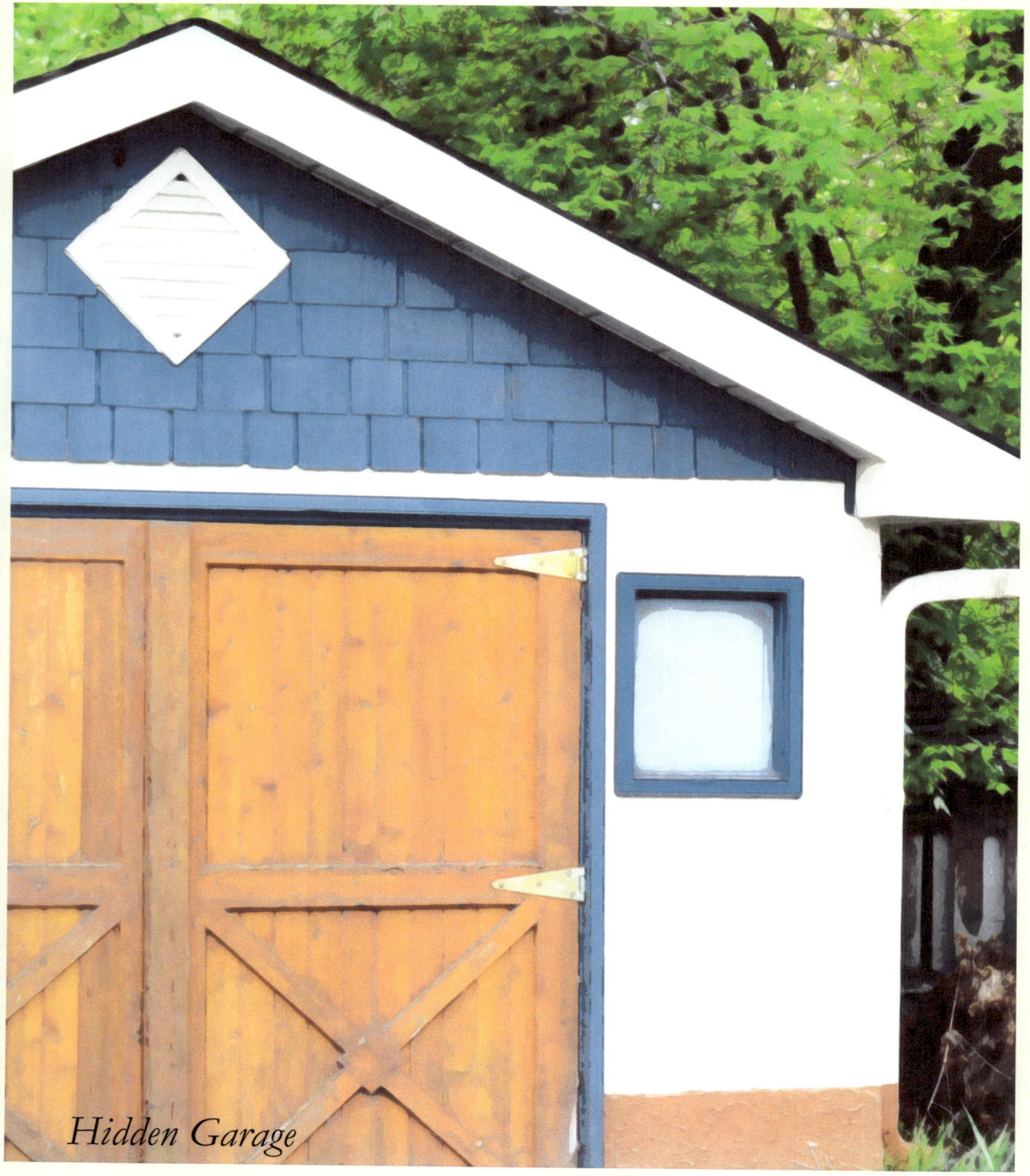

Hidden Garage

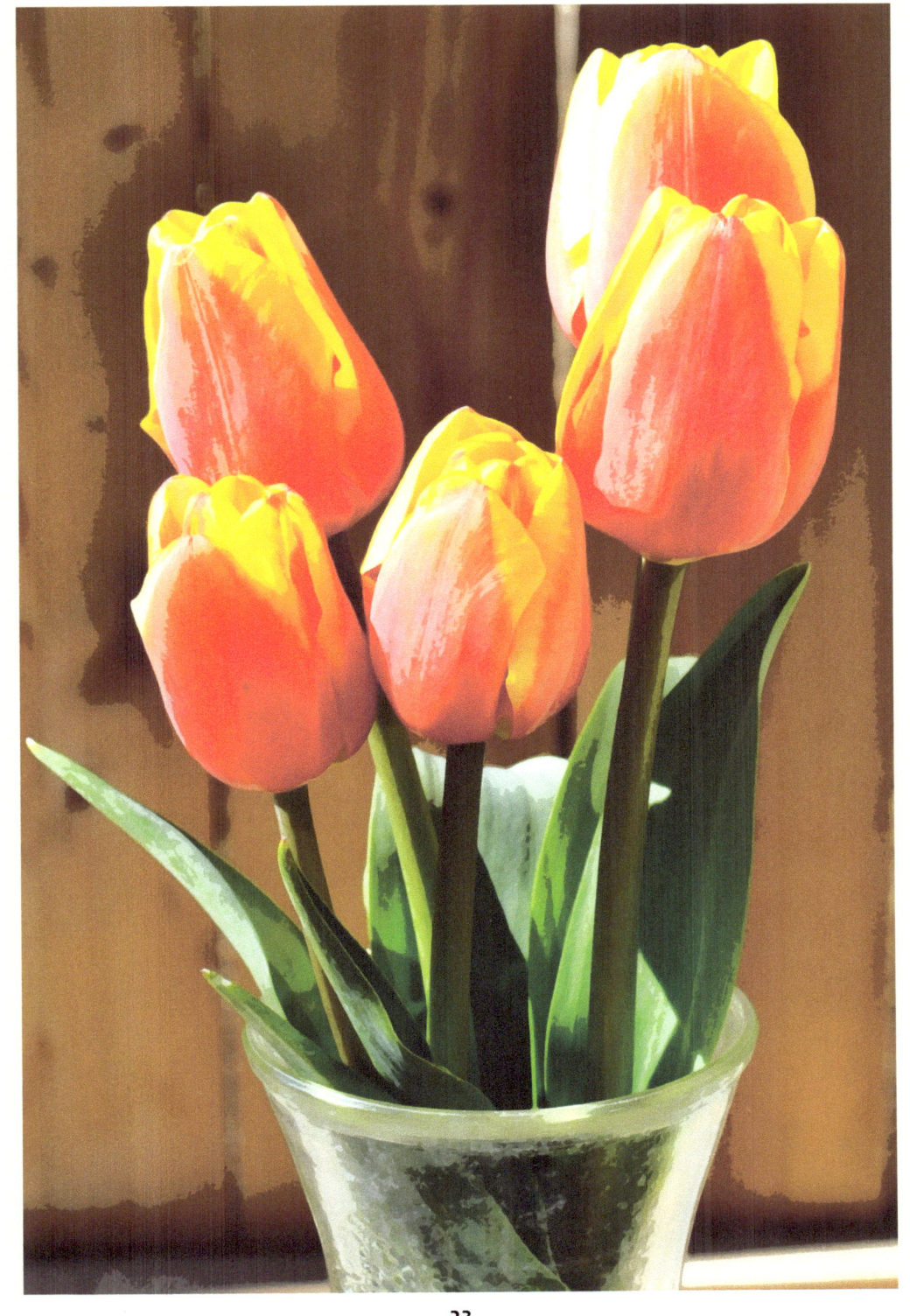

Two
Lips

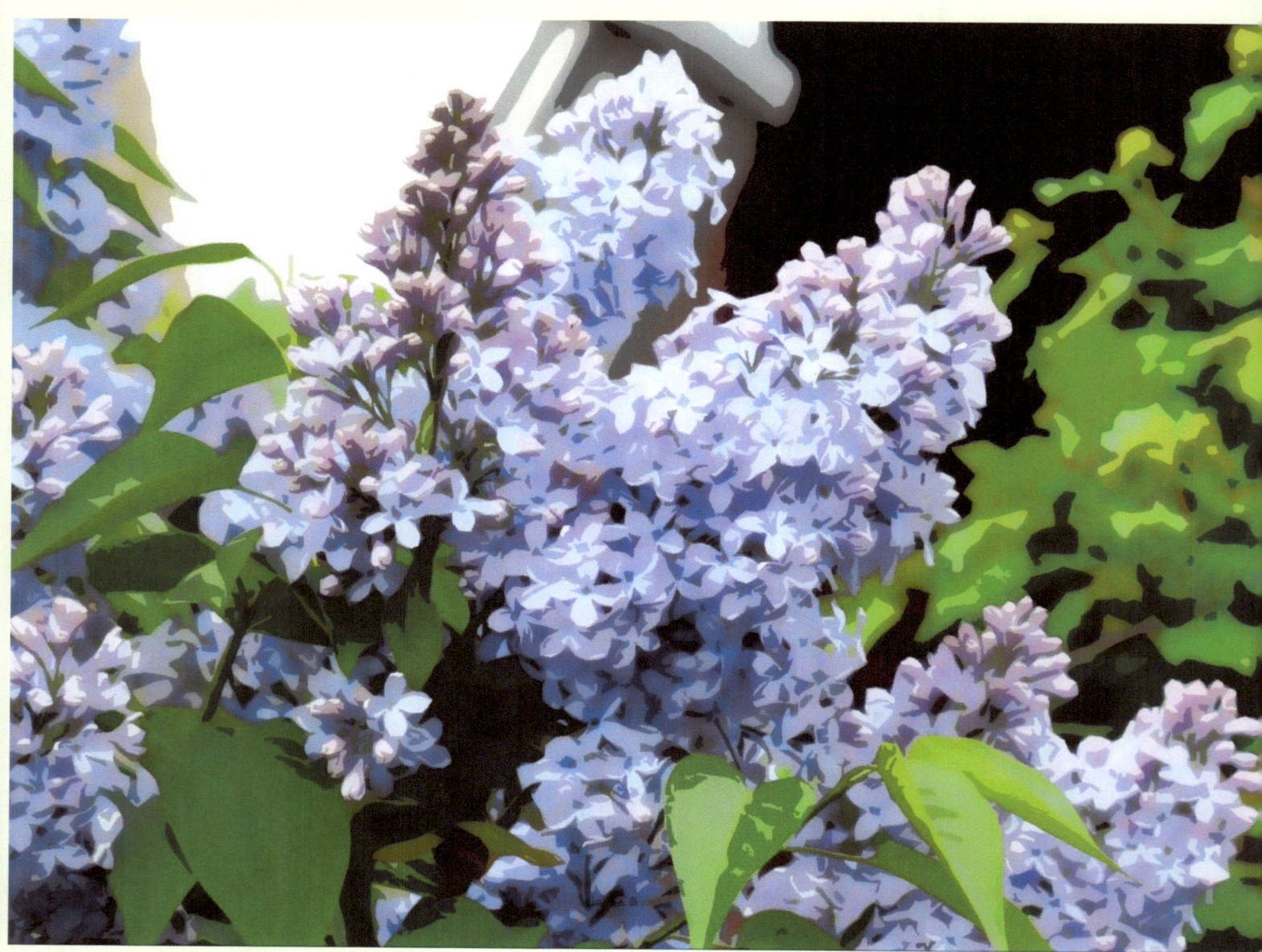

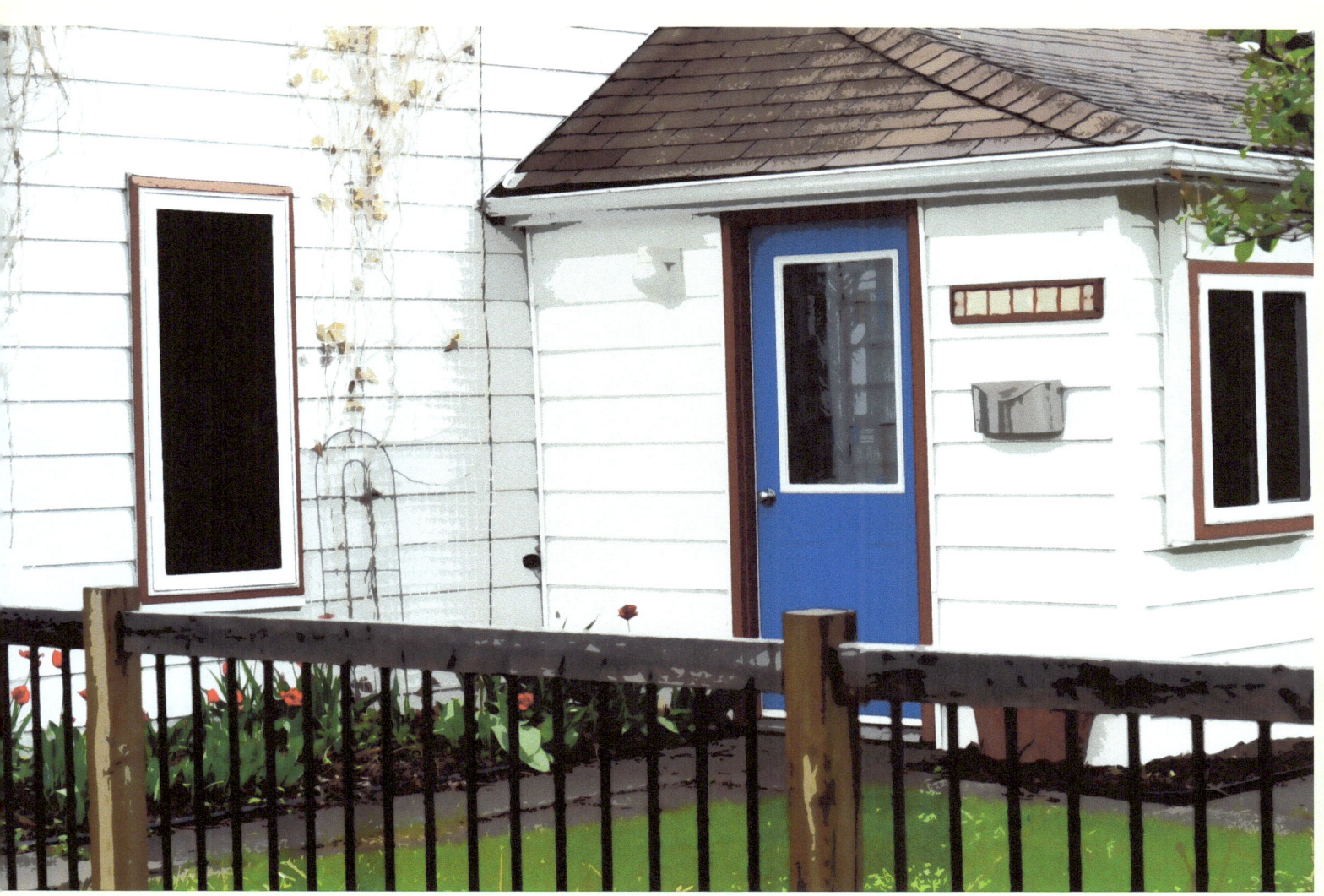

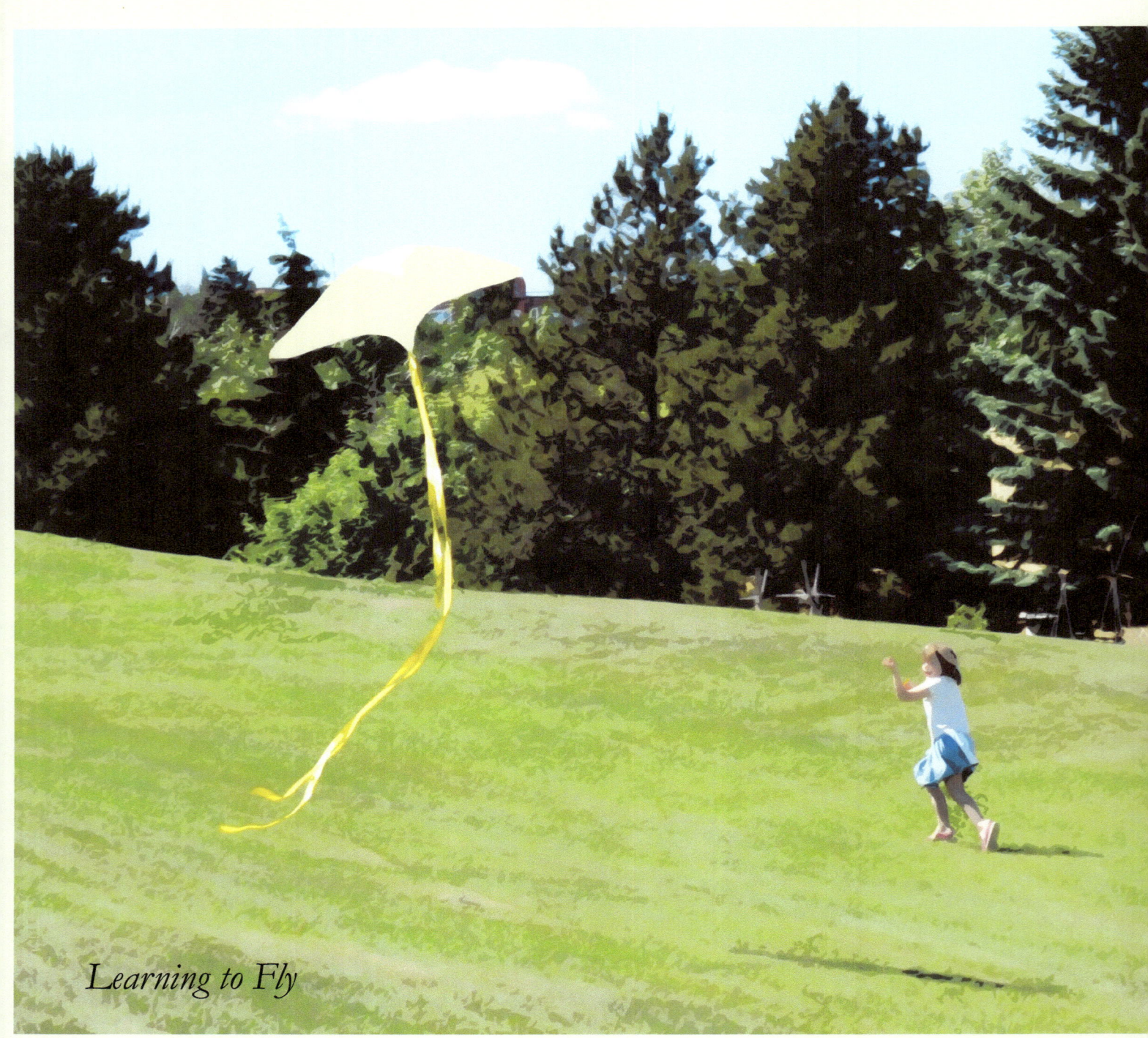

Learning to Fly

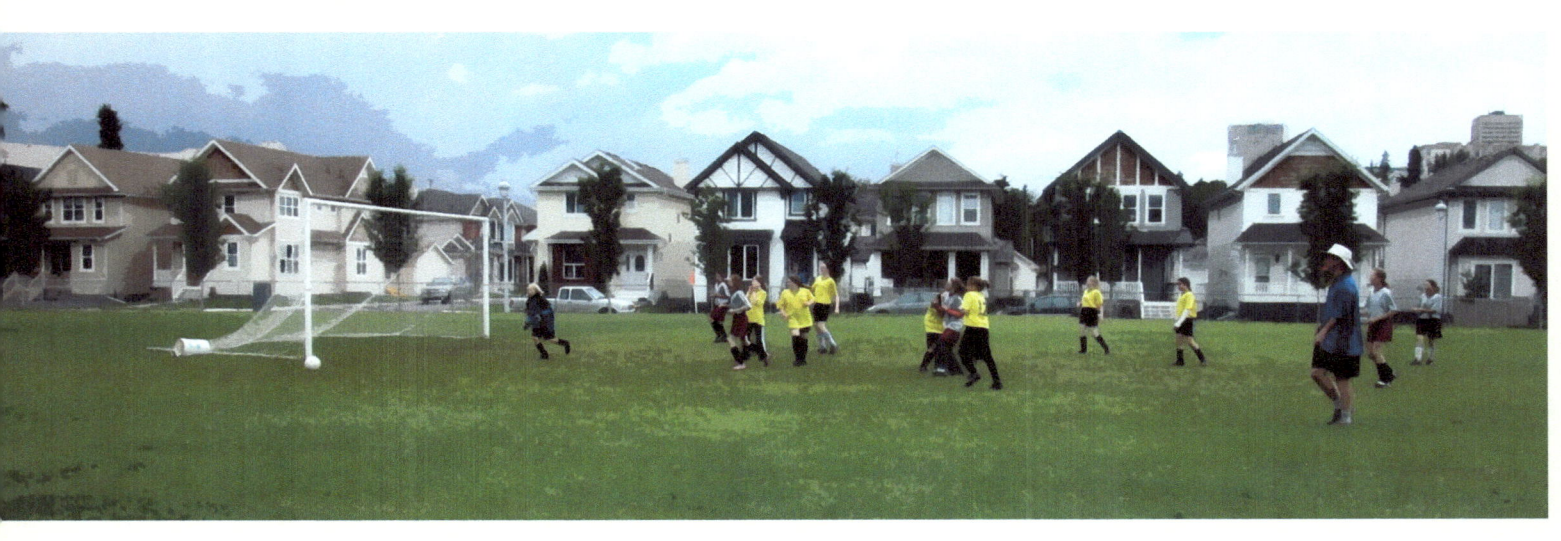

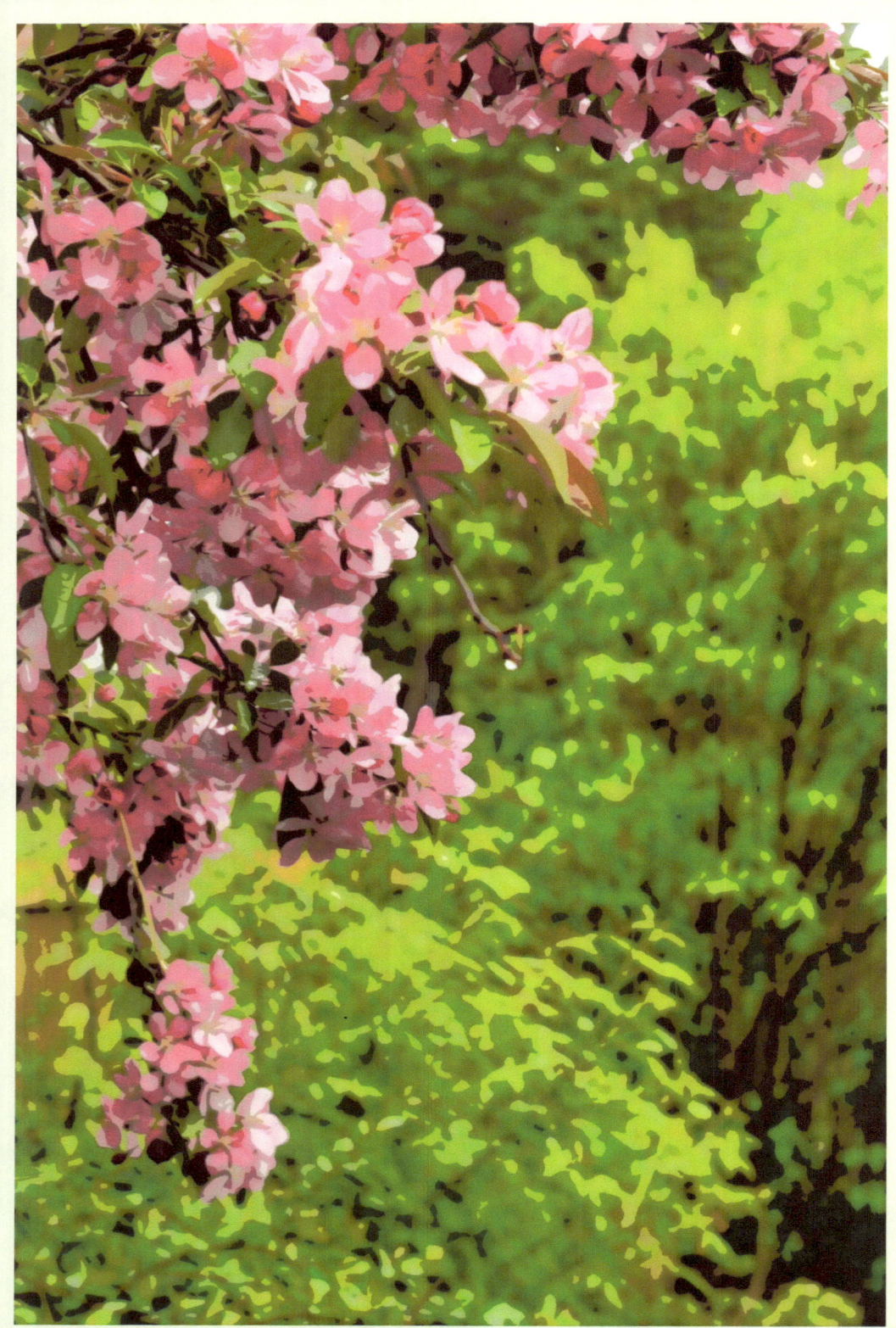

Apple
Blossoms

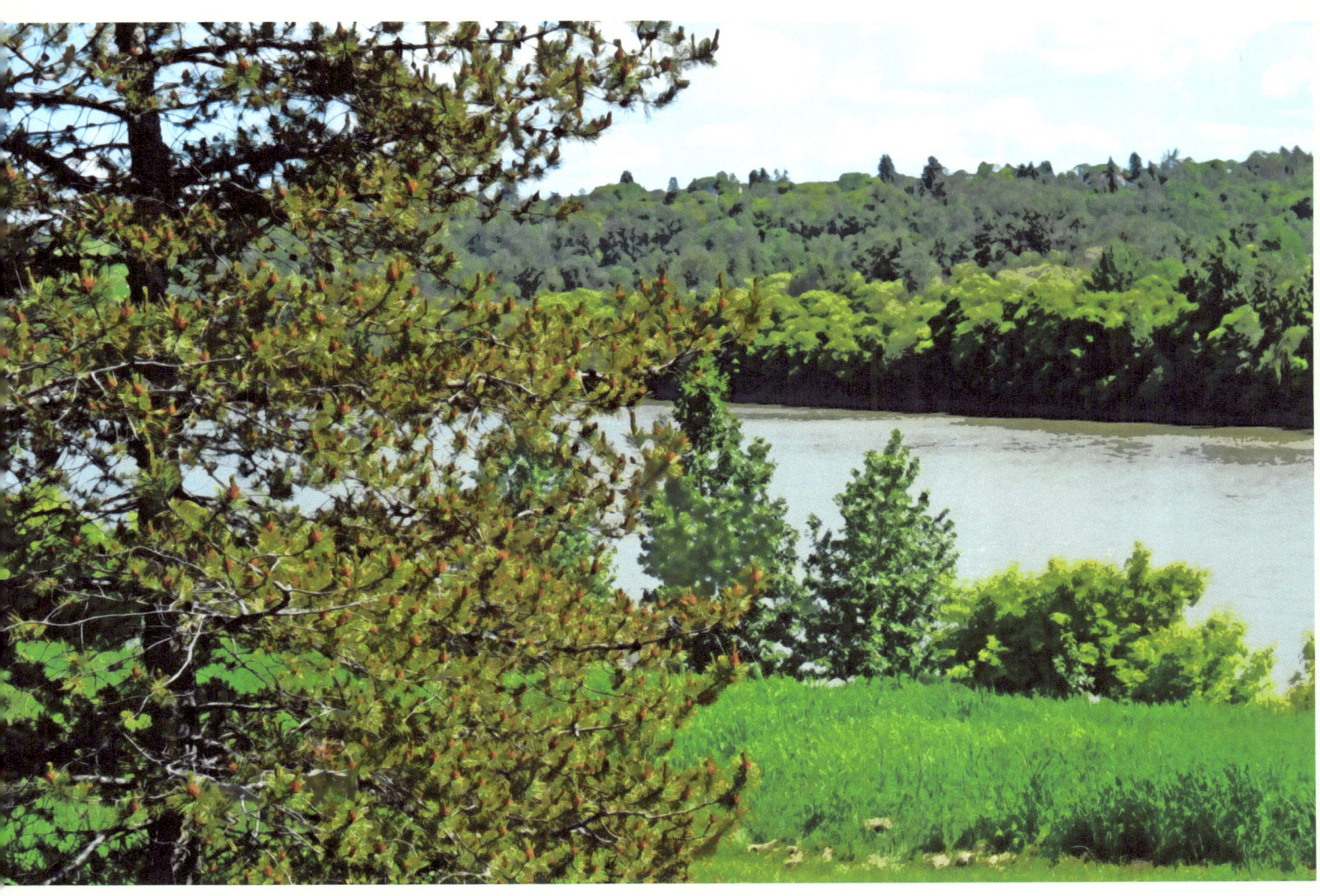

River
Rising

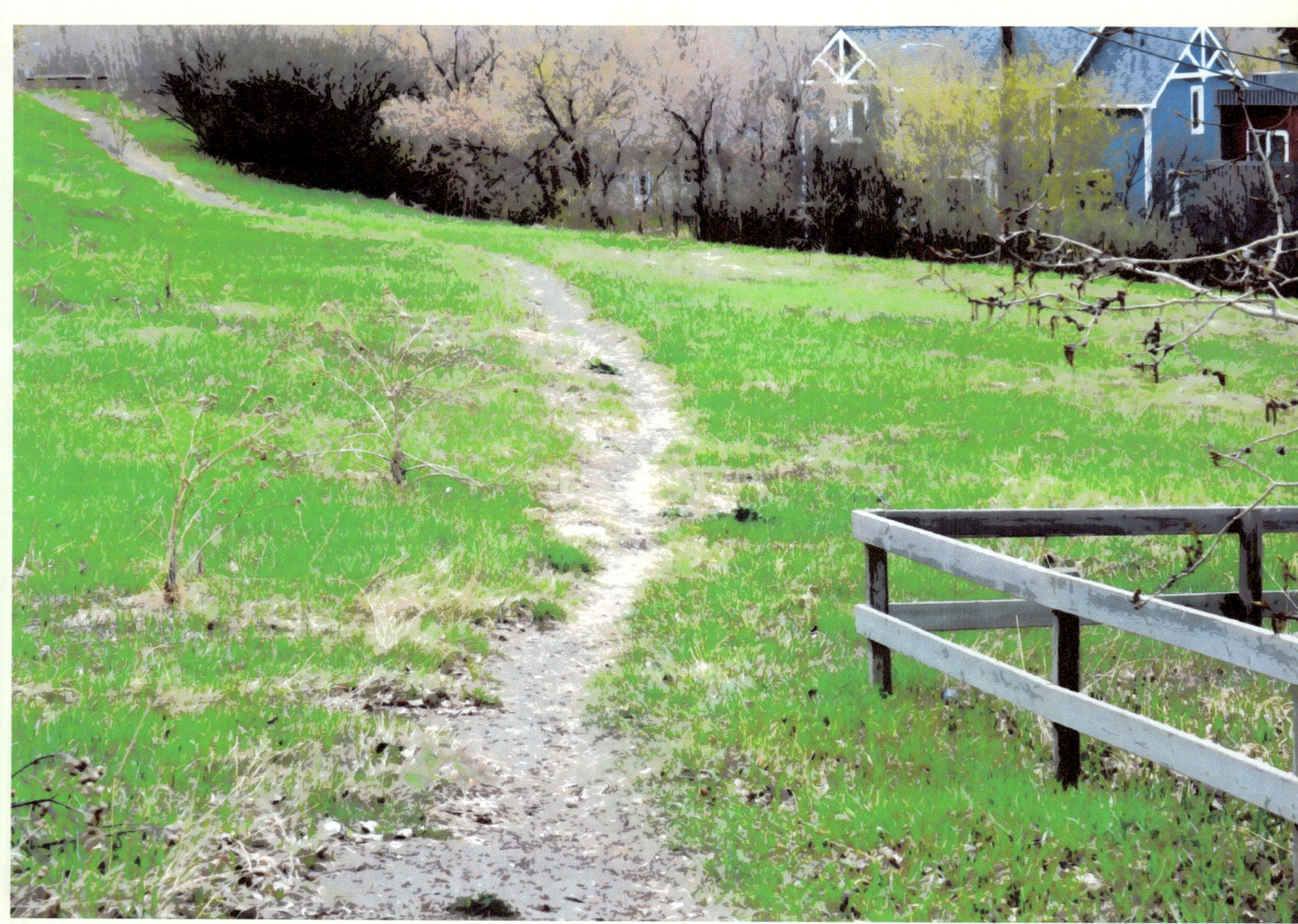

Early Spring

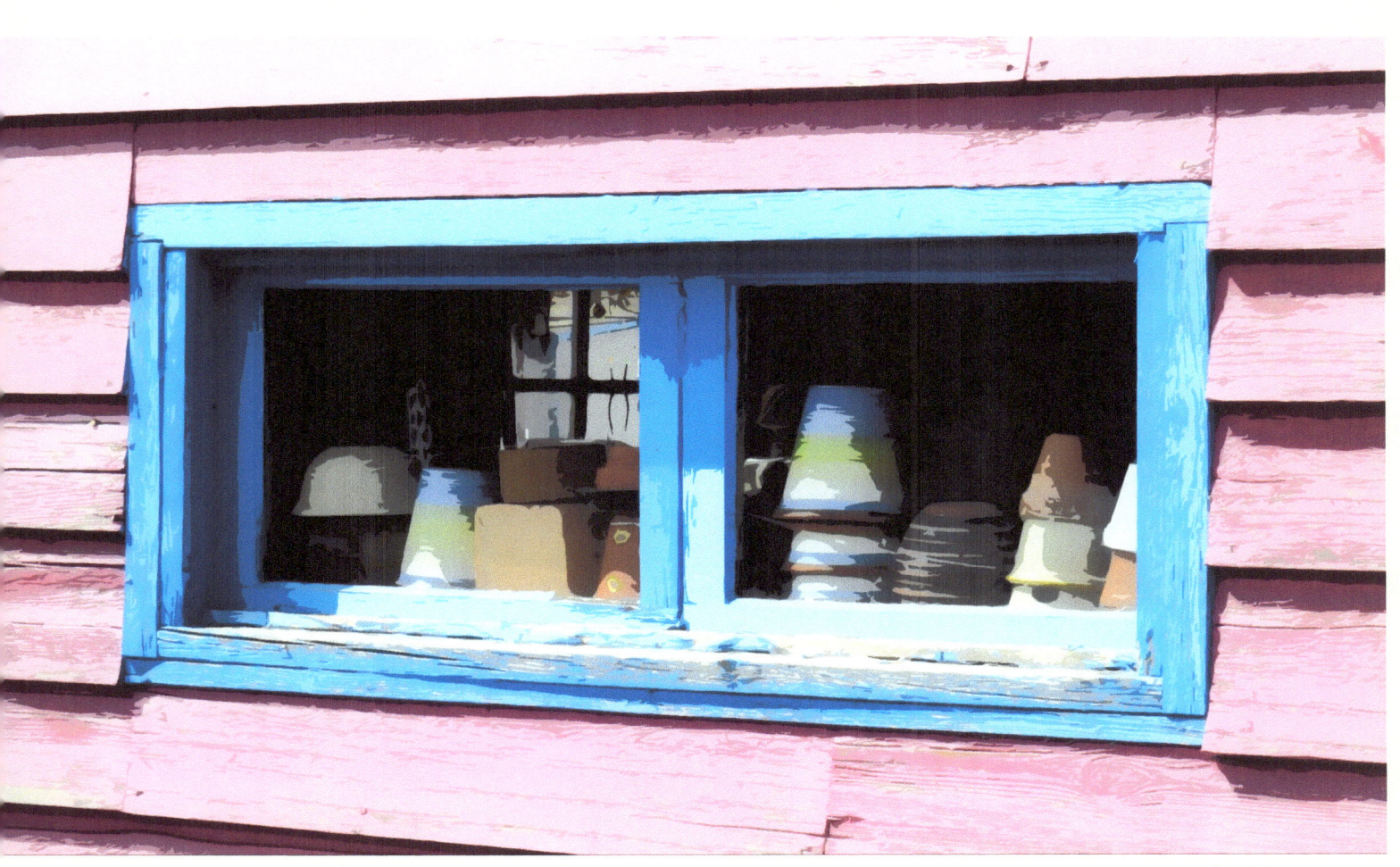

Framing the Pots

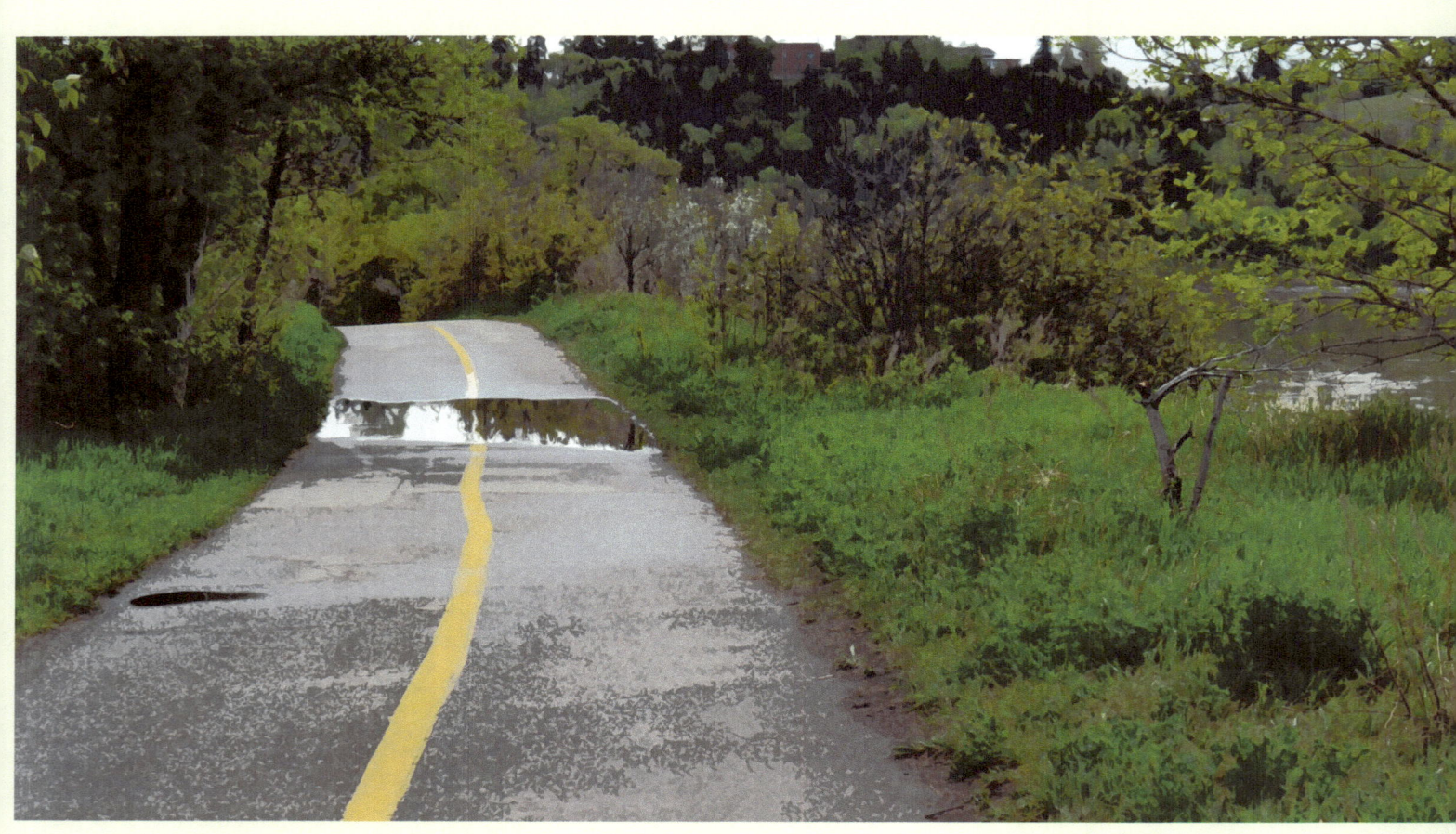

Watch for the Puddle

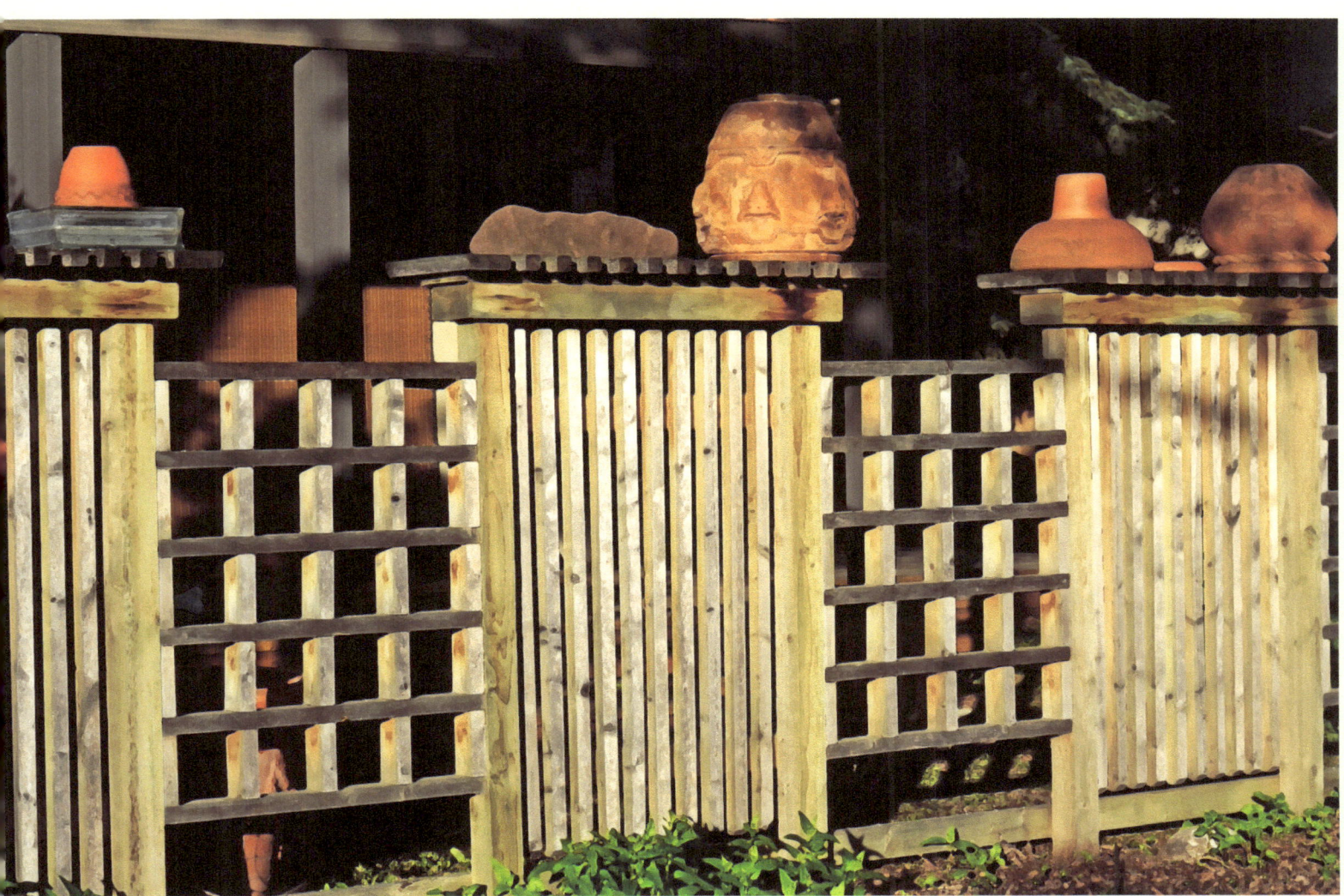

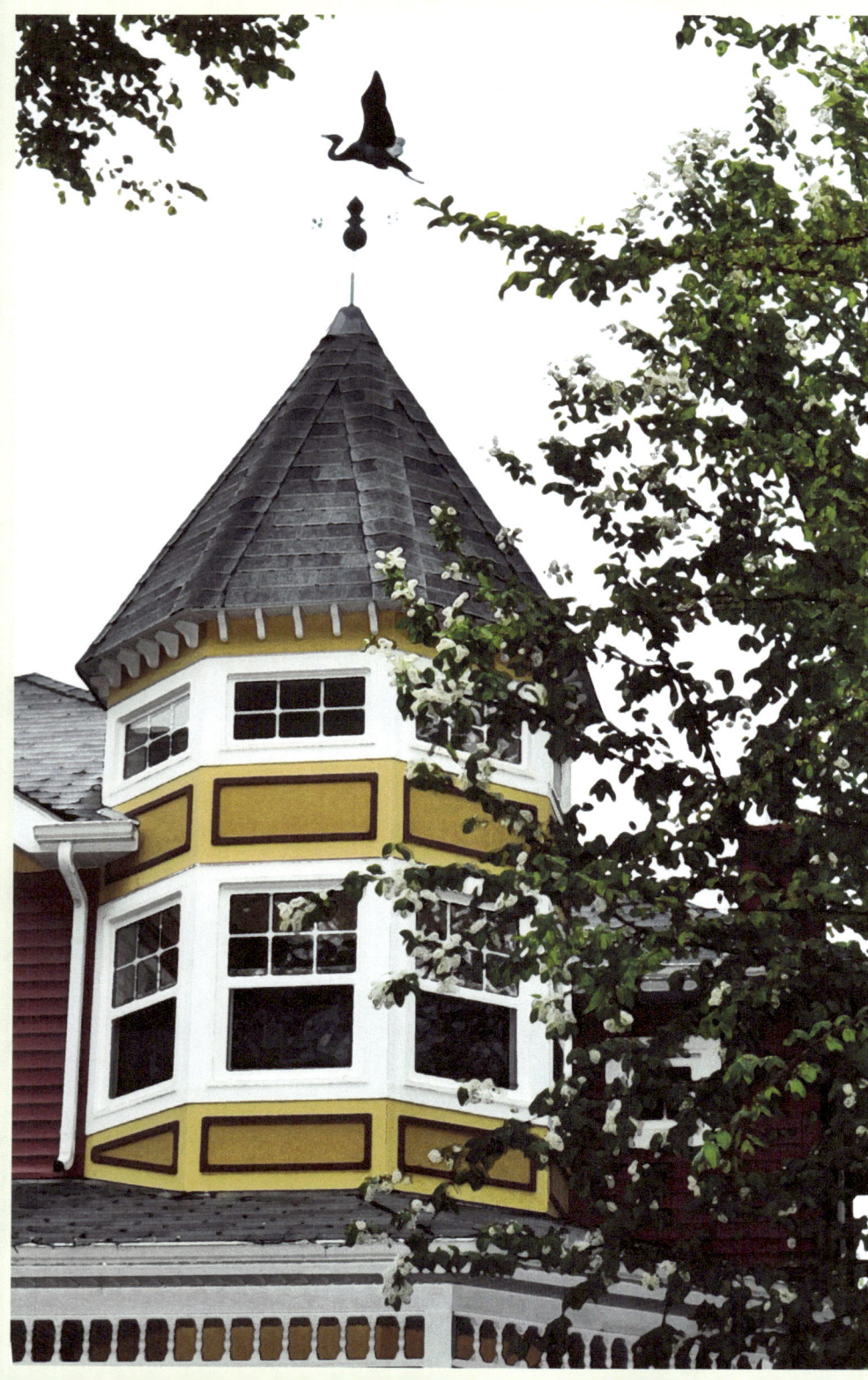

Weather Vane

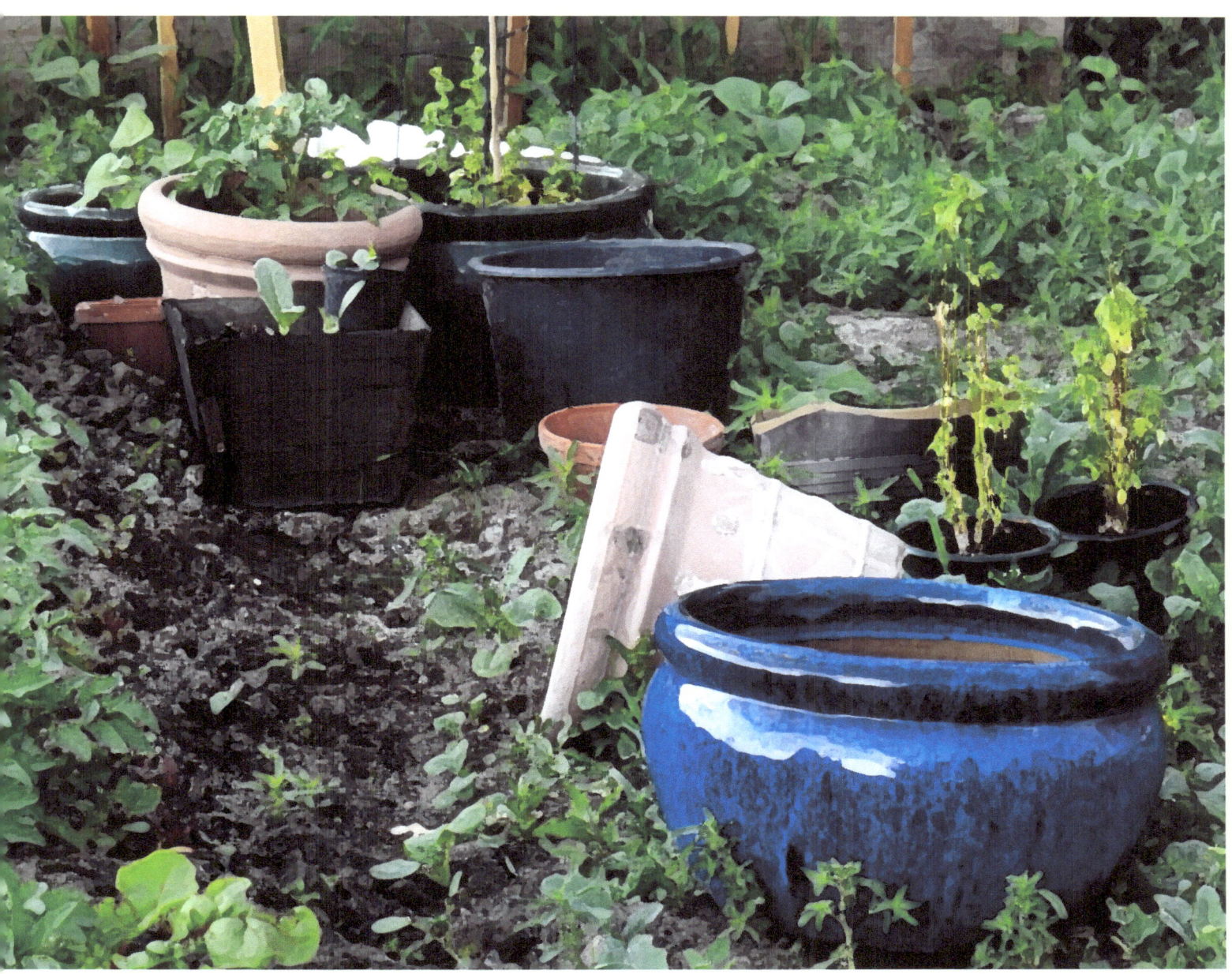

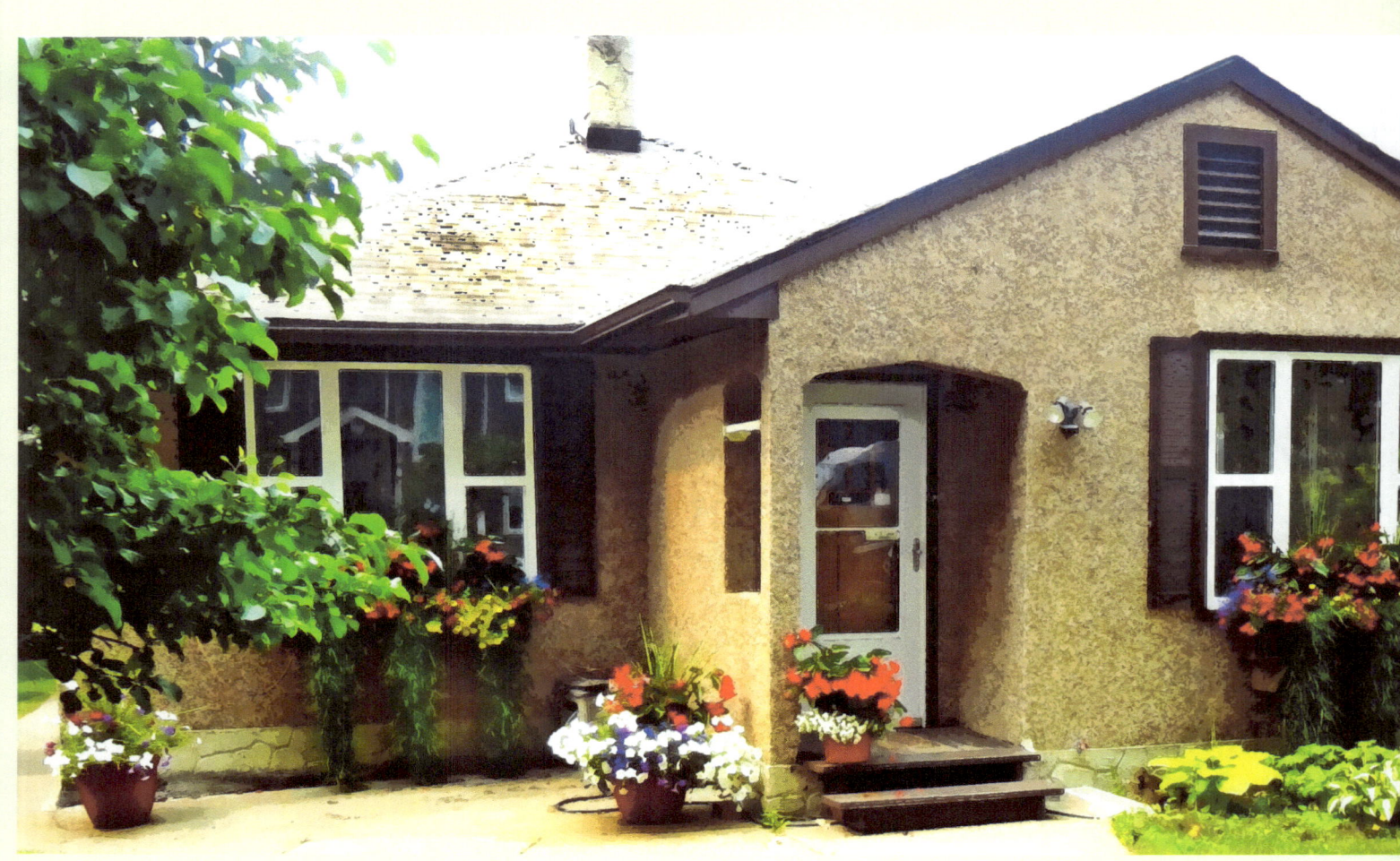

Just Down the Street

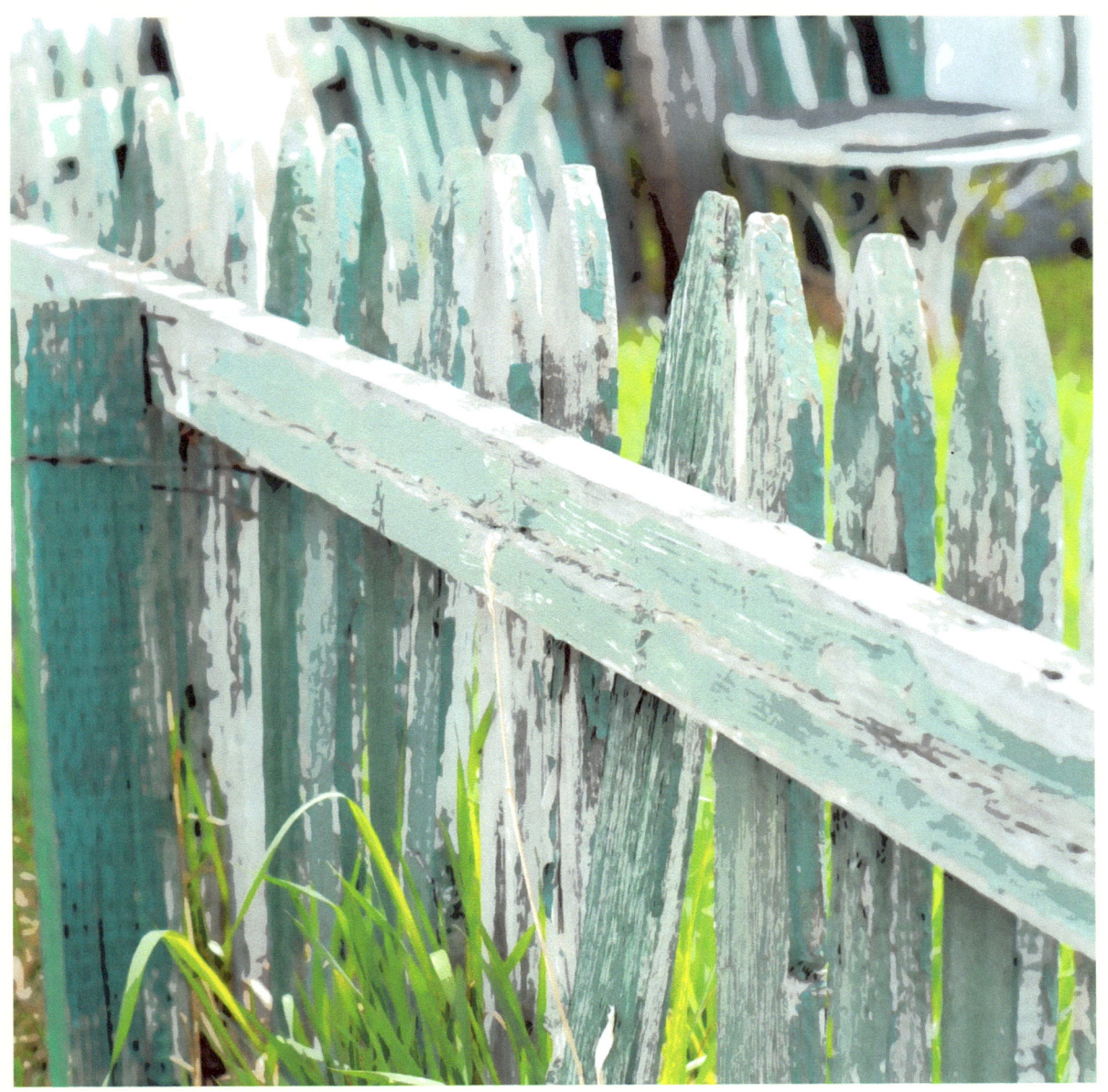

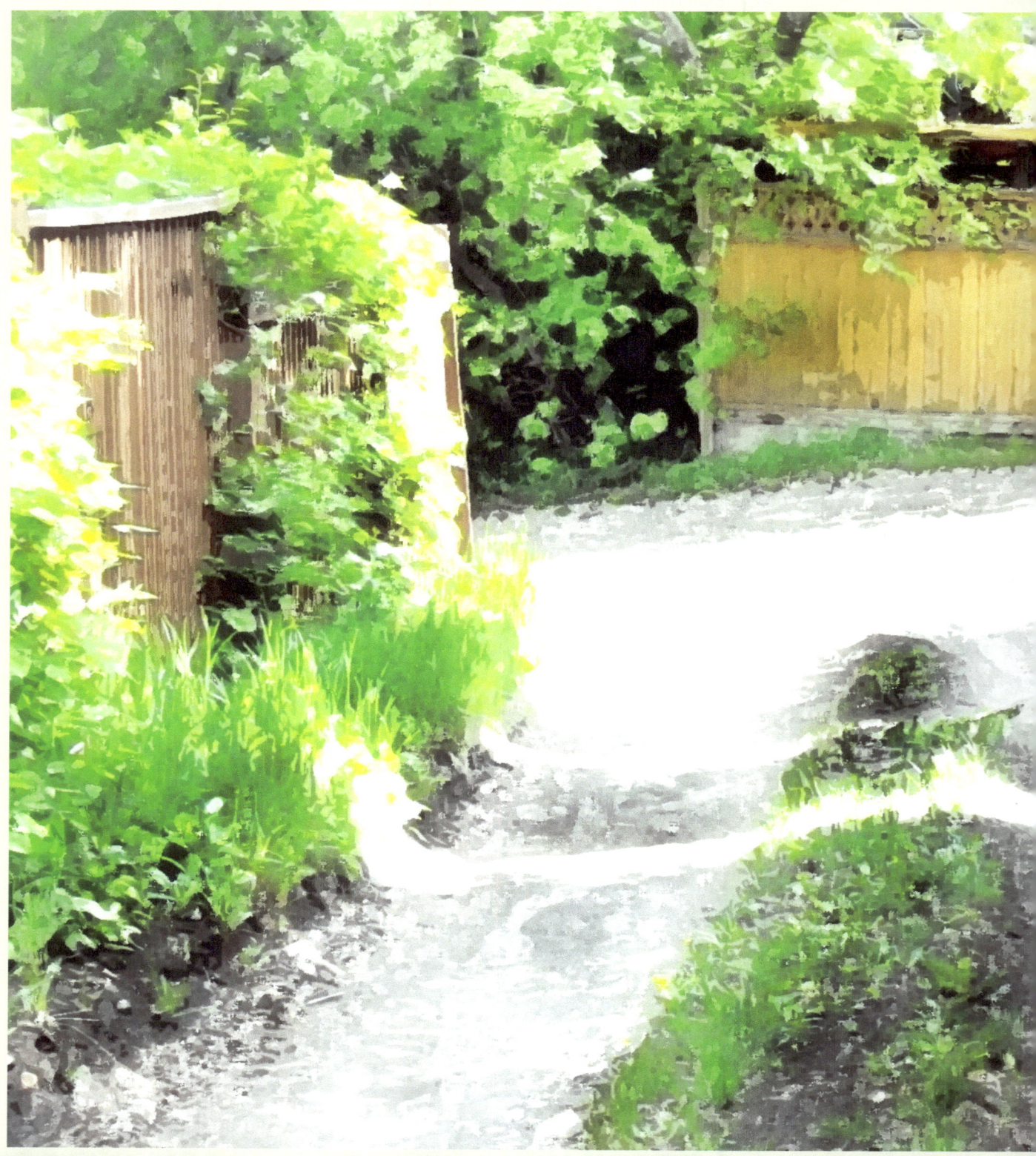

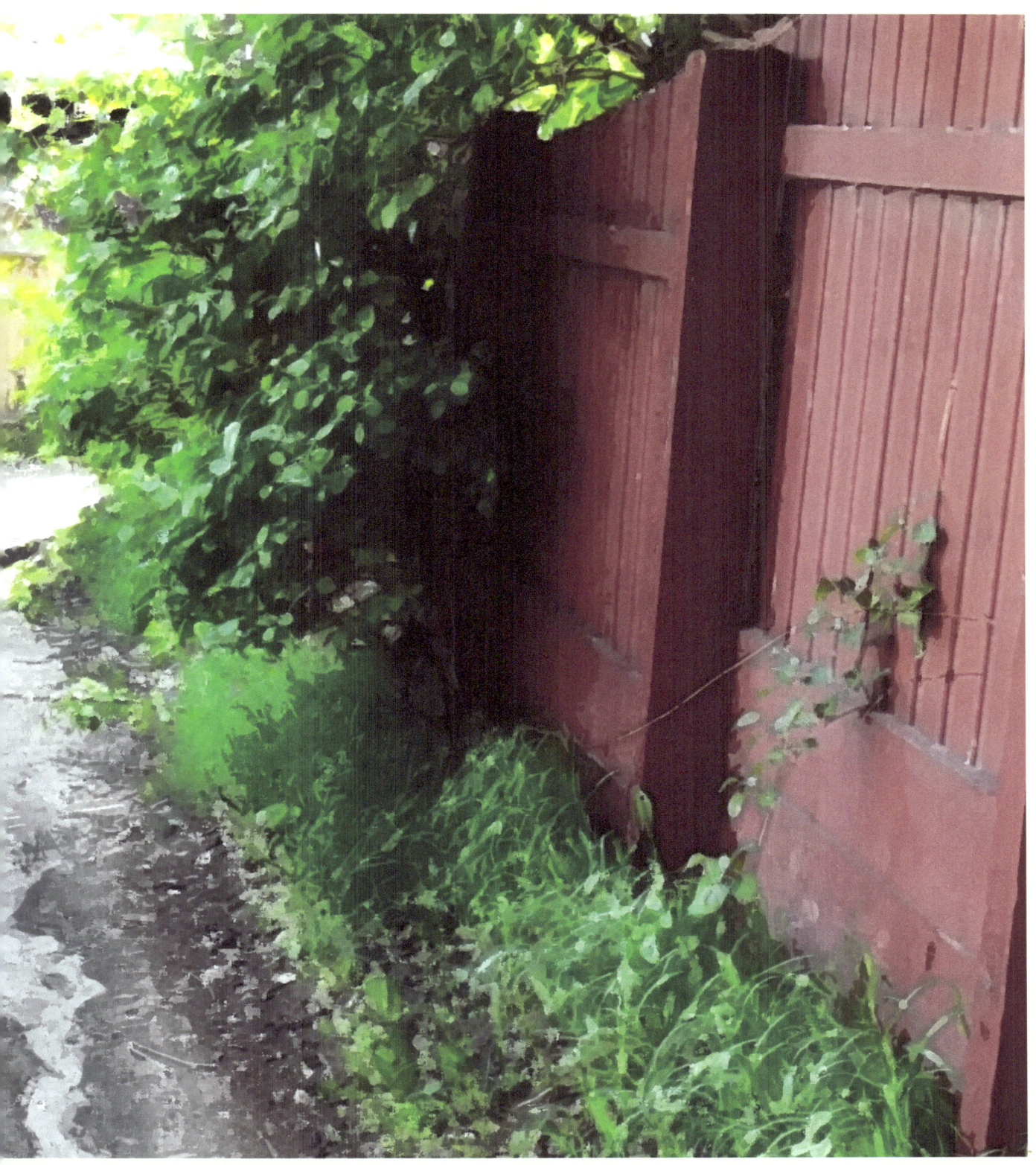

Summer

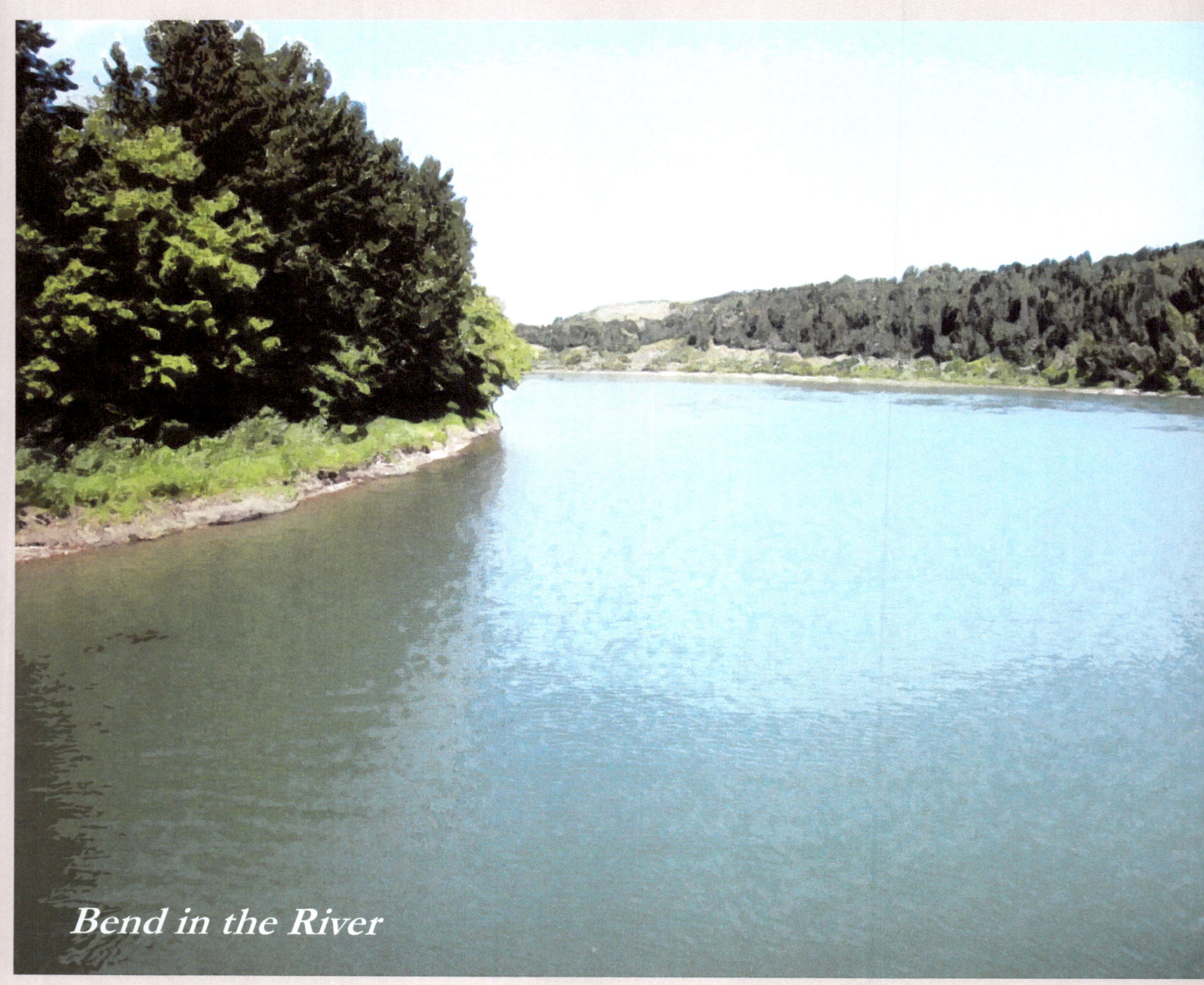

Bend in the River

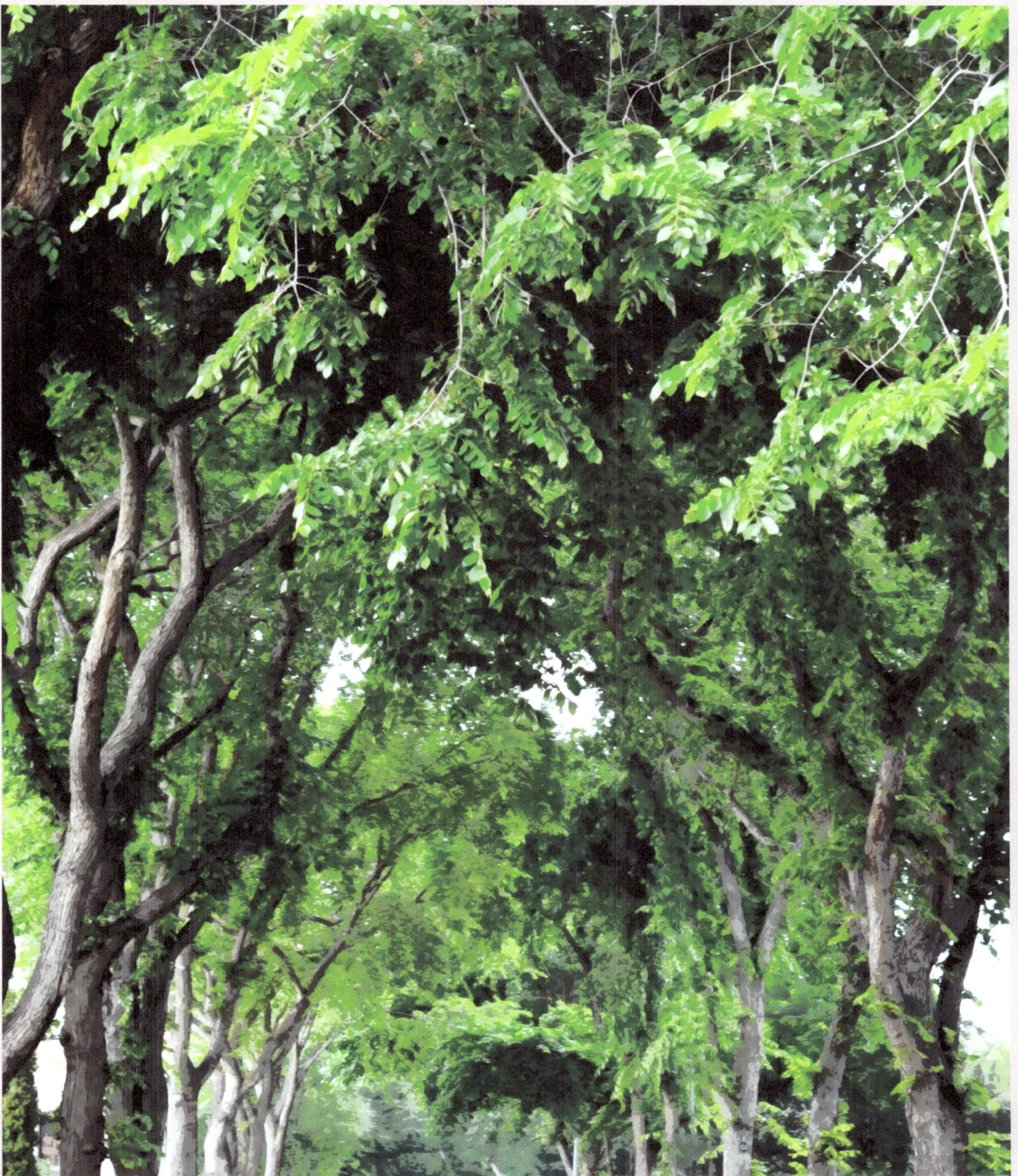

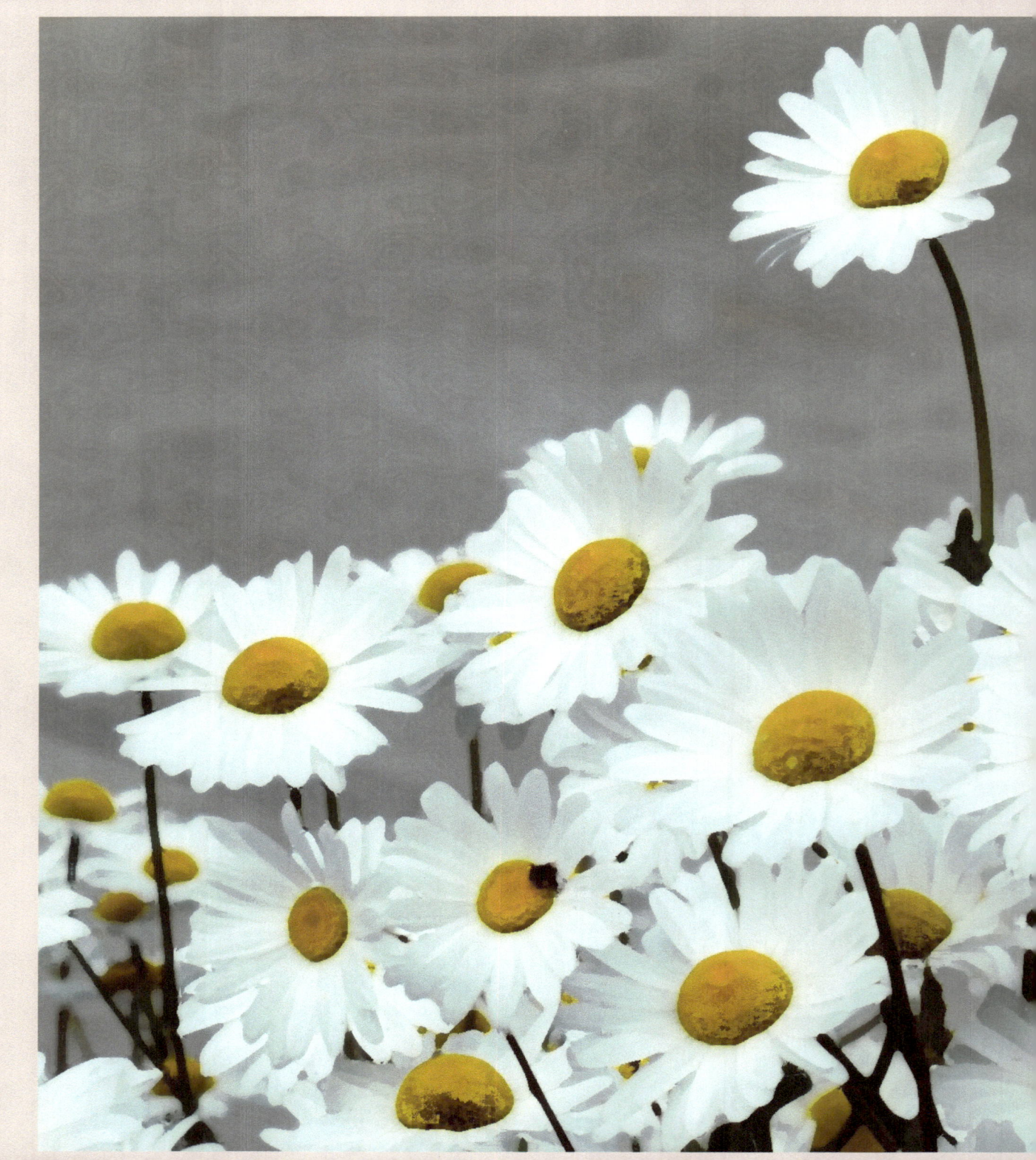

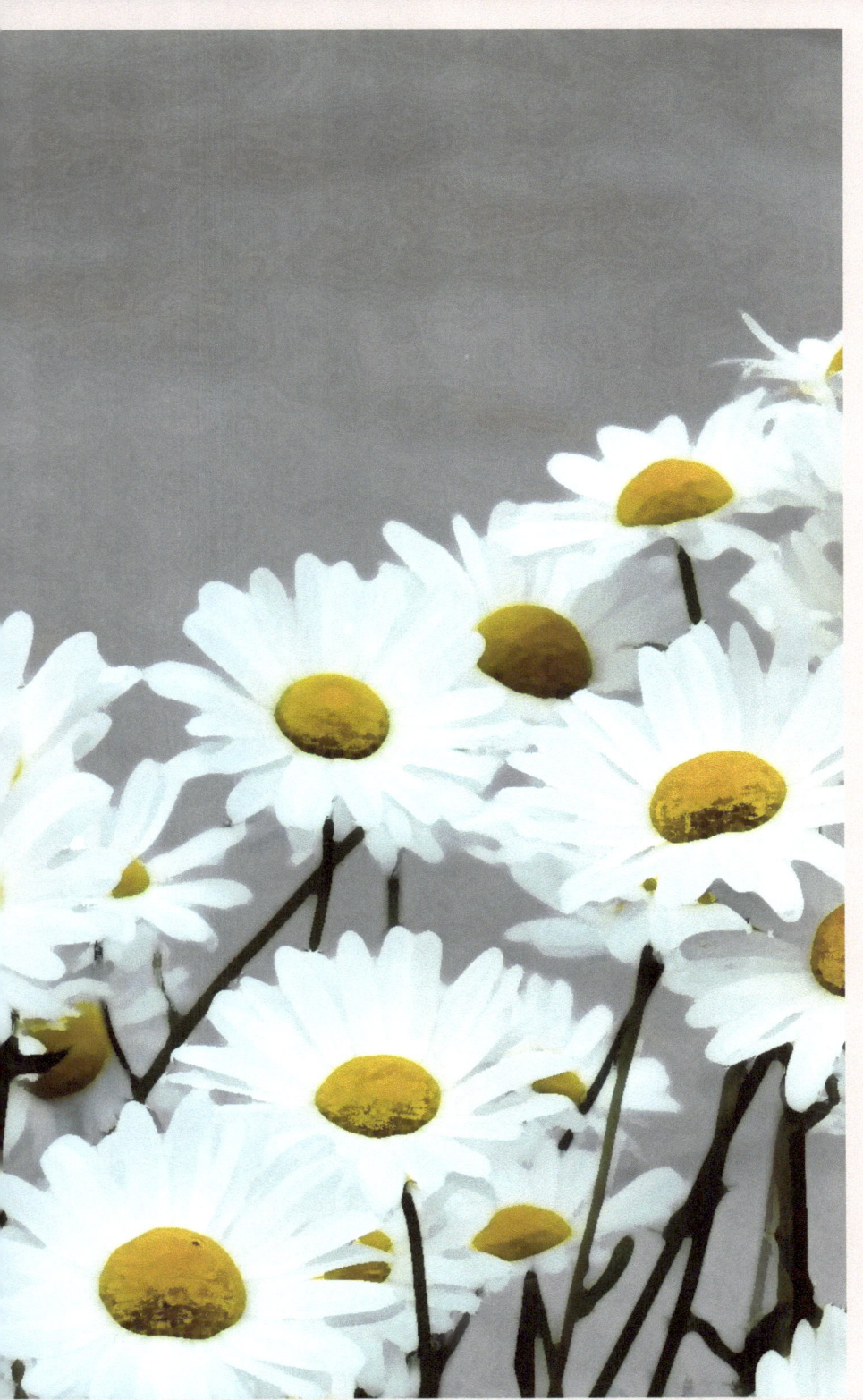

Pick Me!

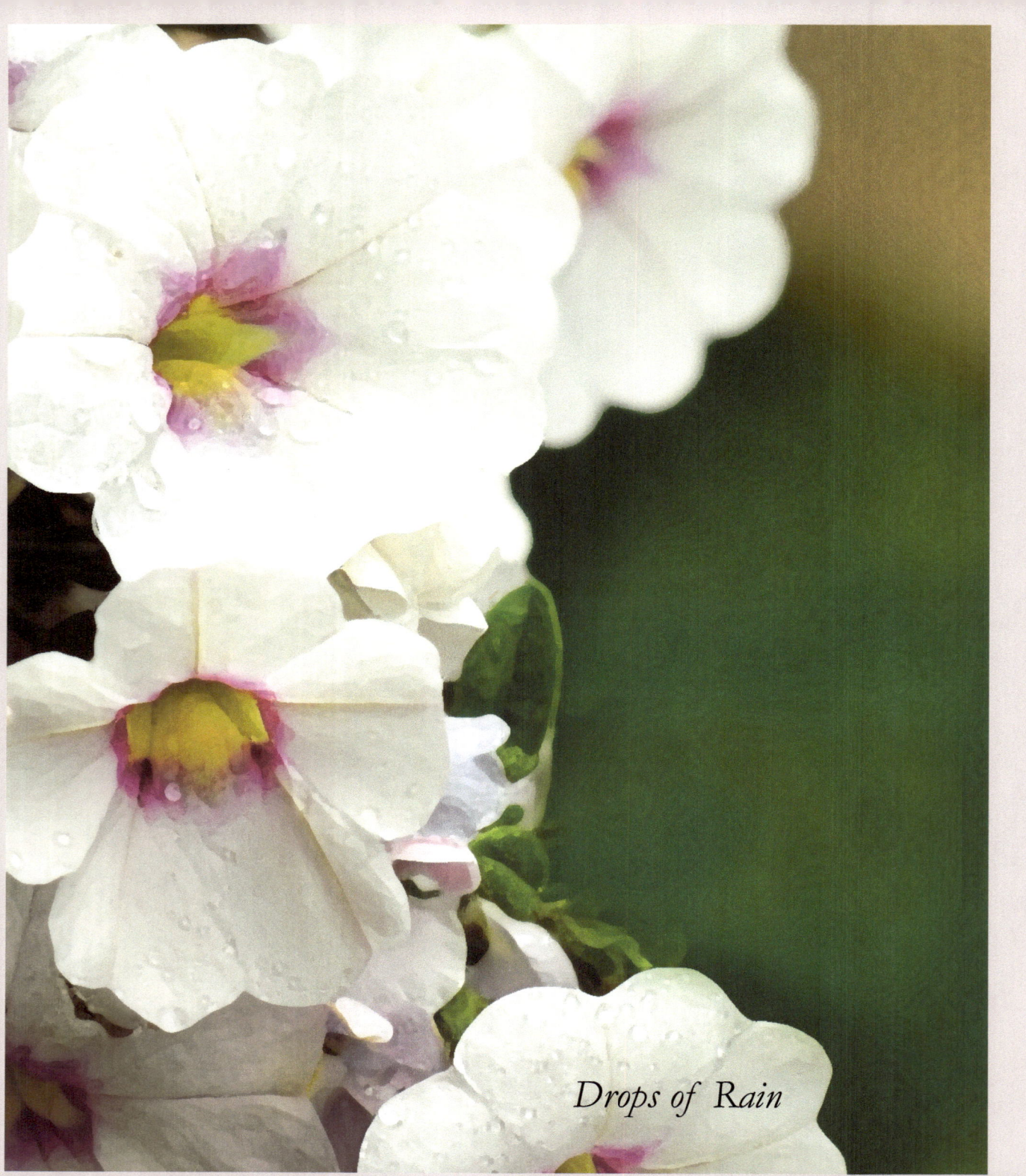

Drops of Rain

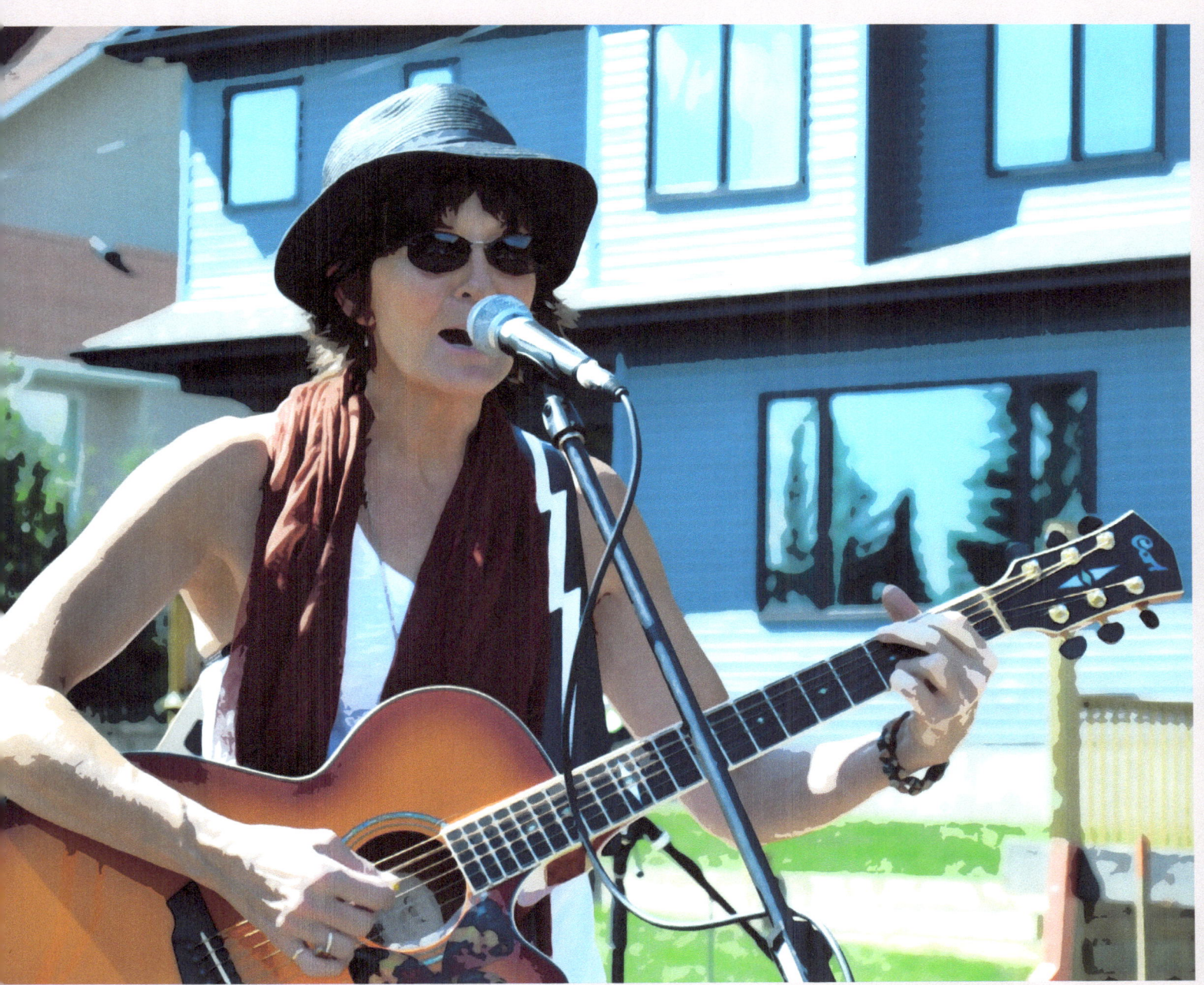

A Riverdale Songbird

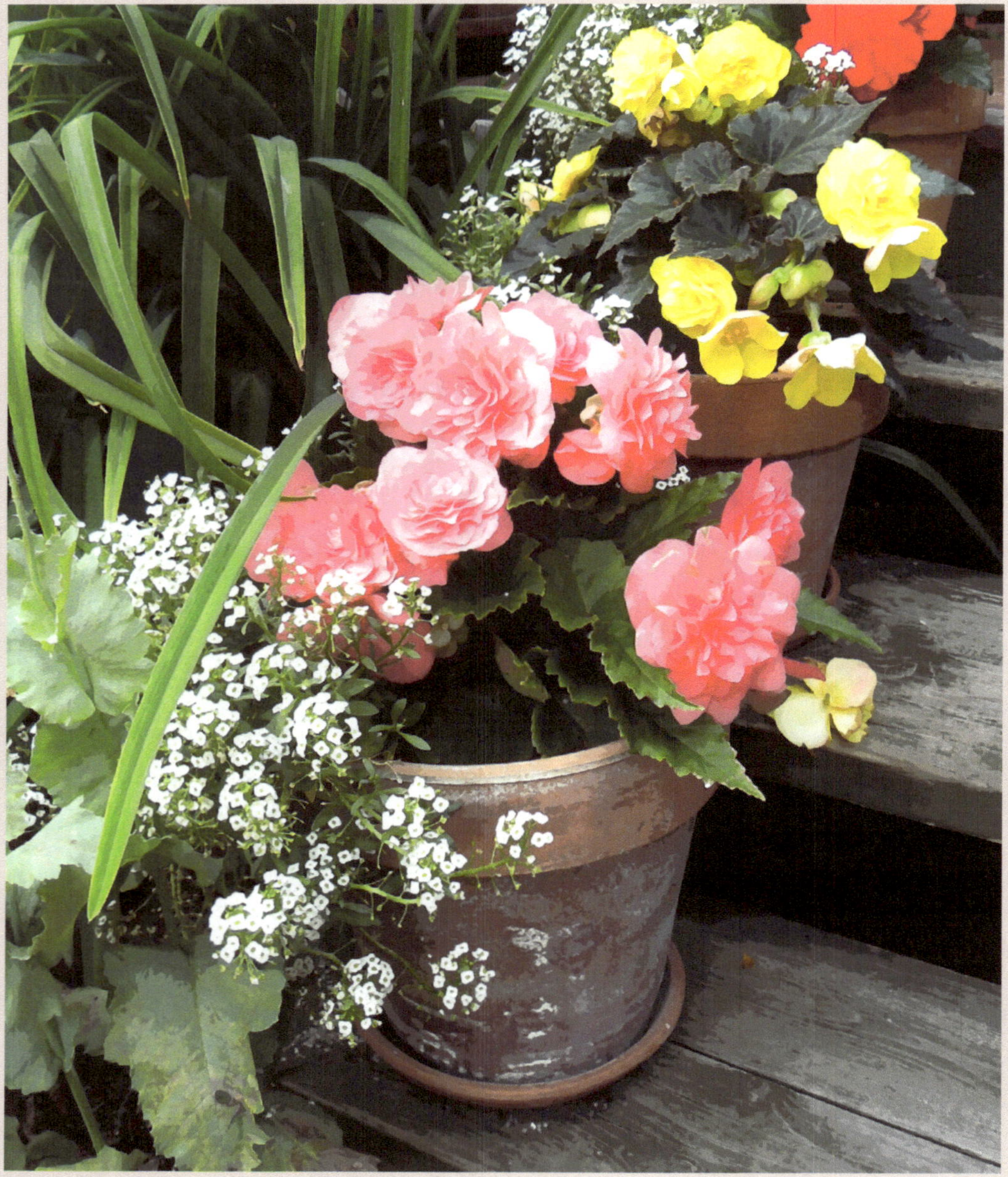

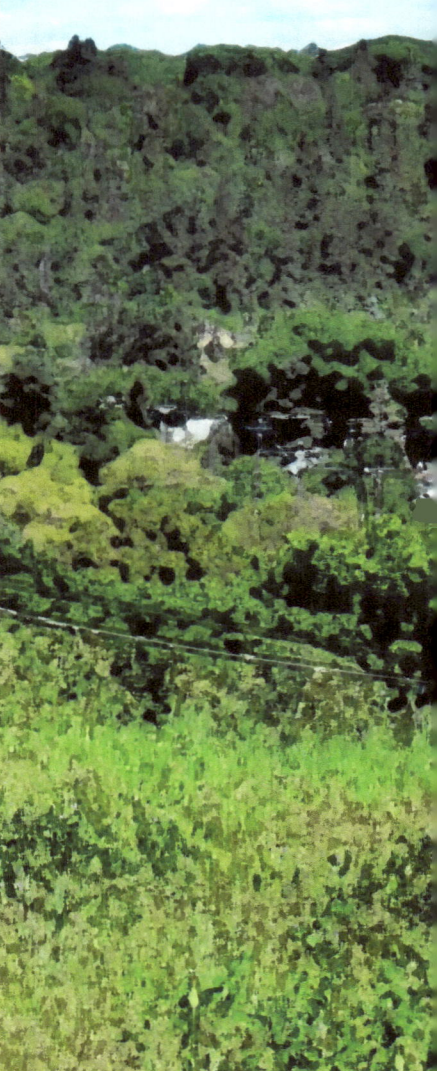

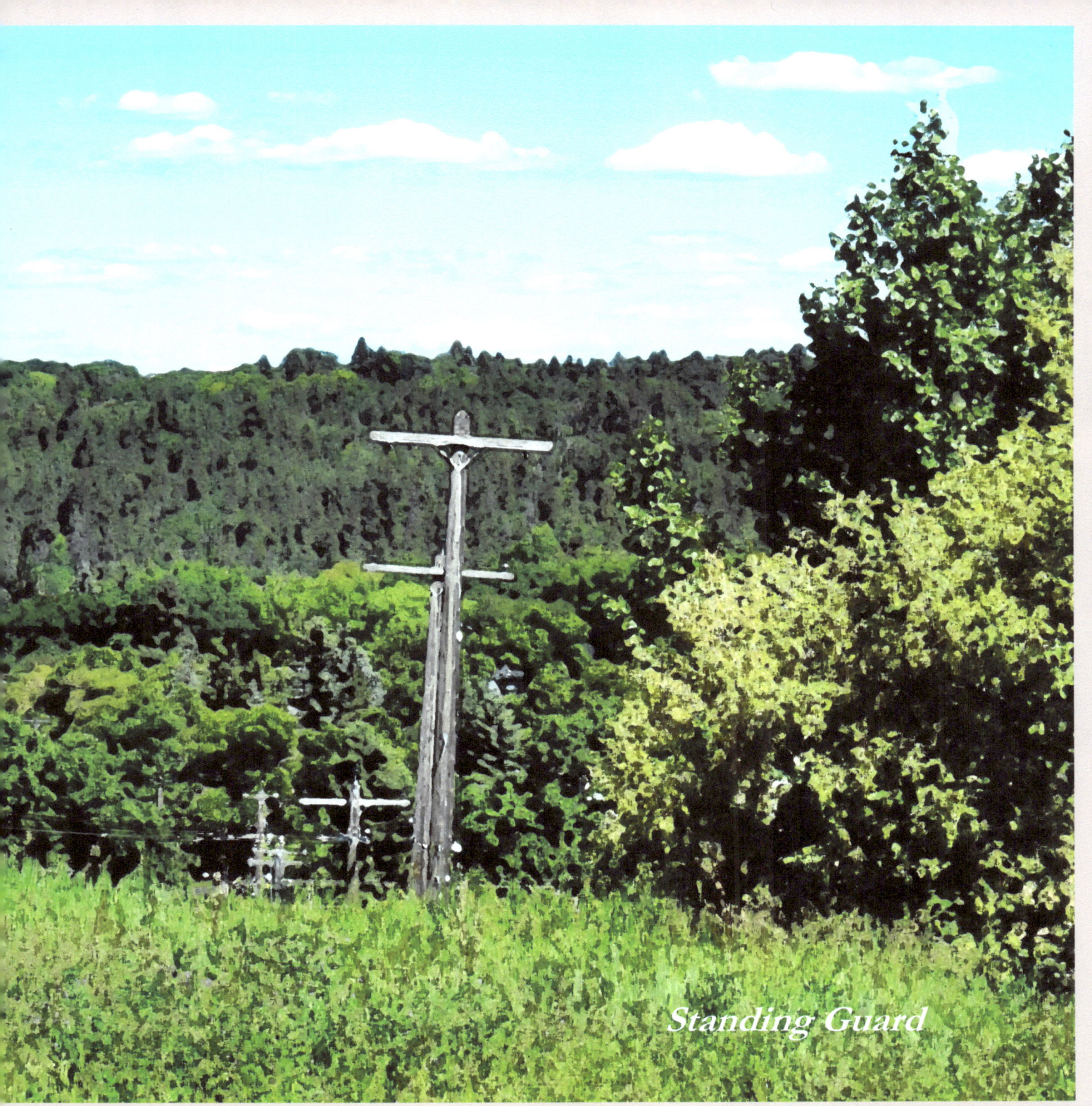

Standing Guard

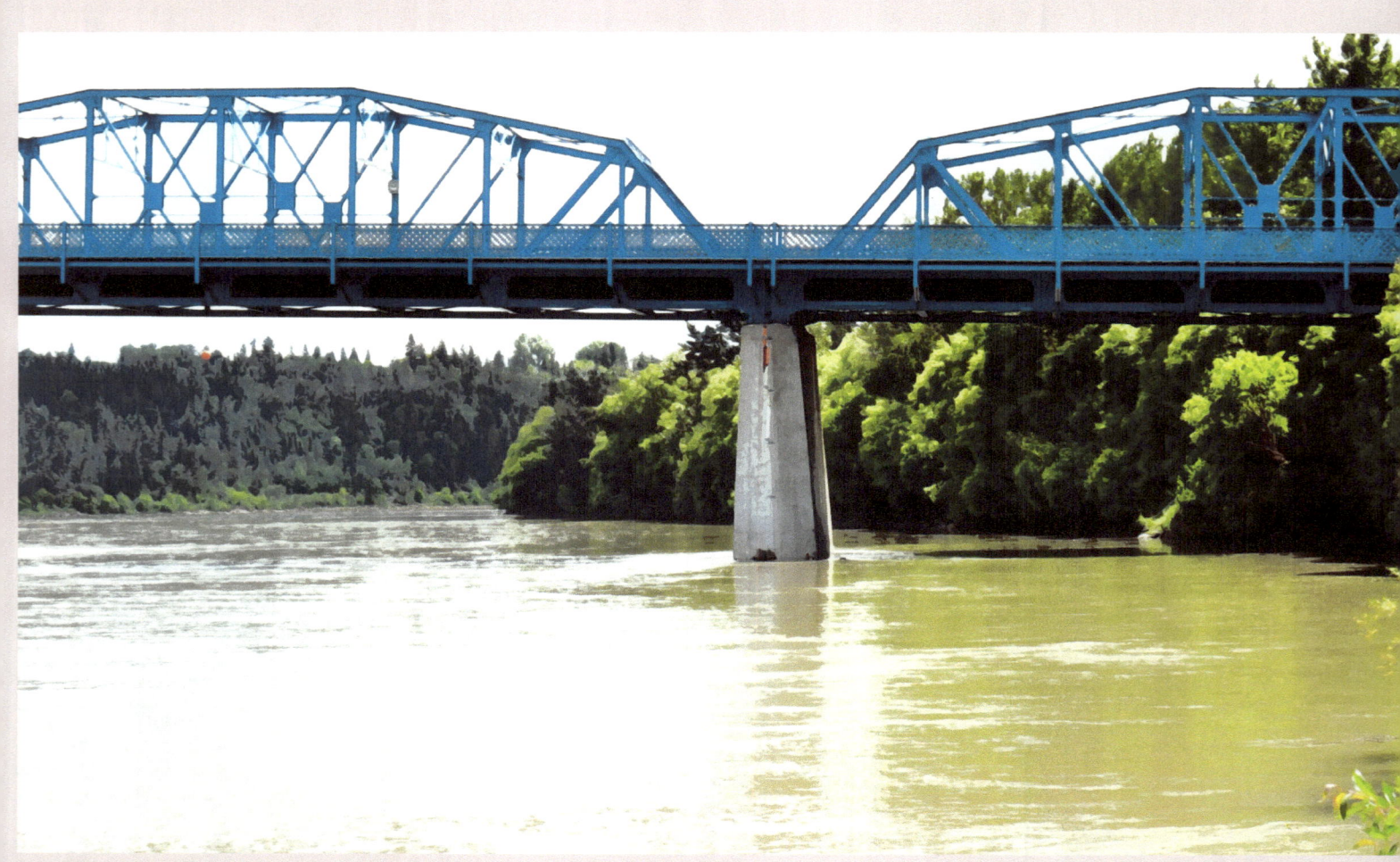

Dawson Bridge

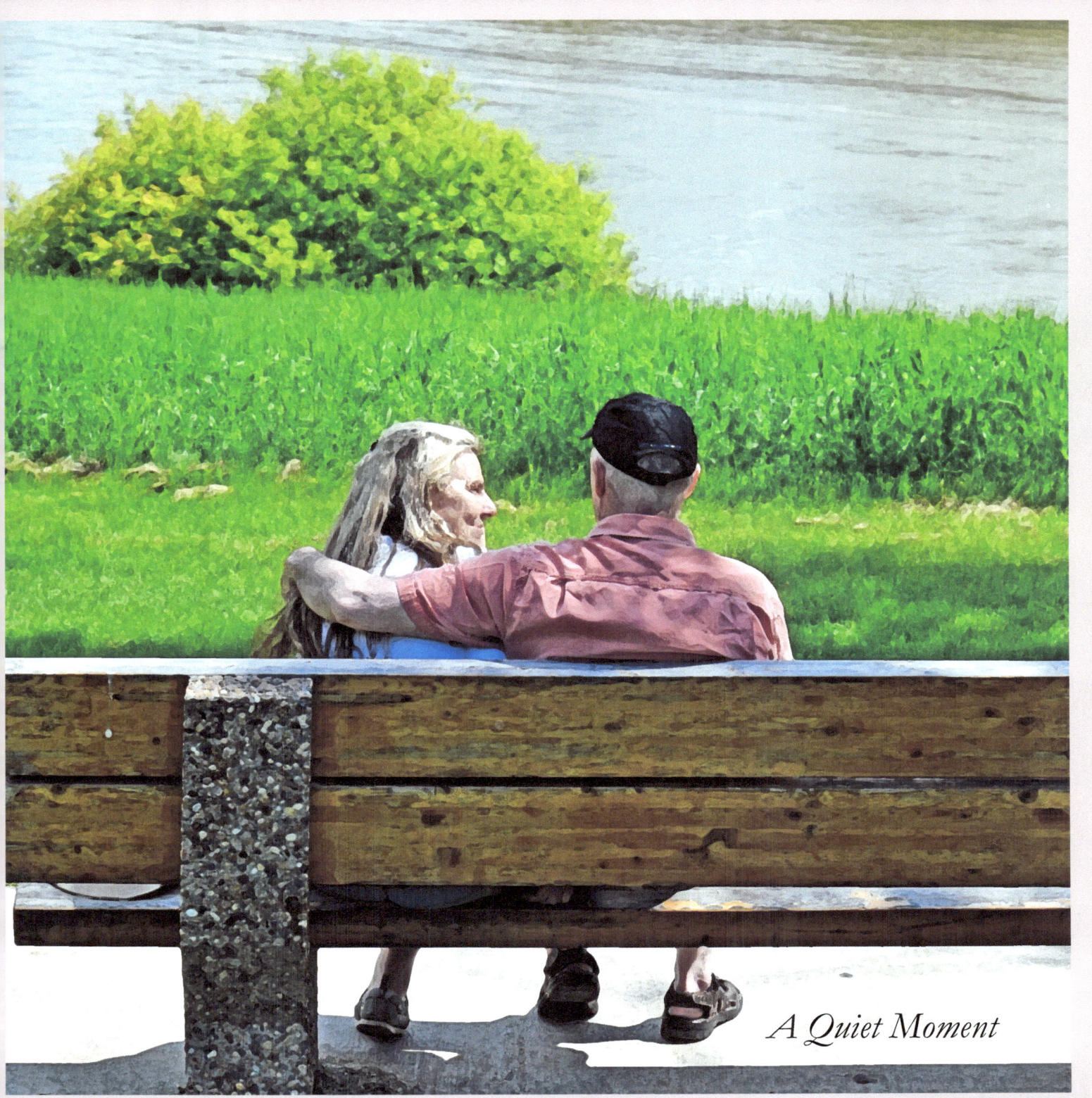

A Quiet Moment

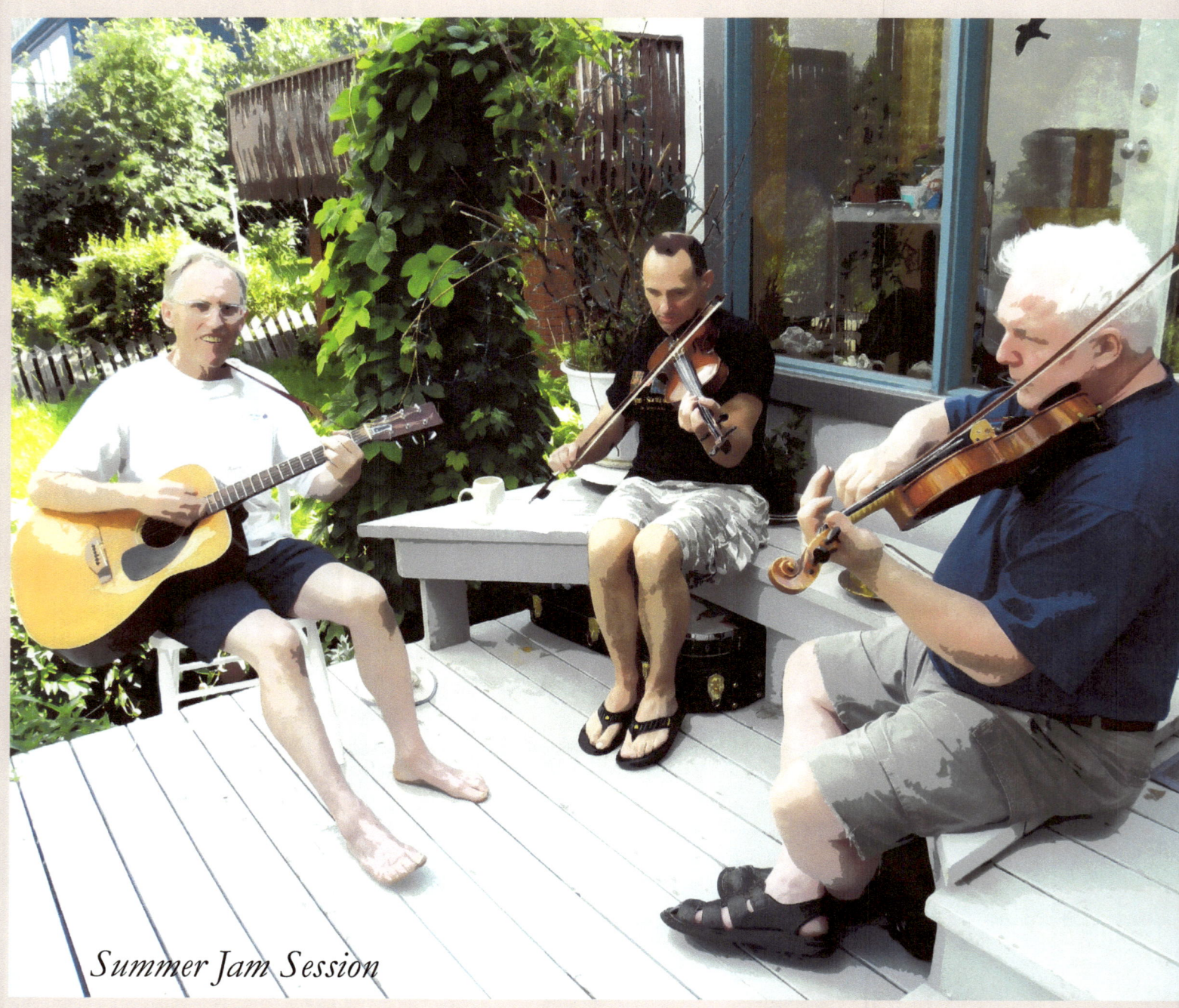

Summer Jam Session

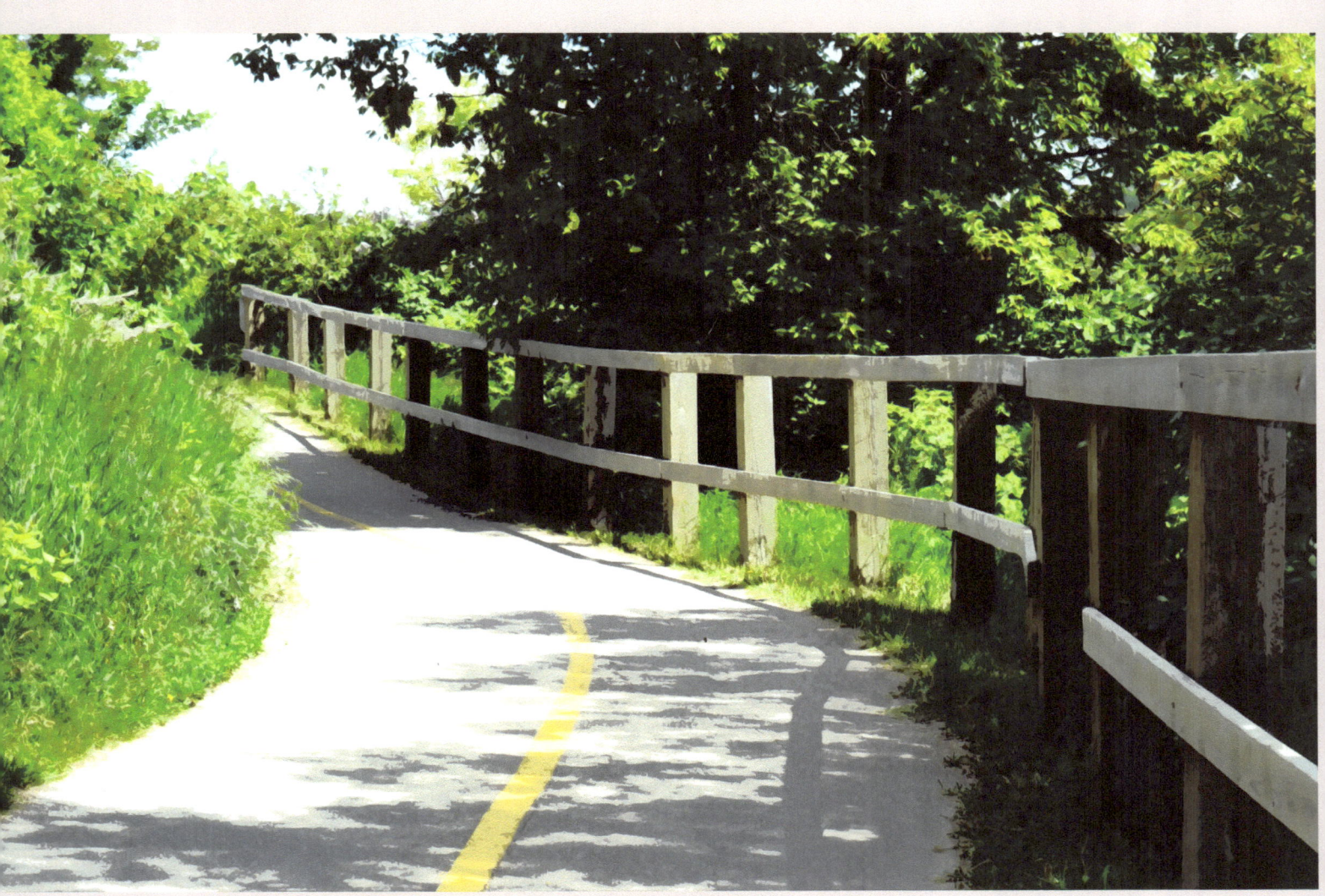

Who's around the corner?

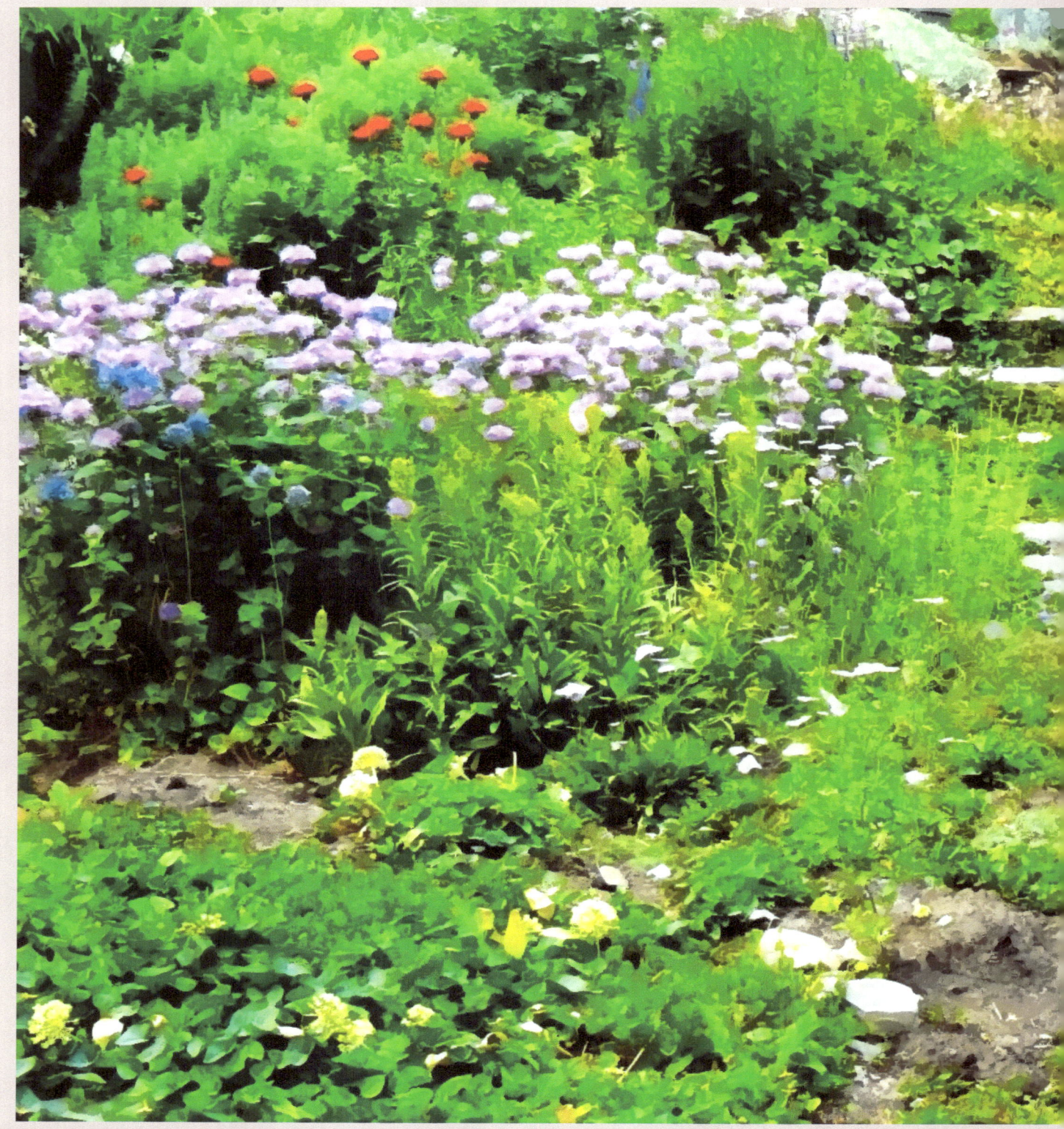

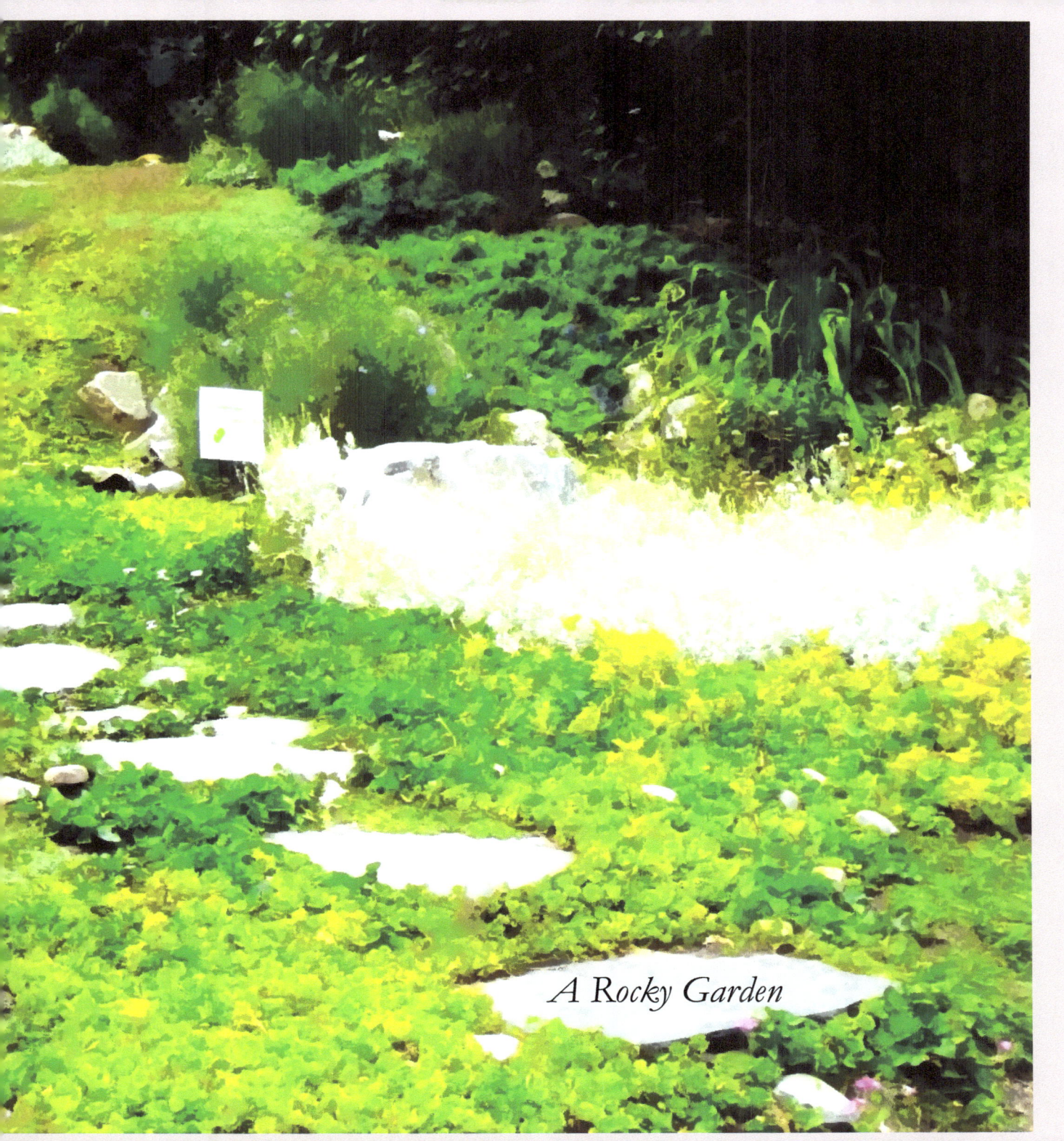

A Rocky Garden

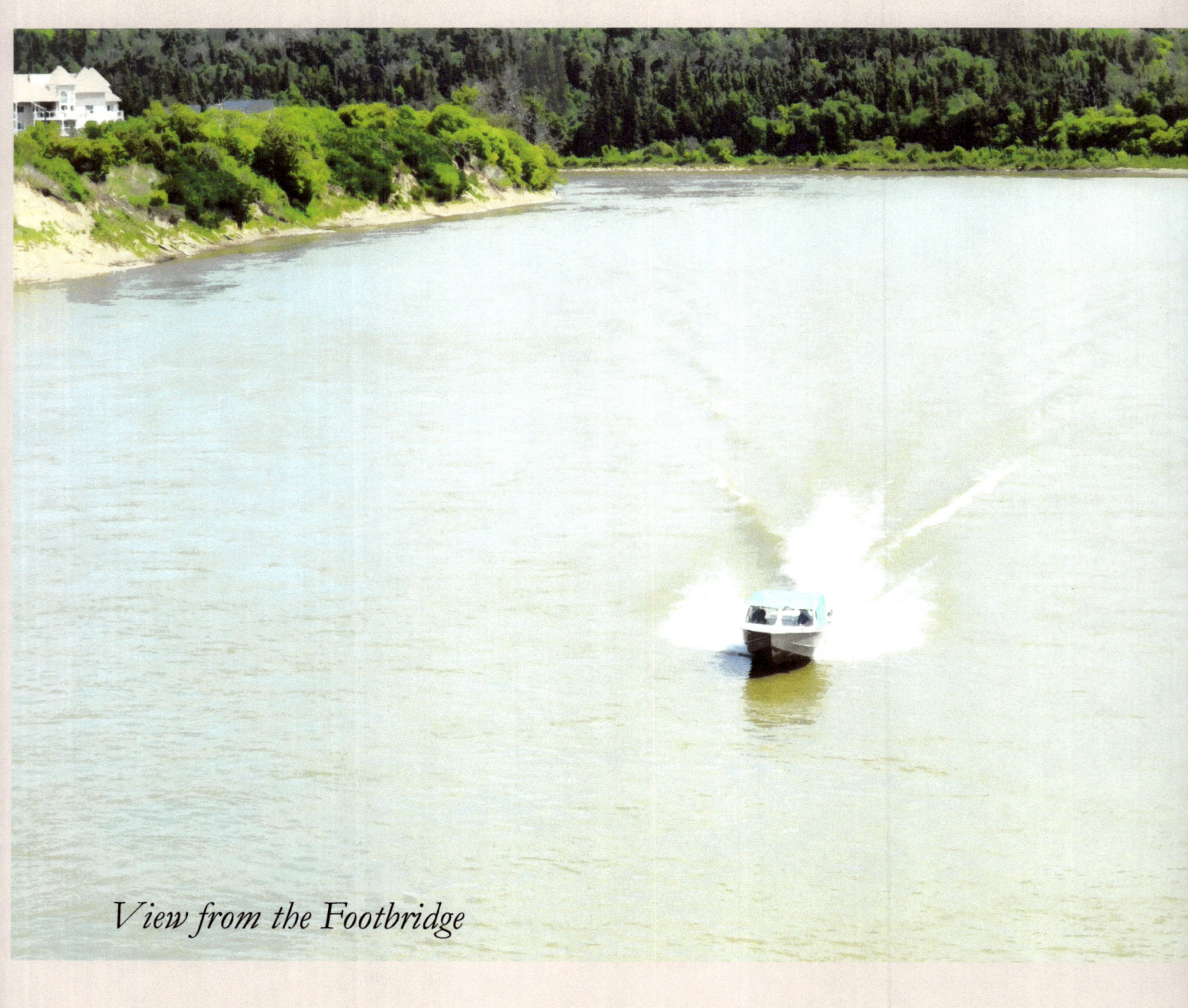

View from the Footbridge

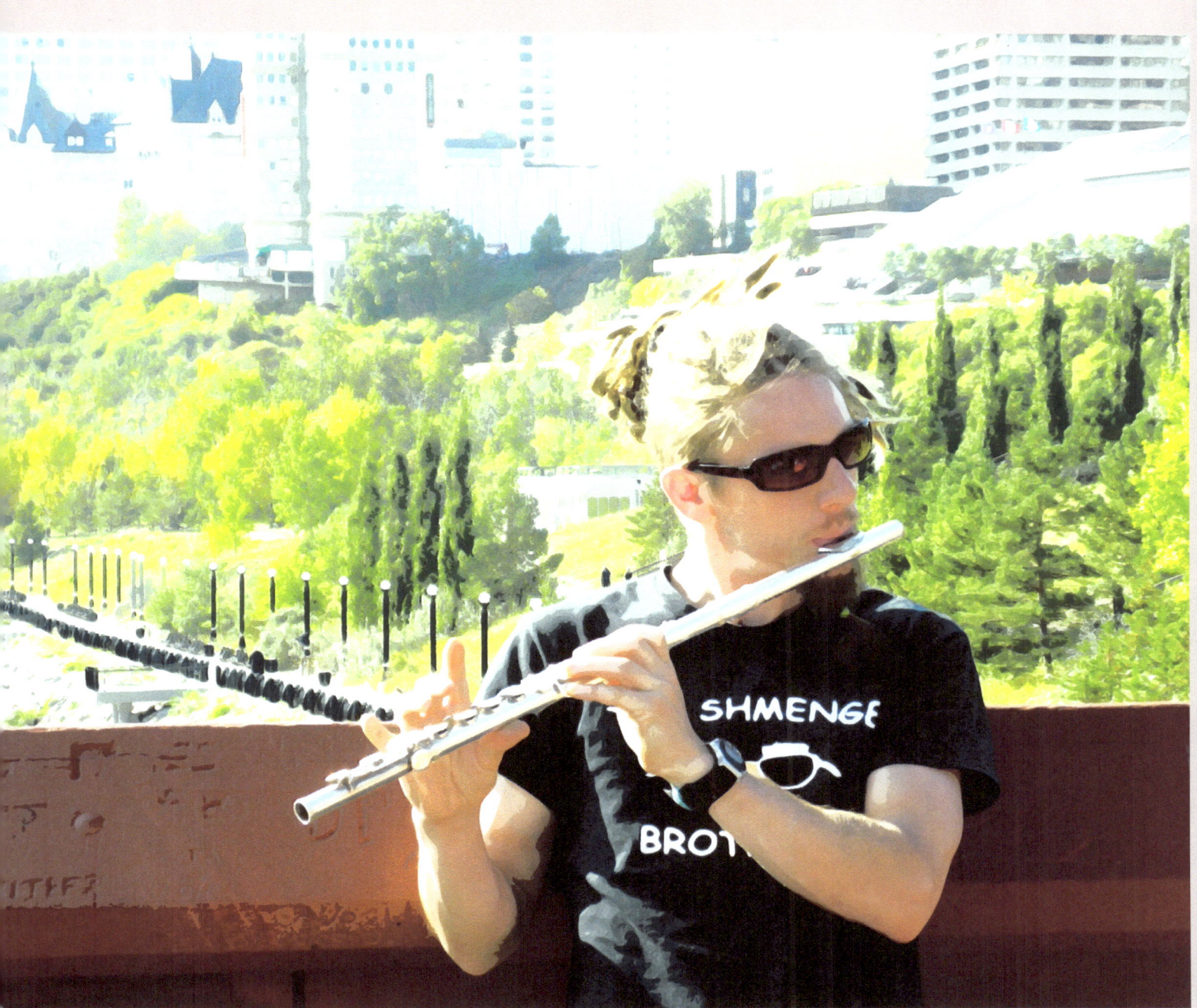

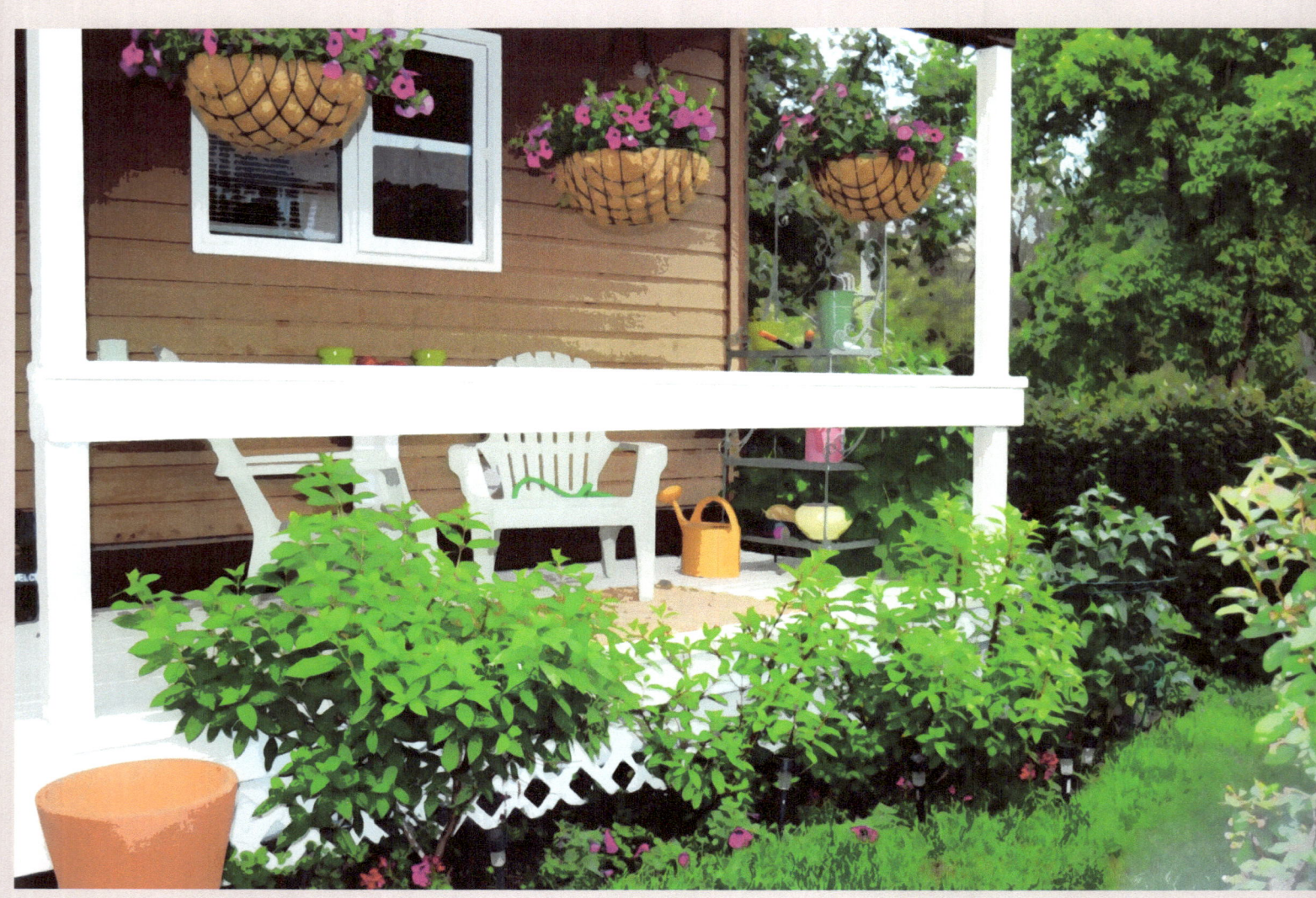

Old Country Porch

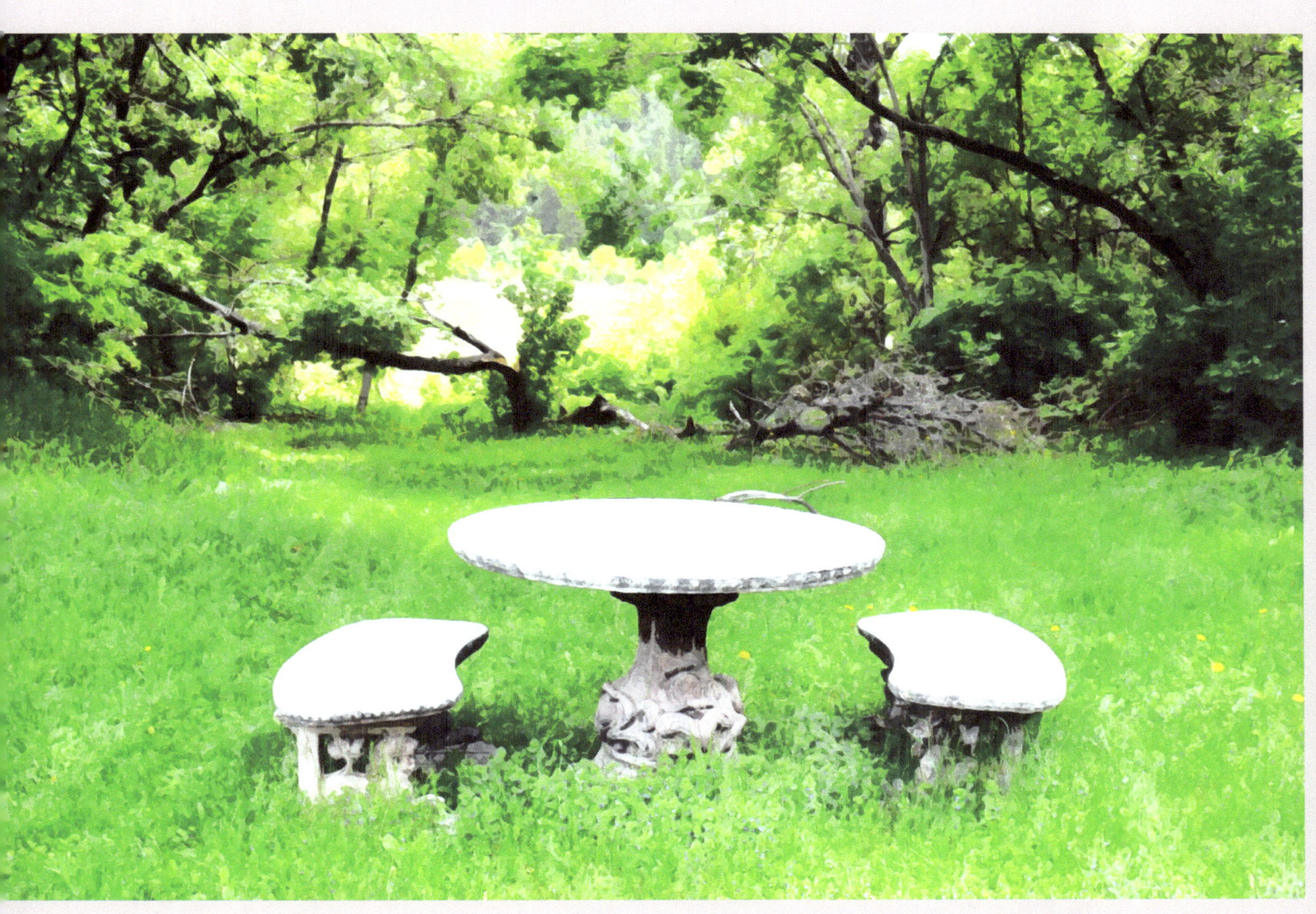

Resting Spot Near the River

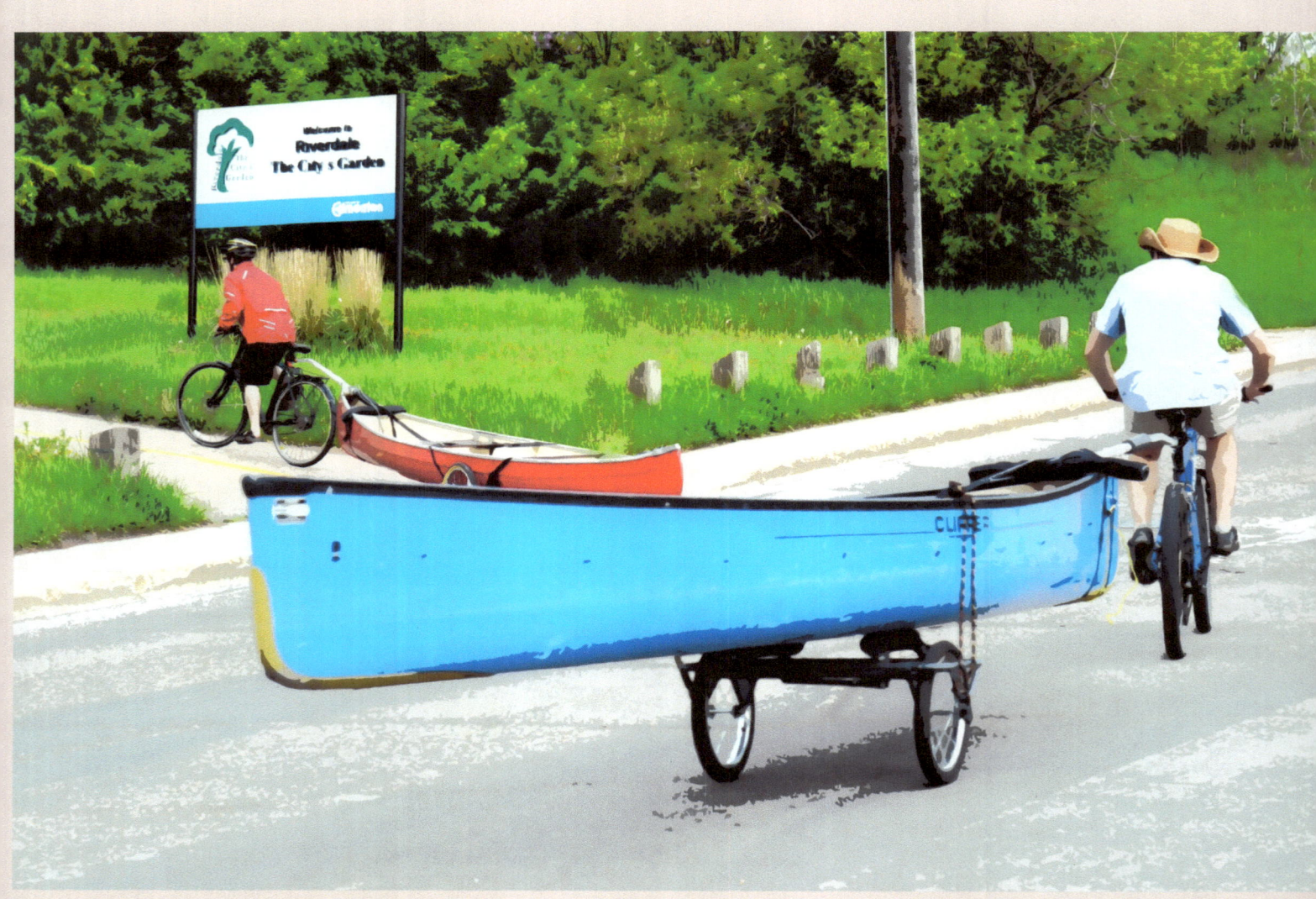

Canoes on Cameron

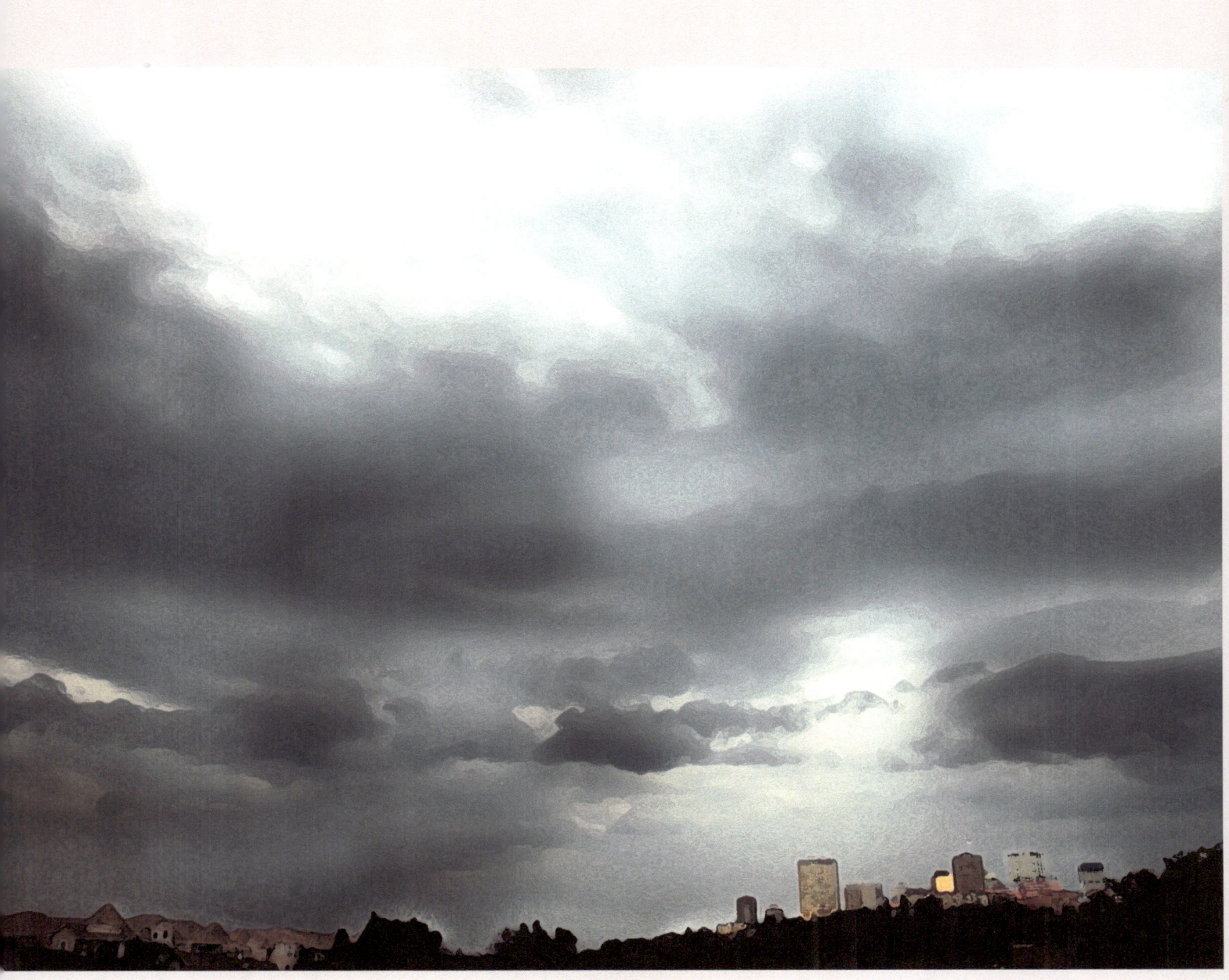

Thunderstruck

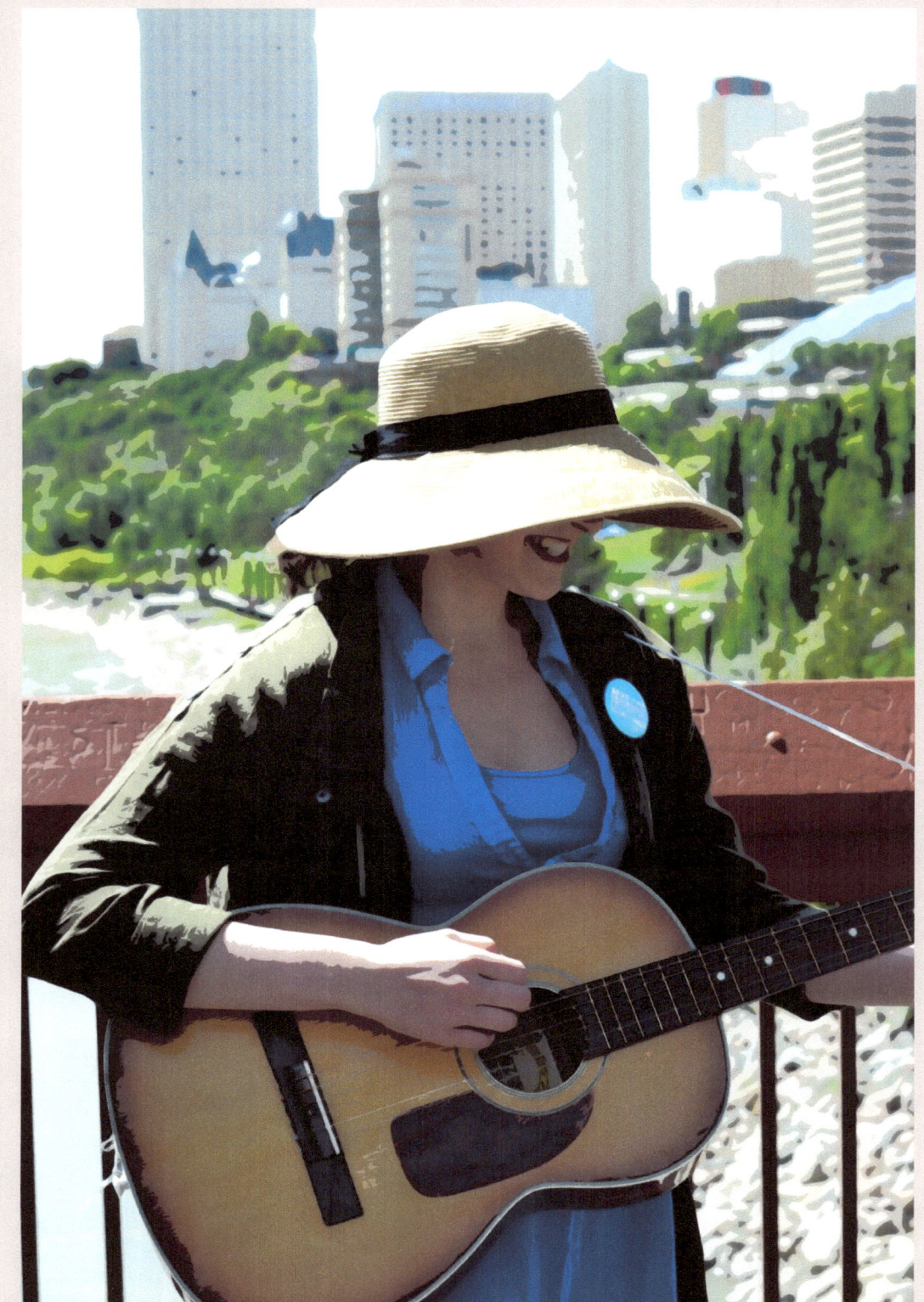

Singing
a Tune

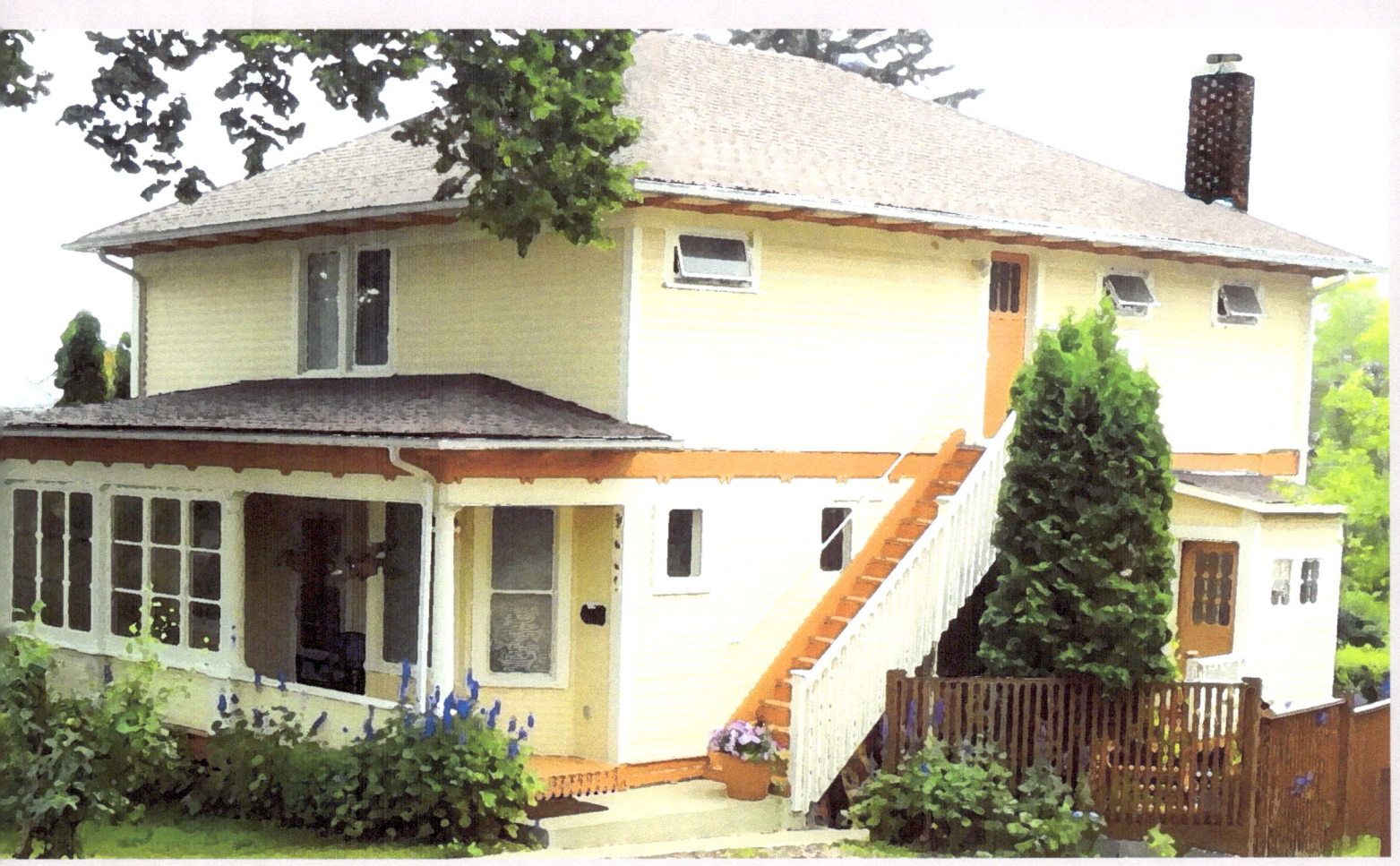

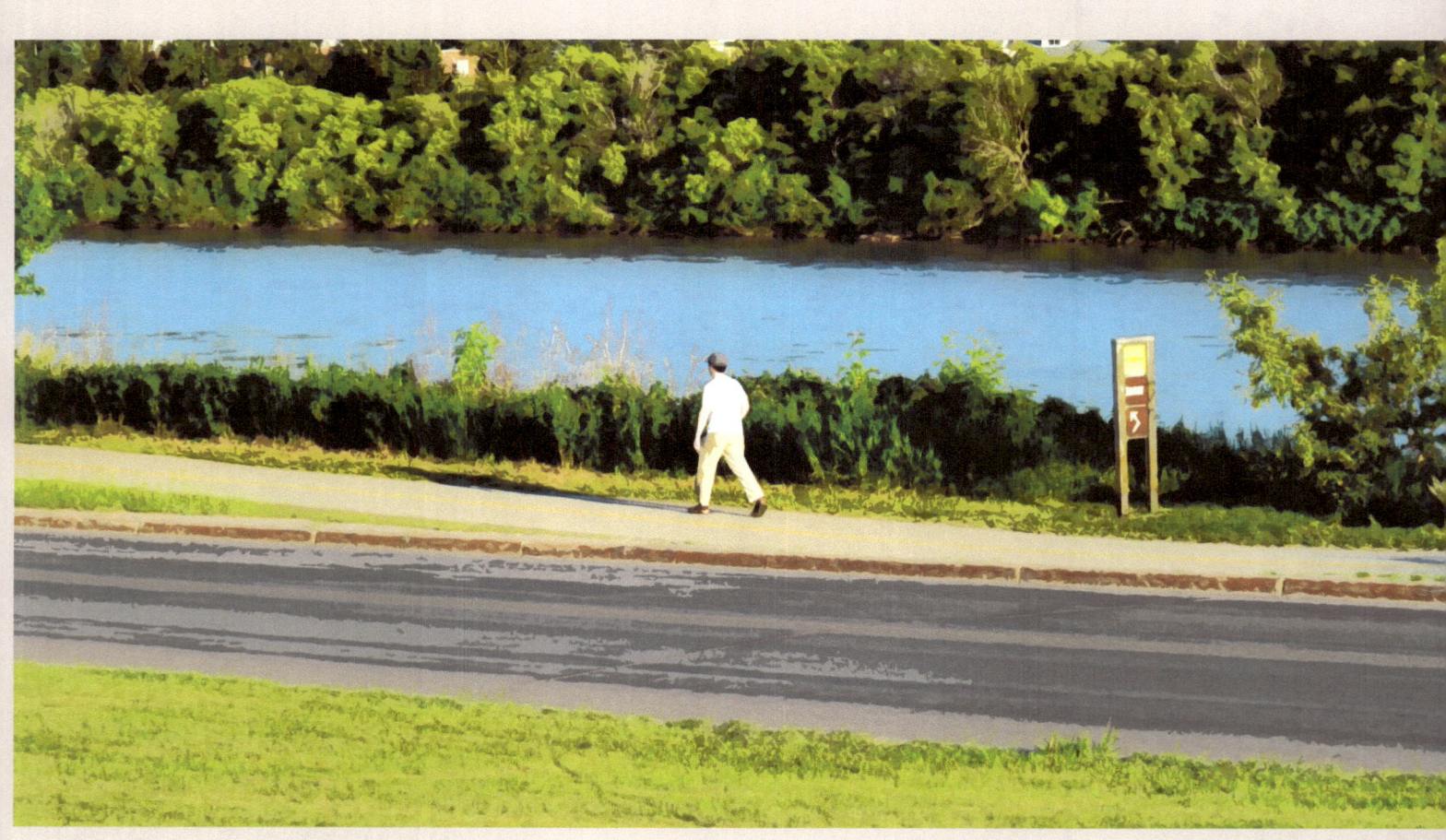

Out for an Evening Walk

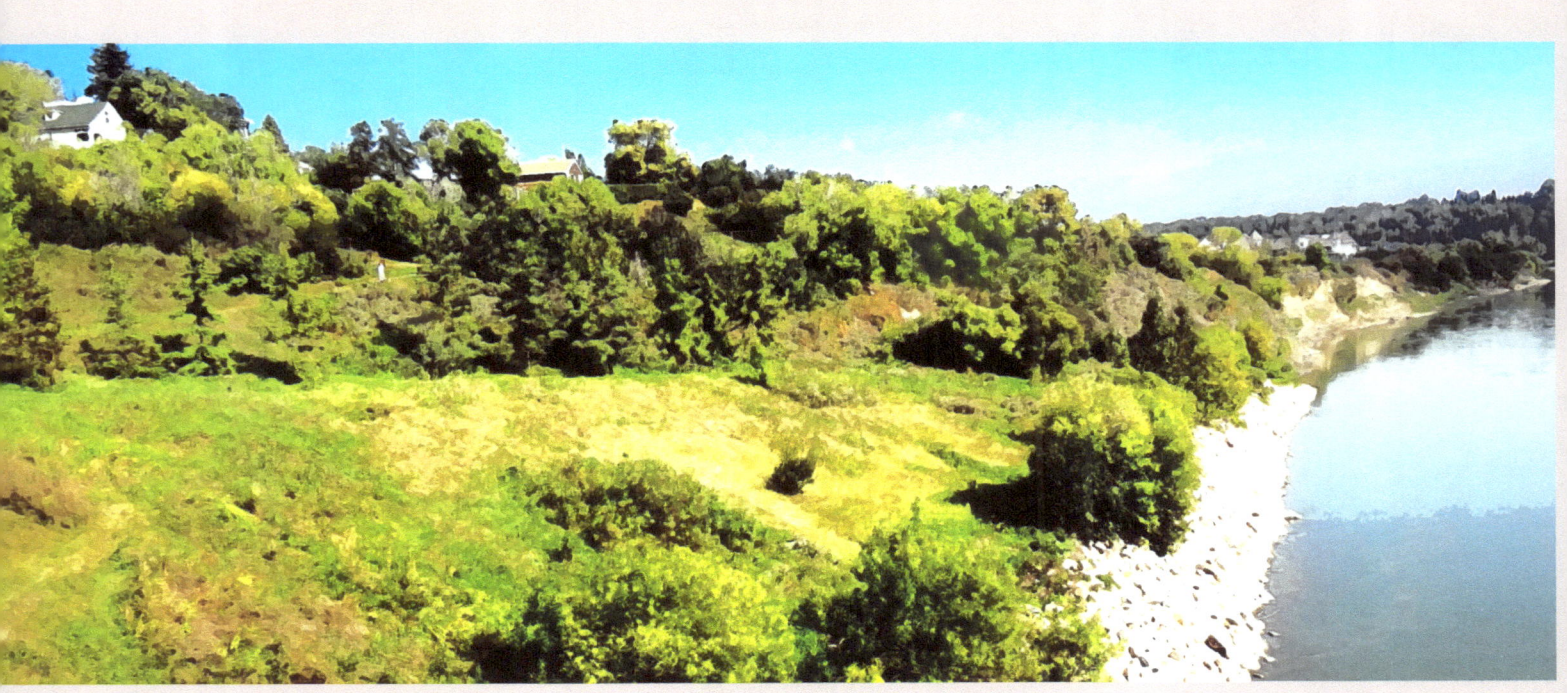

By the Shore

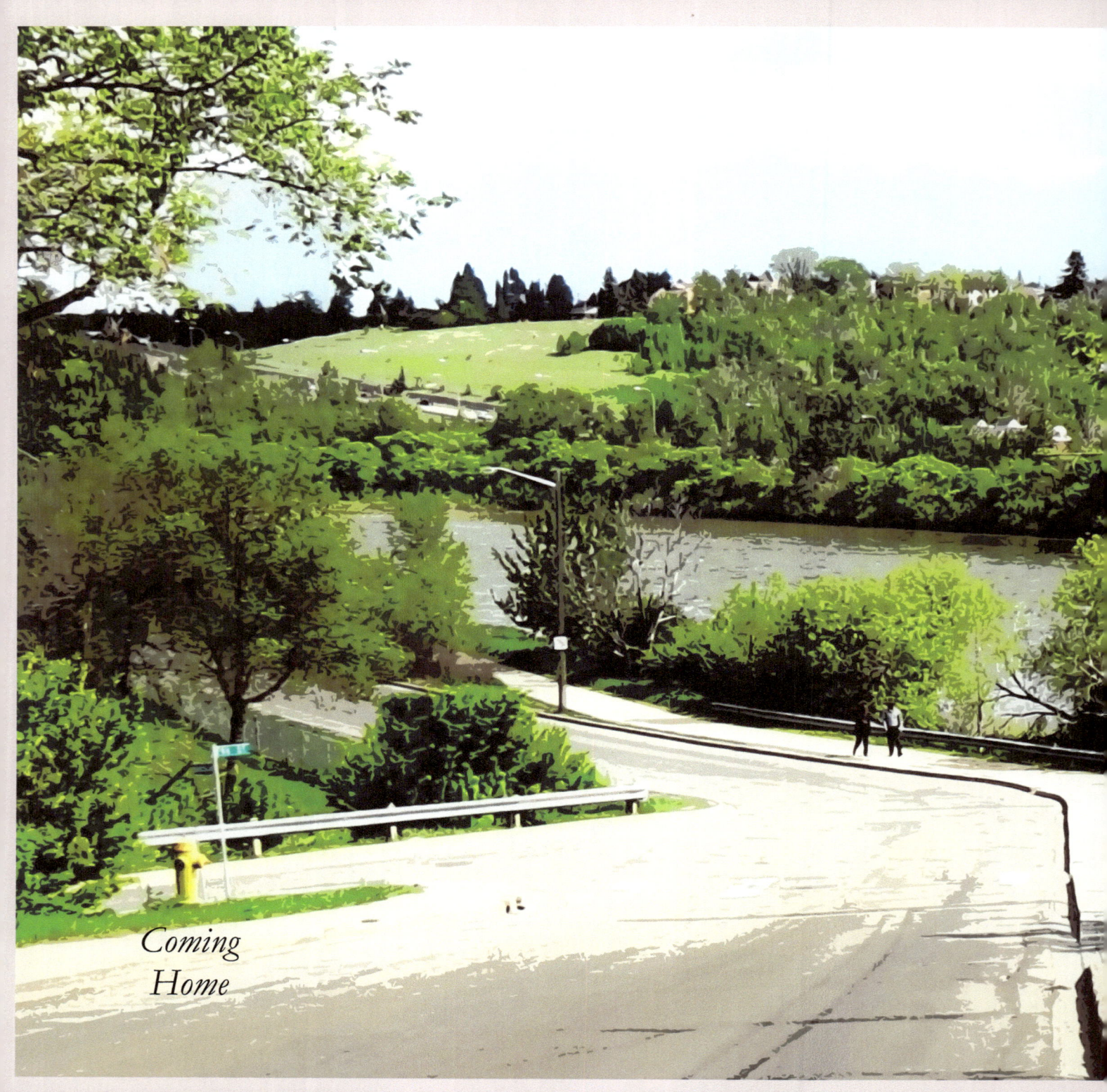

*Coming
Home*

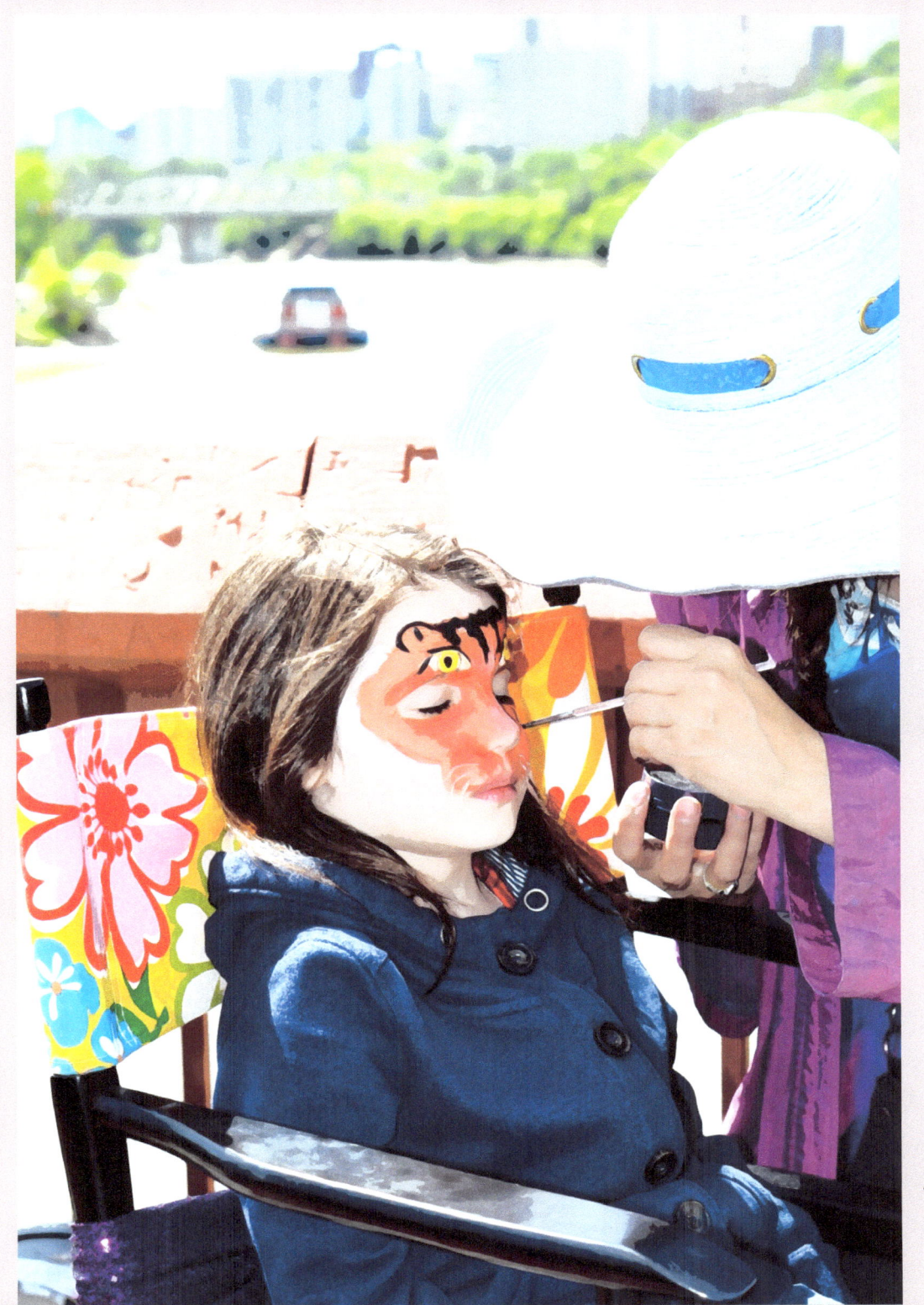

*Facing
the Tiger*

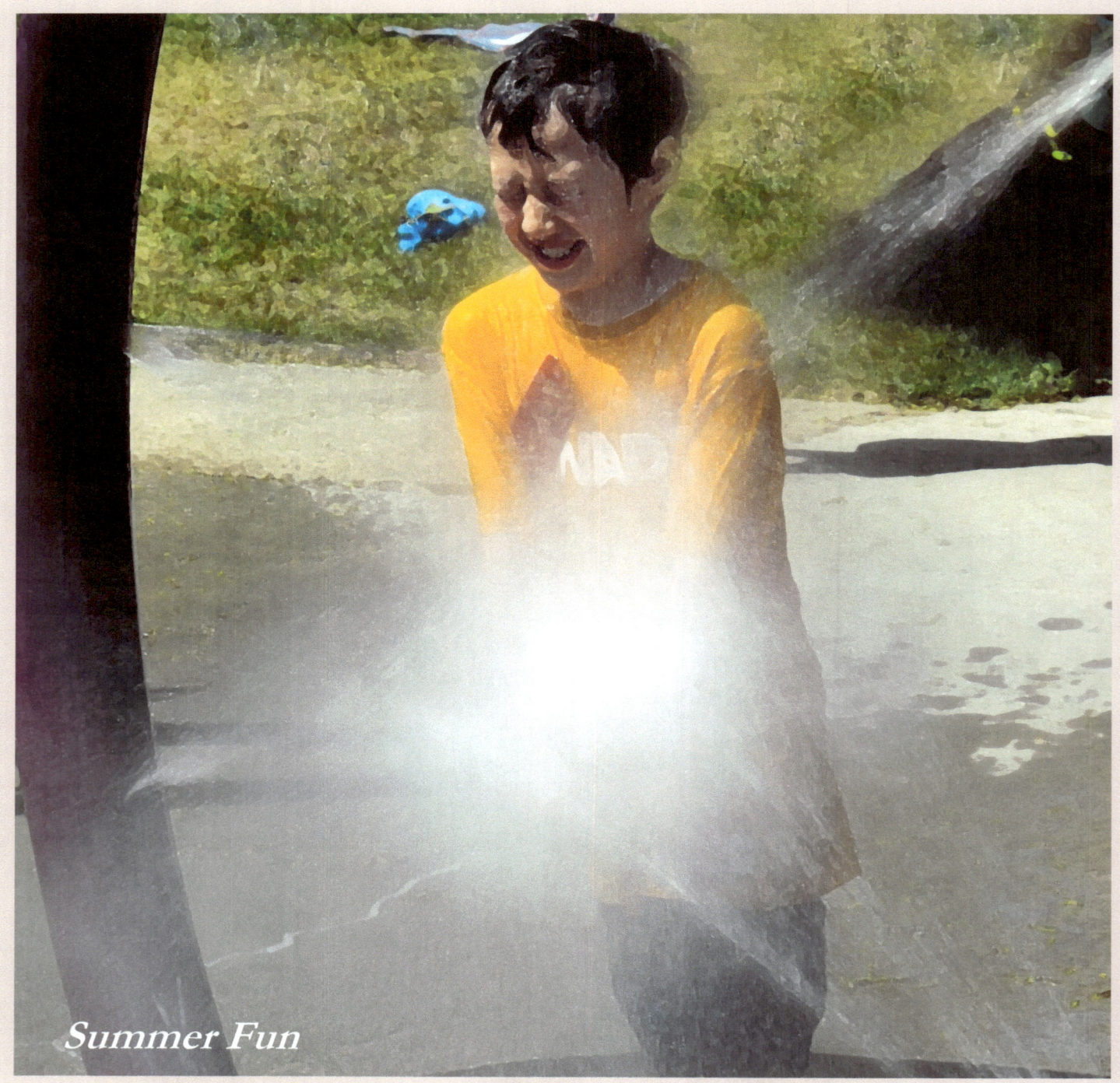

Summer Fun

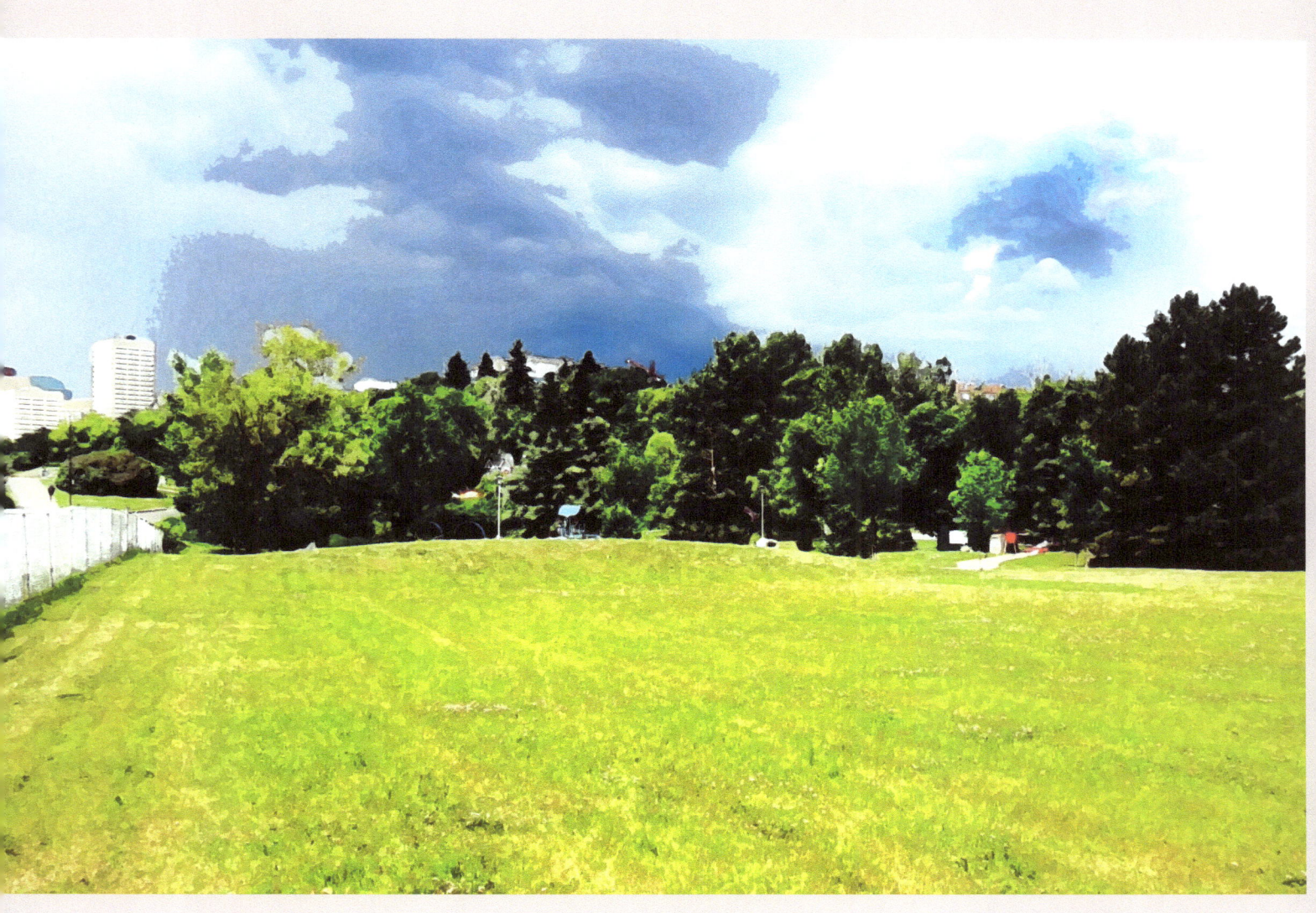

Storm Brewing

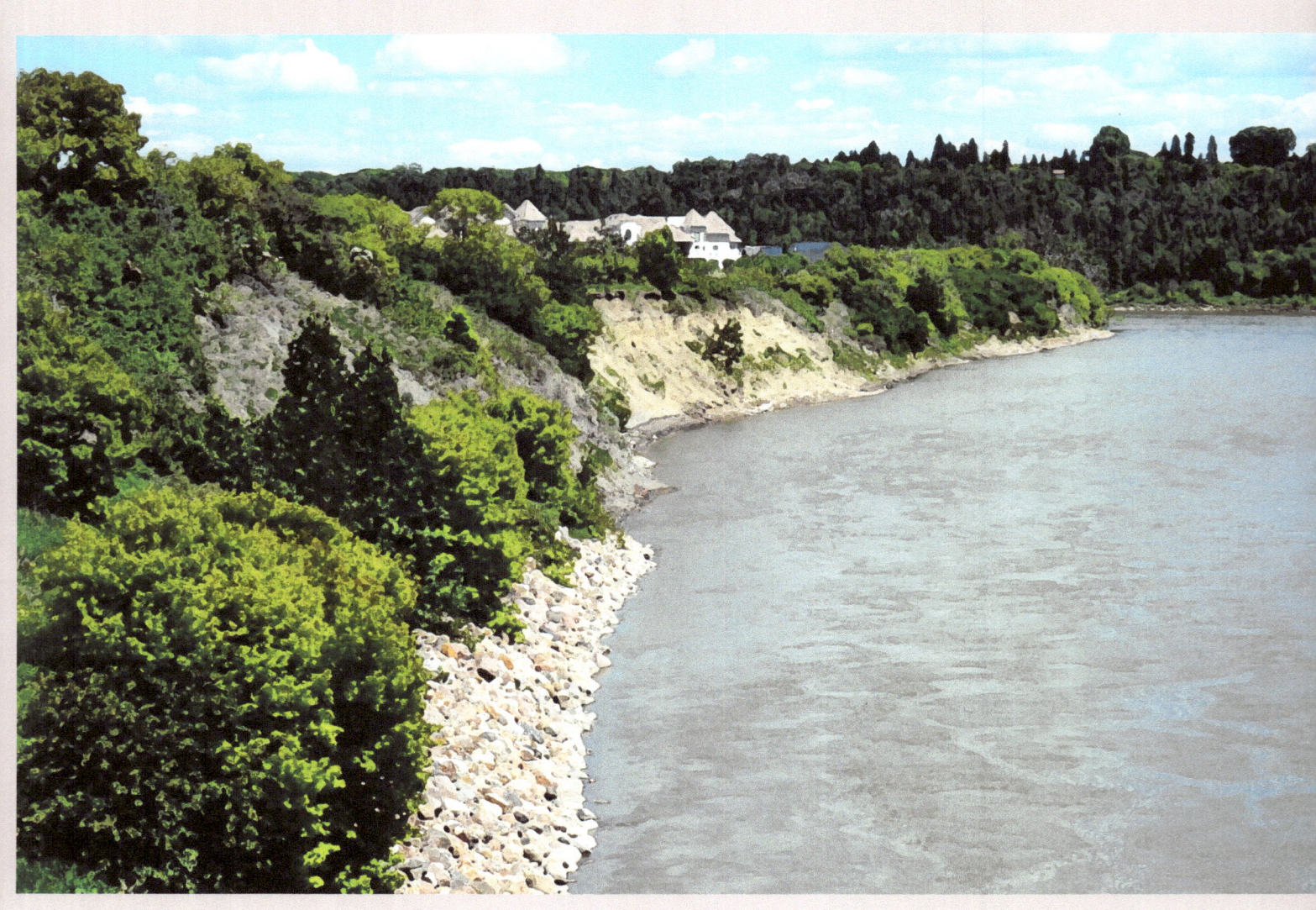

River Cliffs

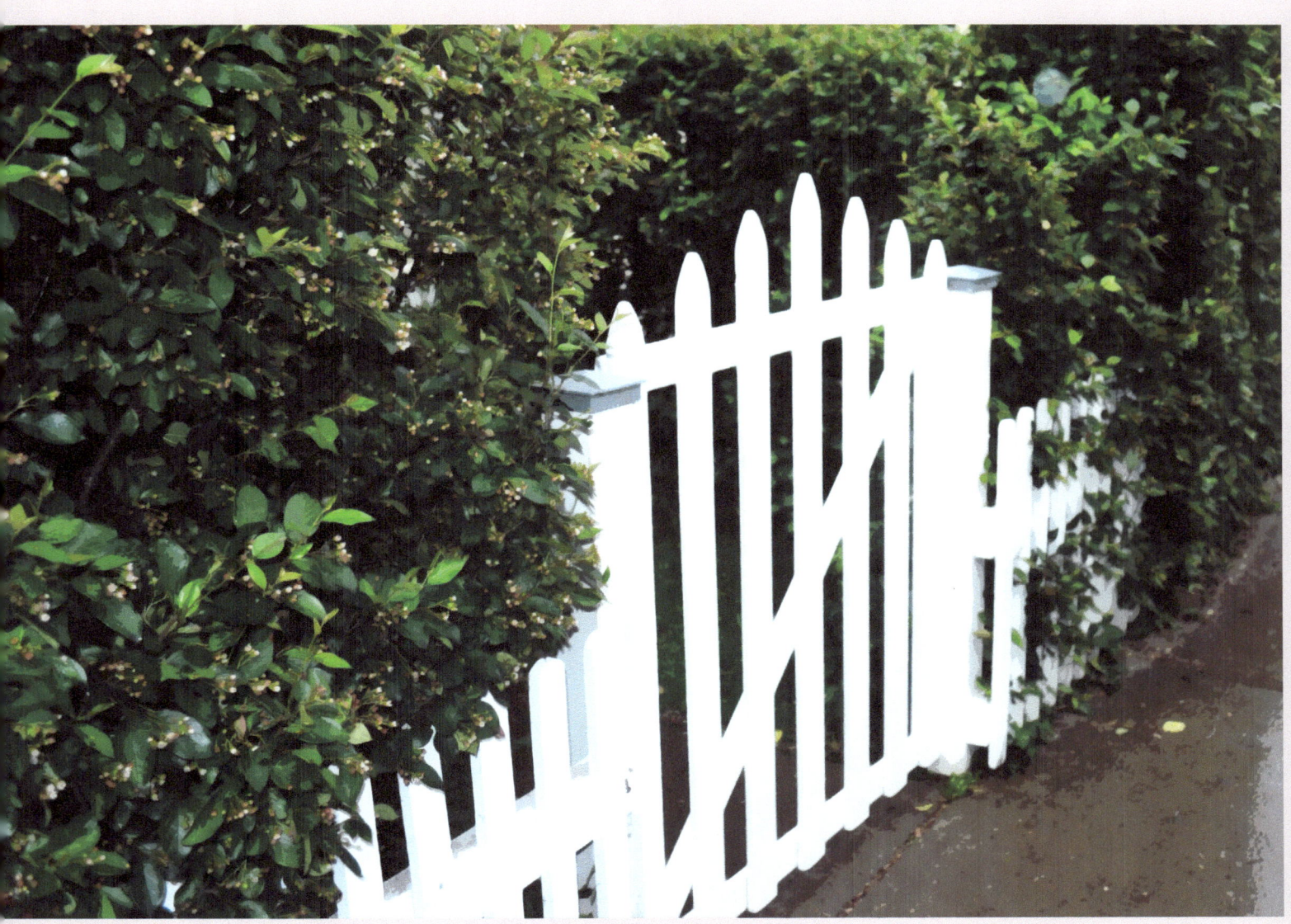

White Picket Fence

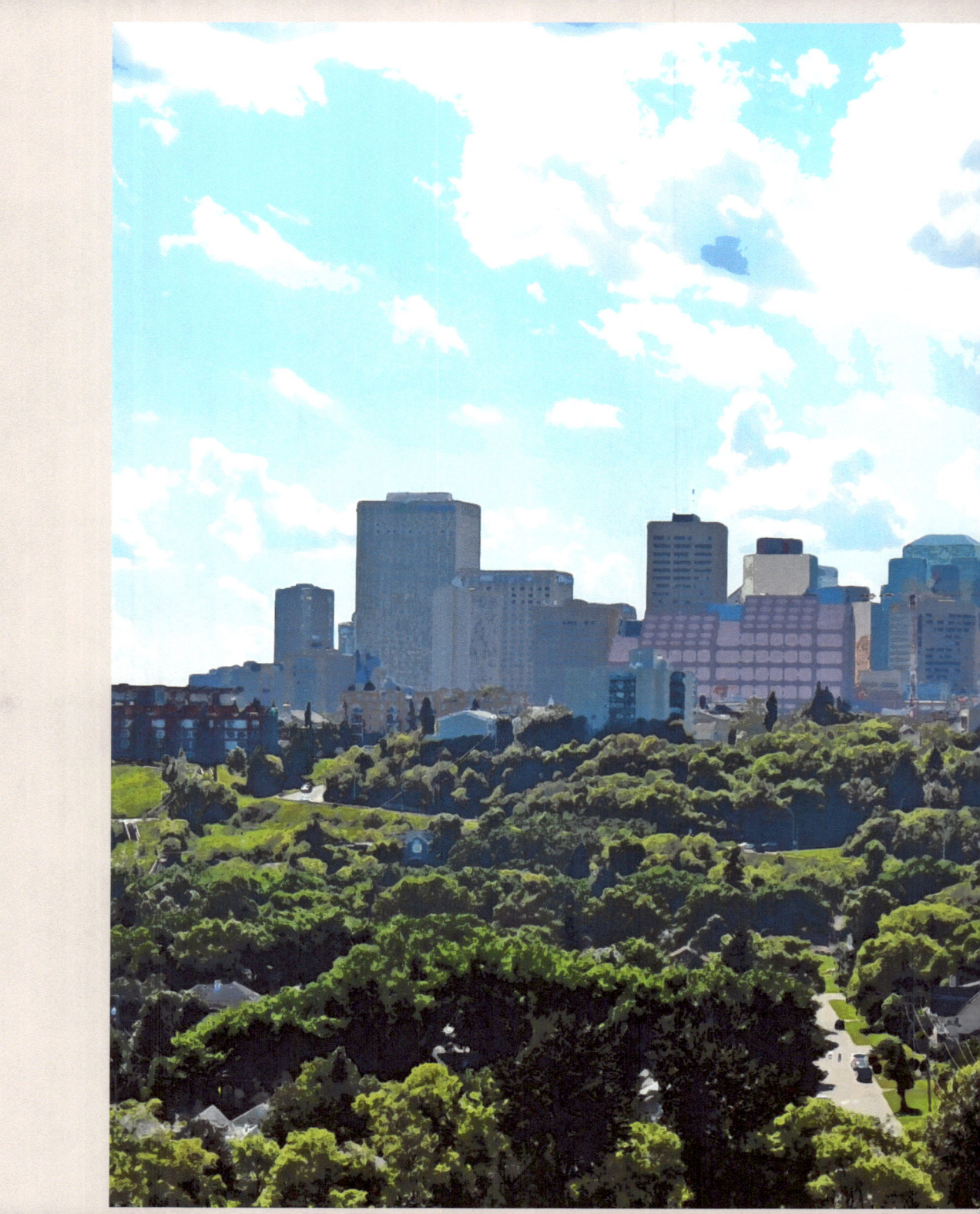

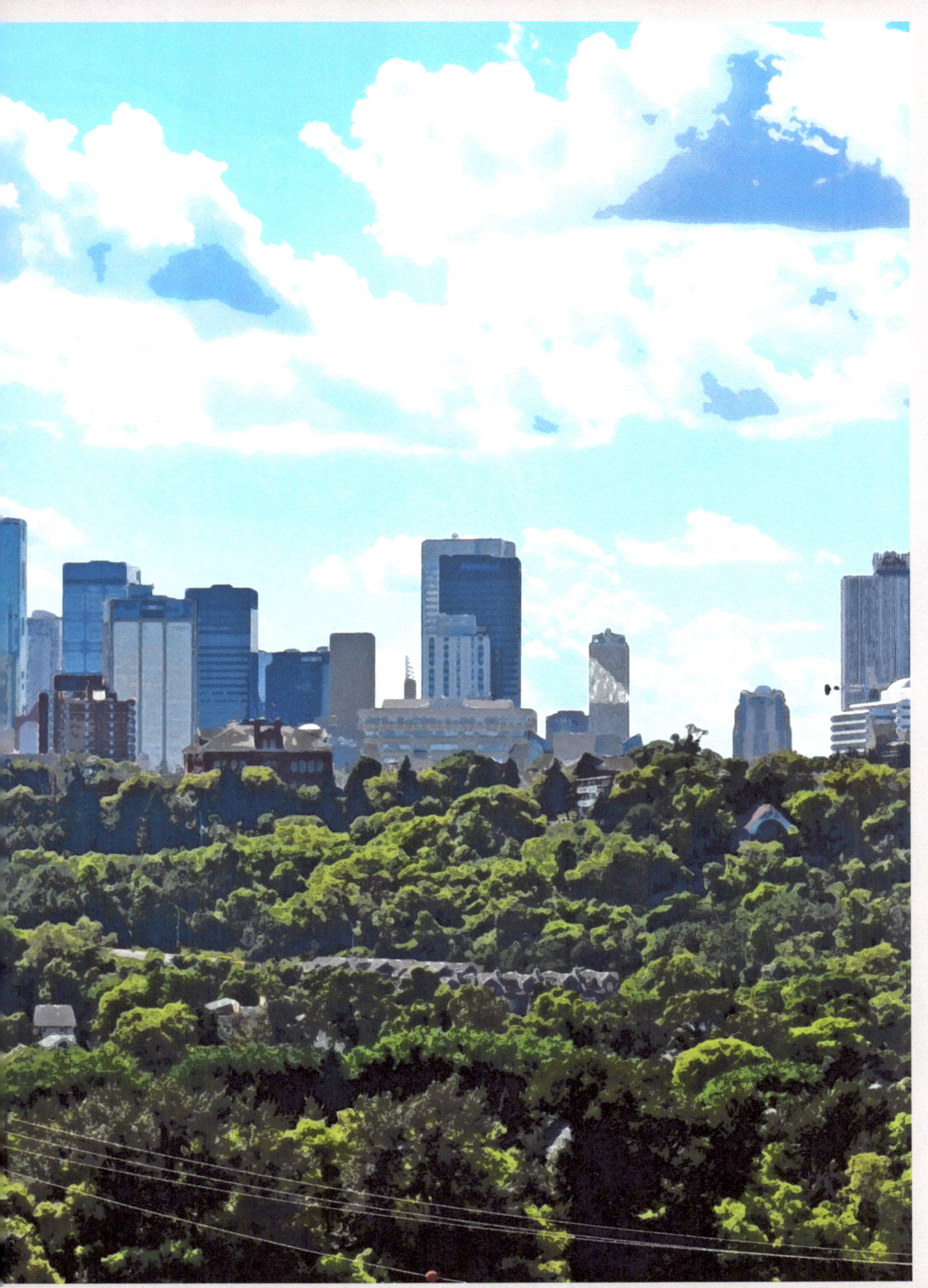

Dog Days of
Summer

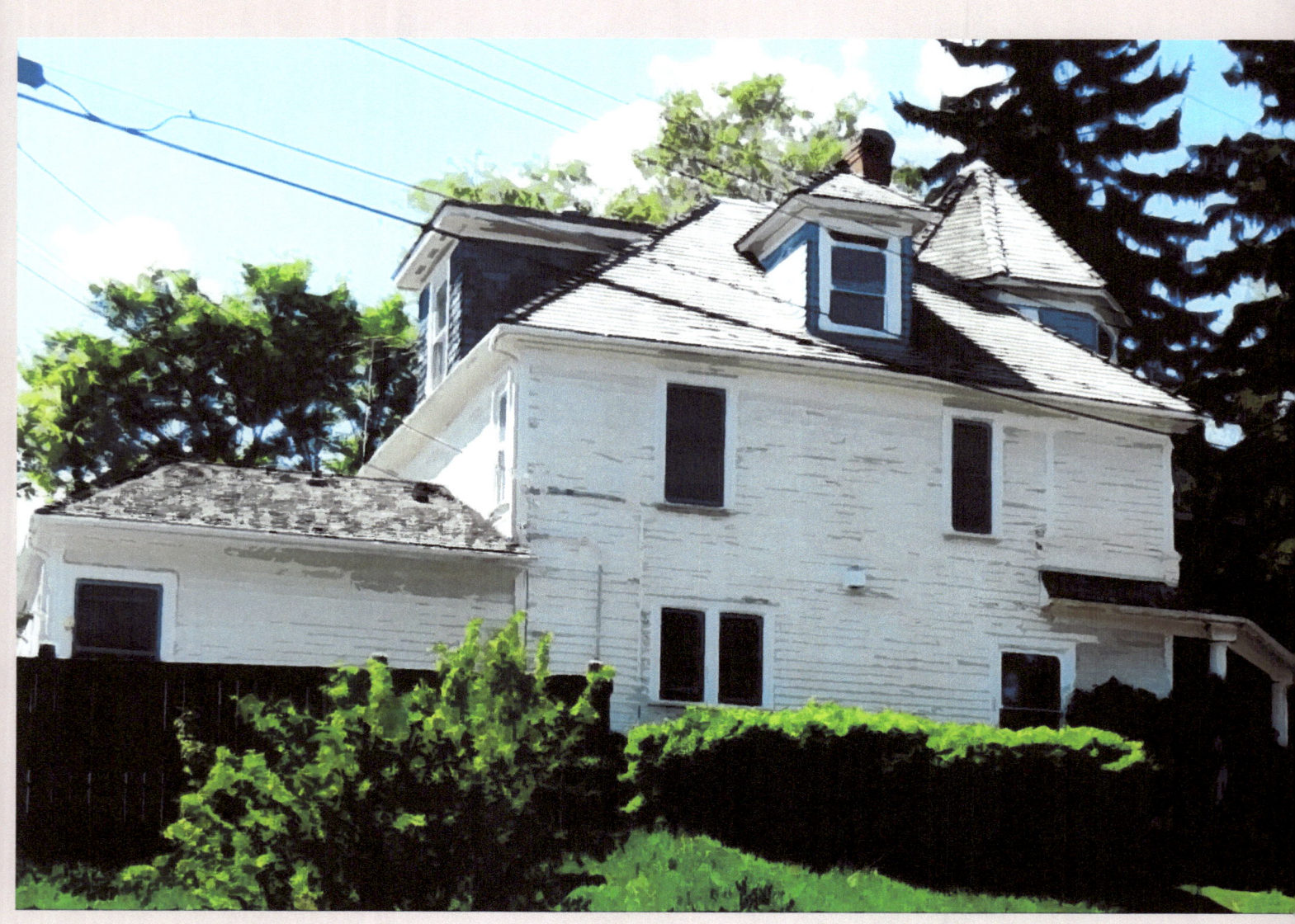

Grand Manor on the Hill

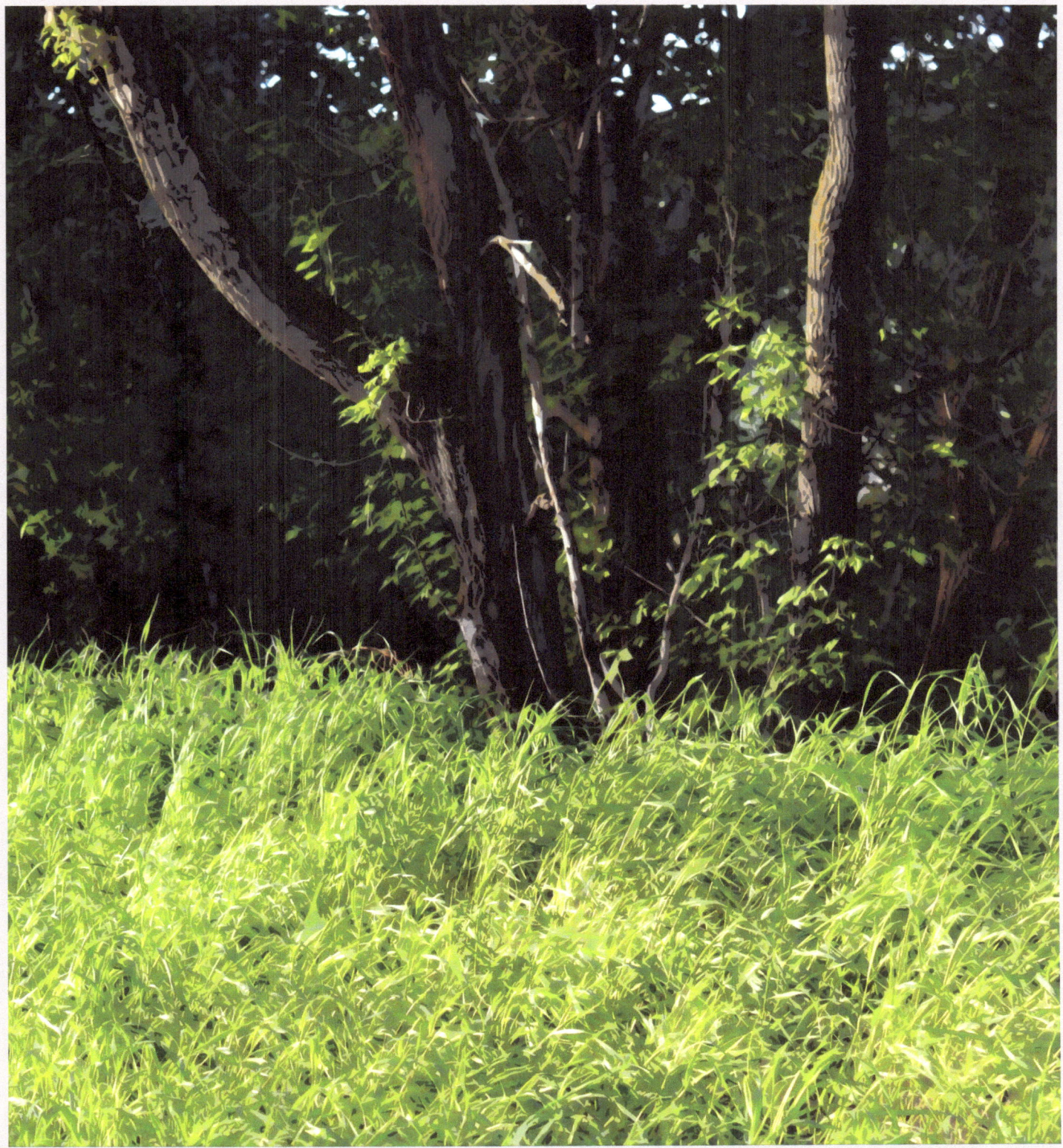

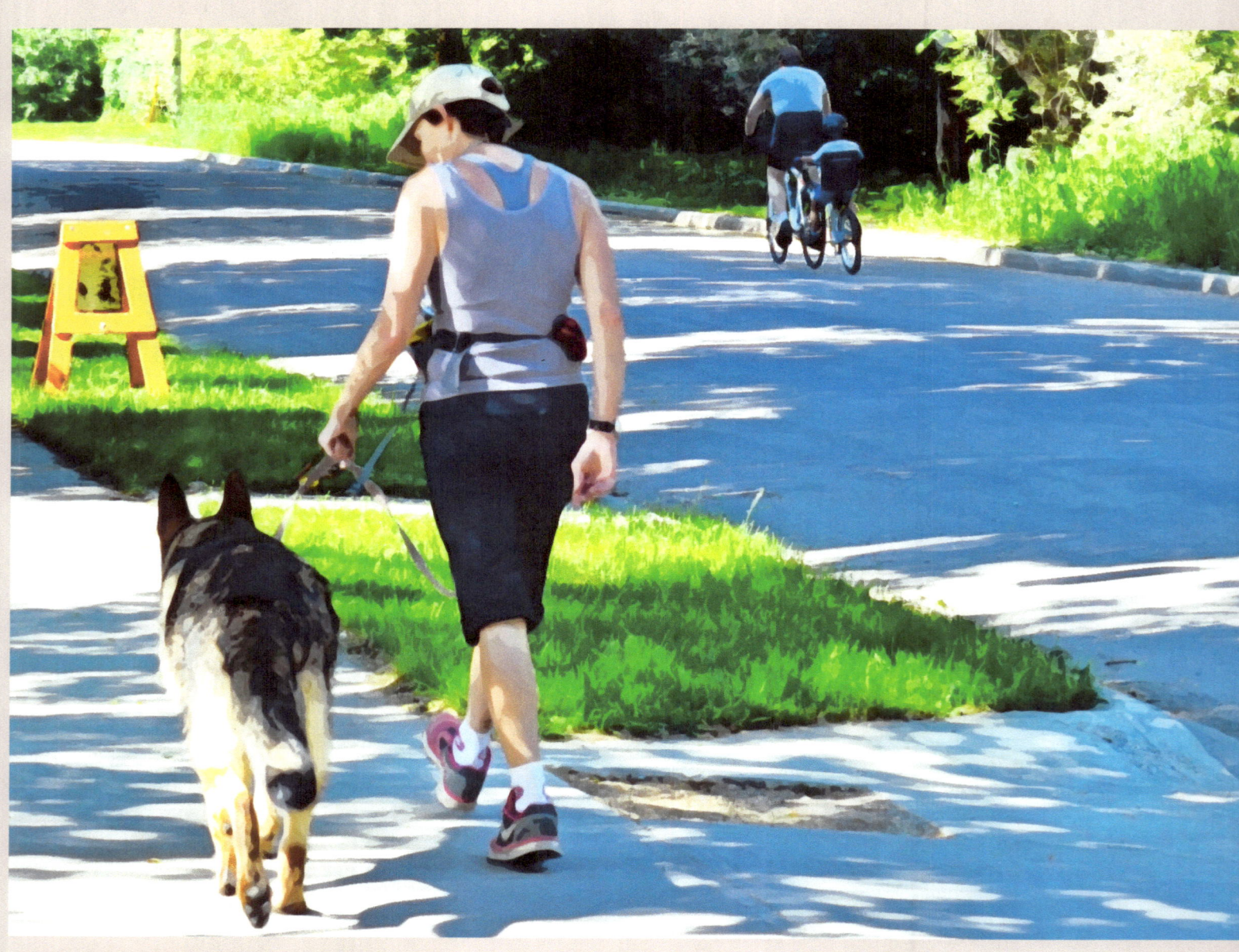

Sunday Afternoon

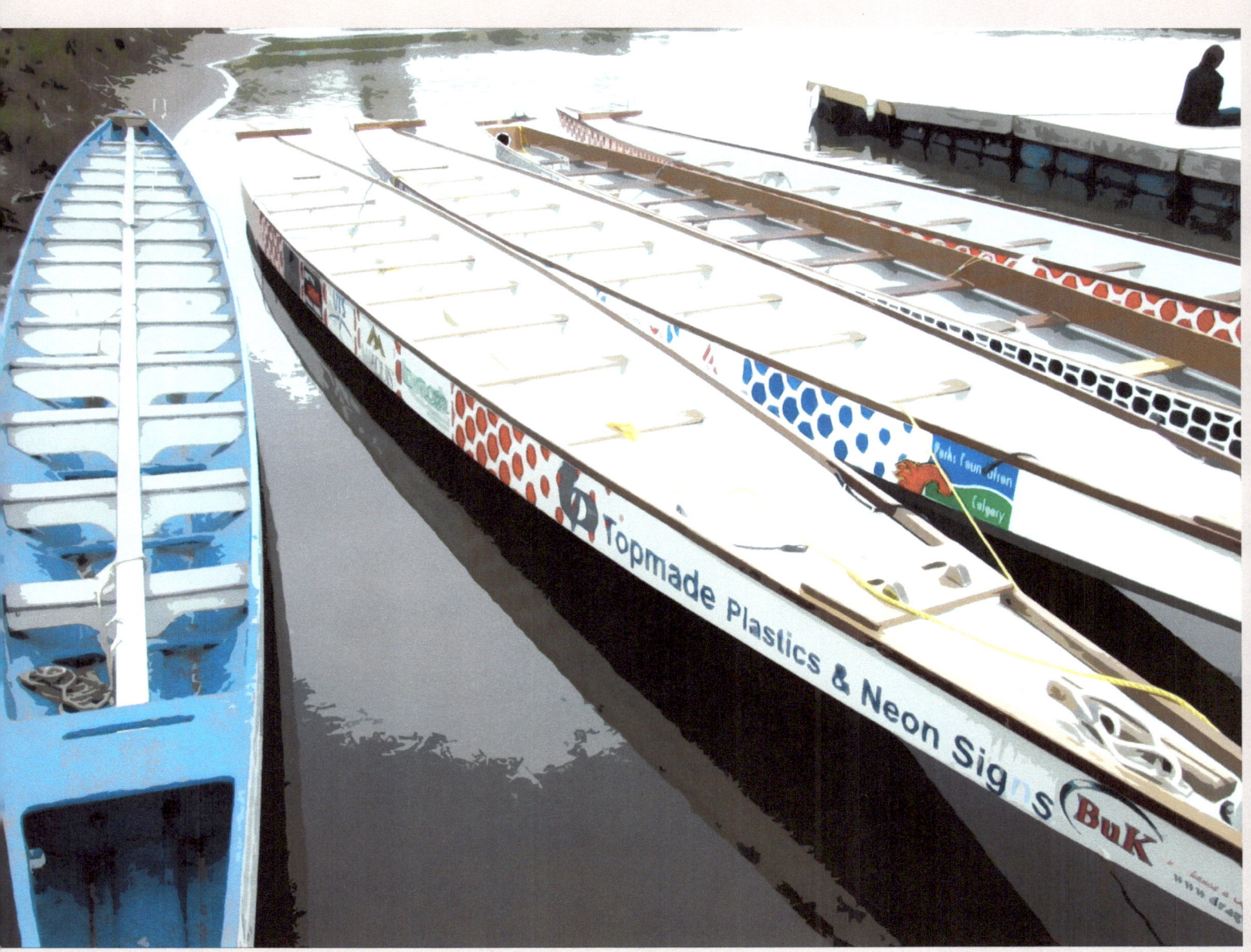

Girl on the Pier

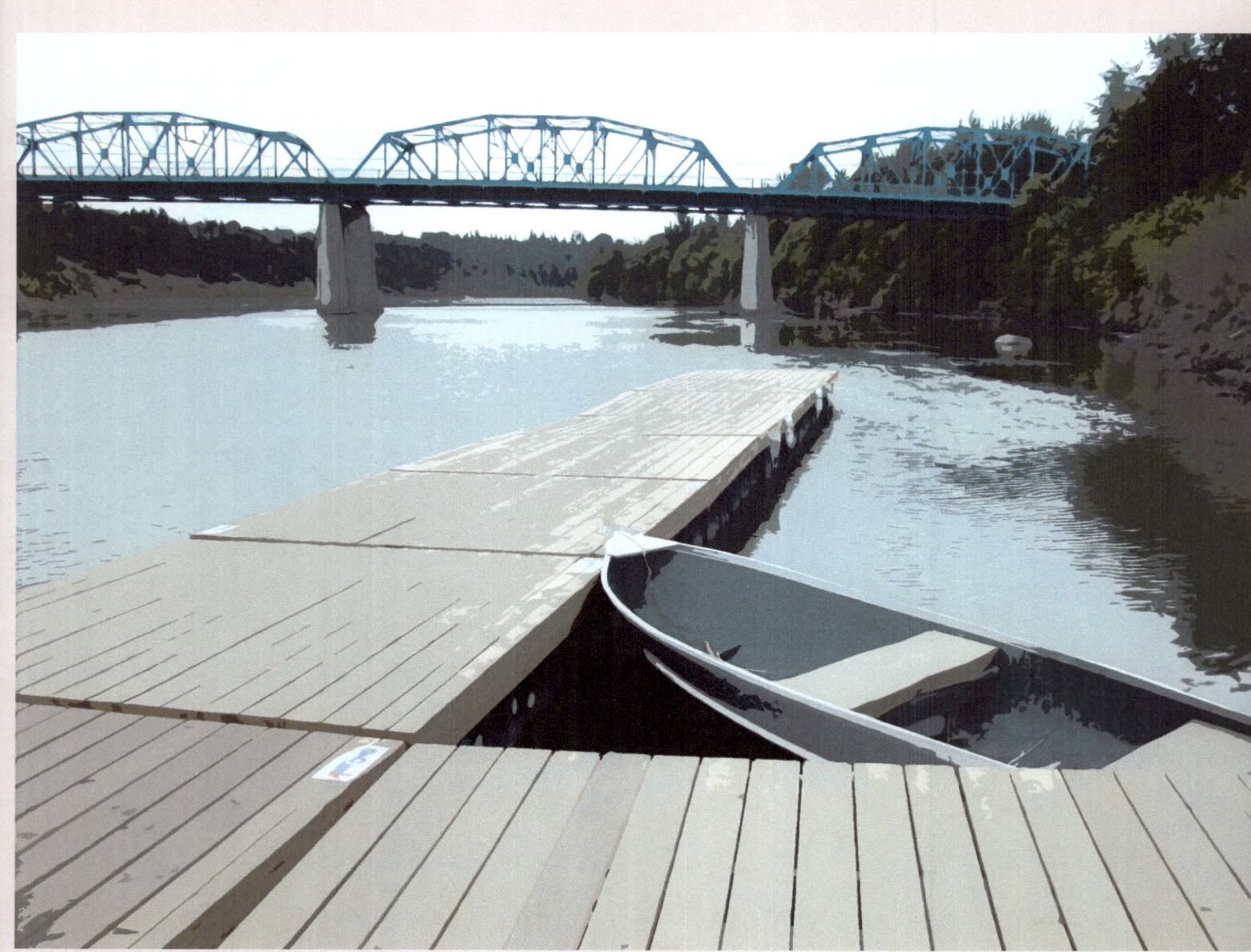

Docked Boat

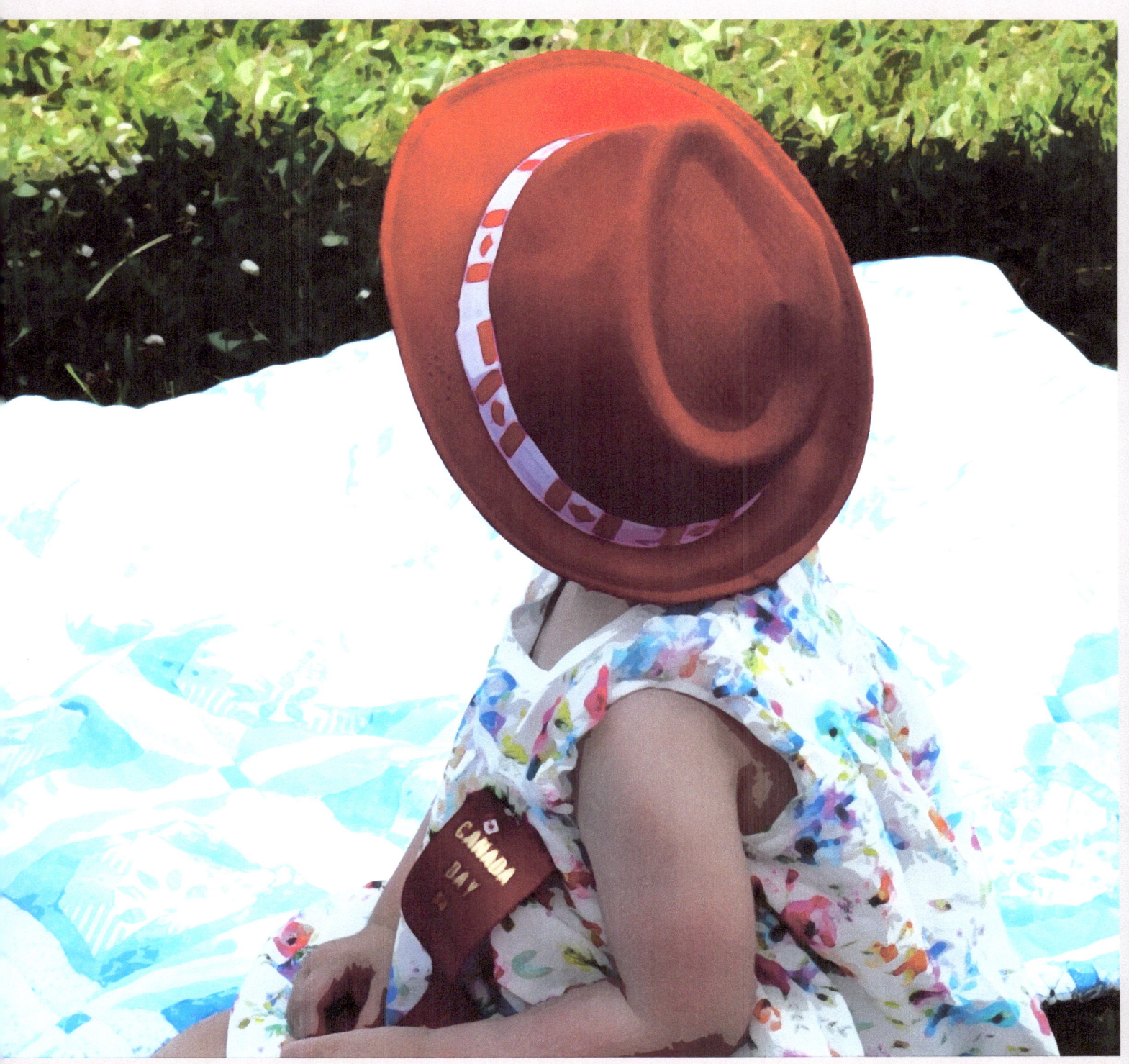

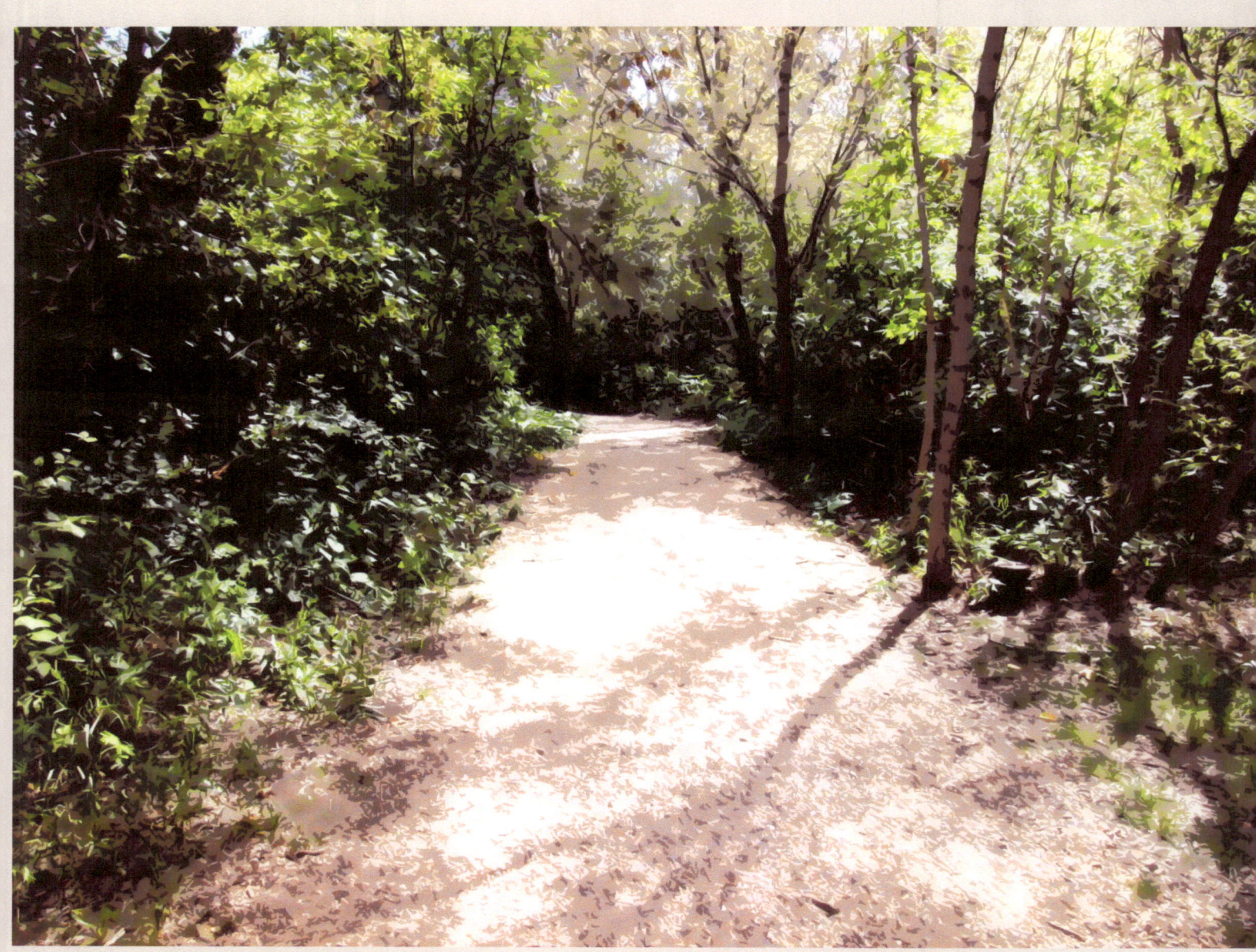

Pink Path

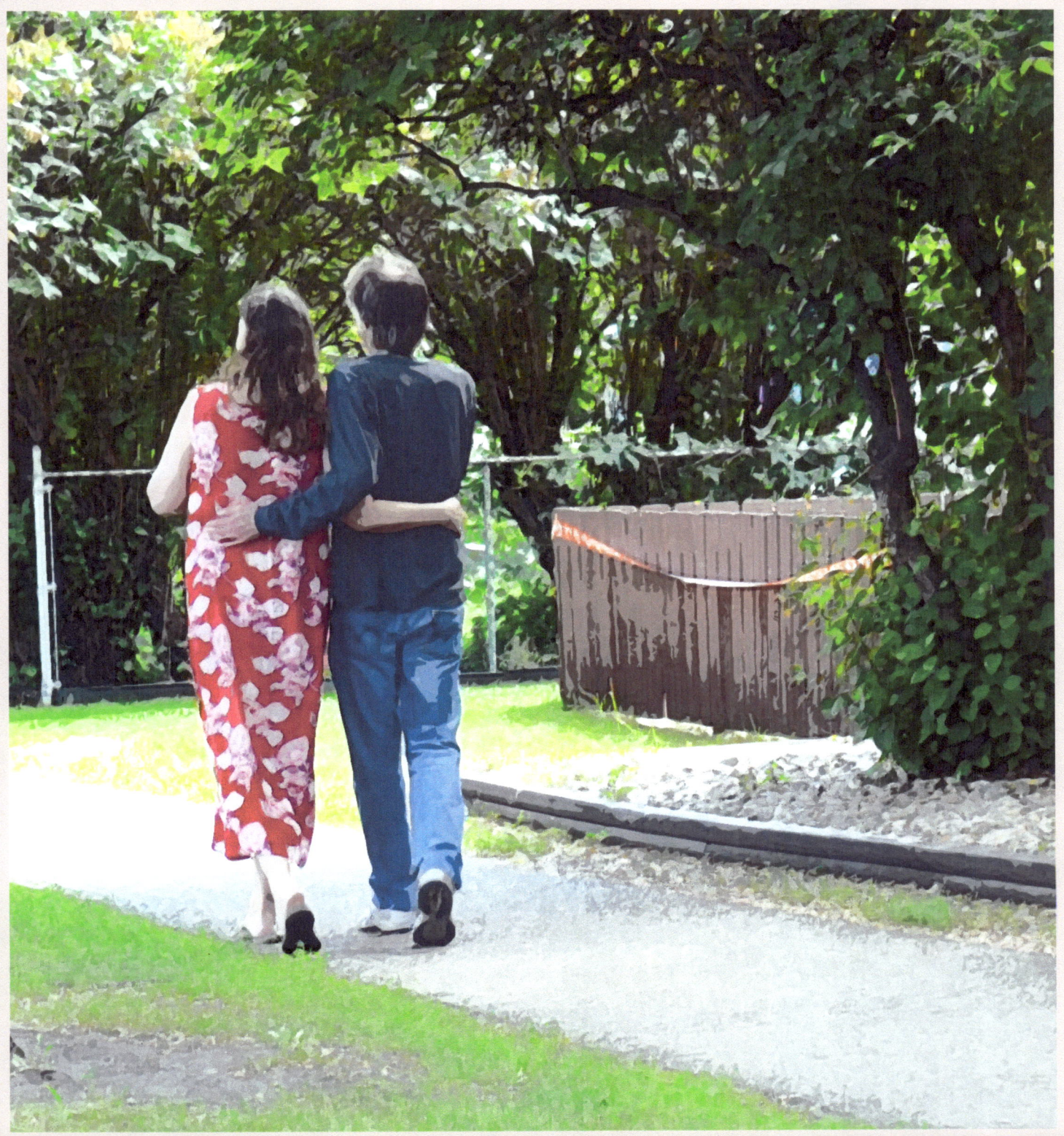

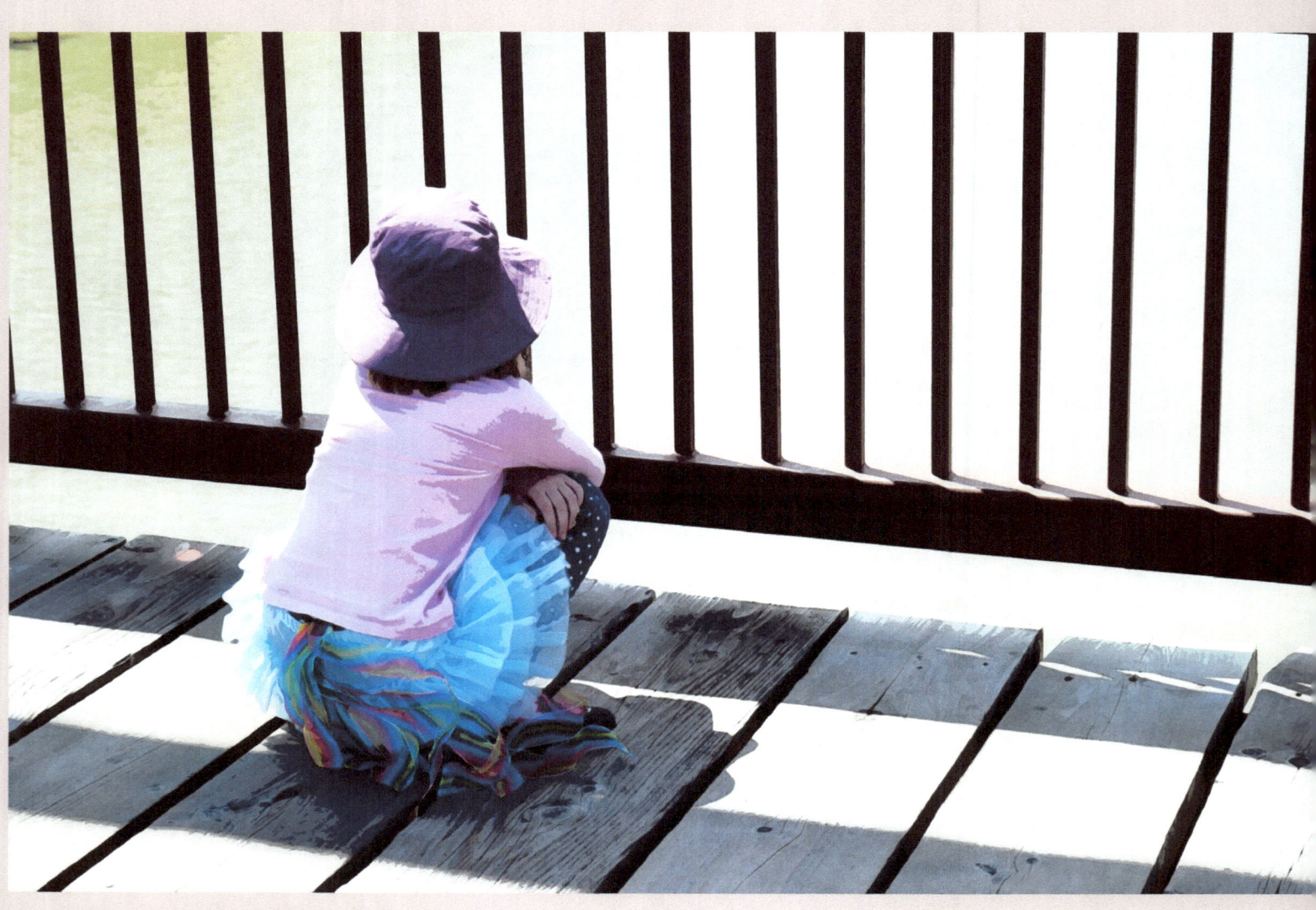

Watching the Waves

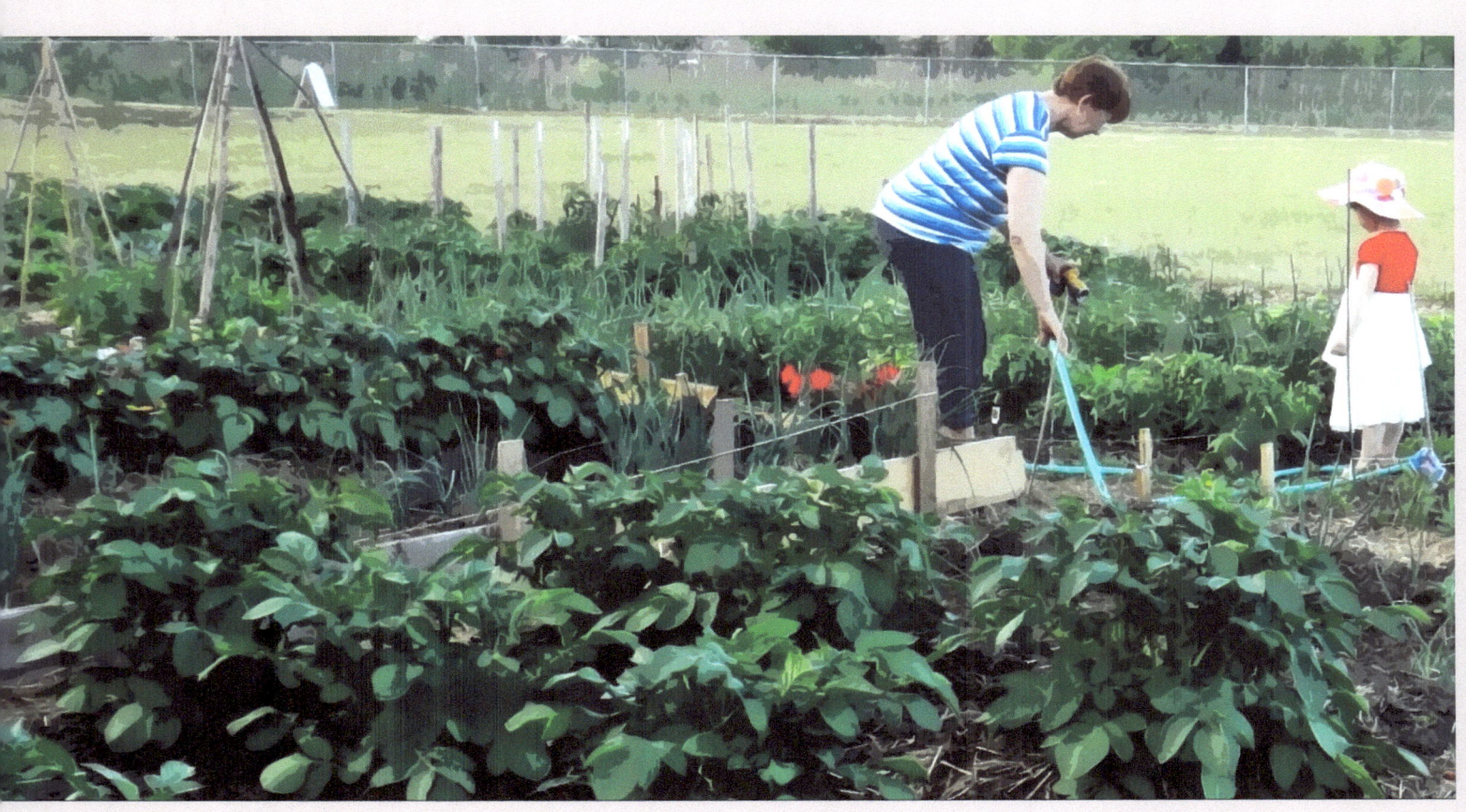

How Does Your Garden Grow?

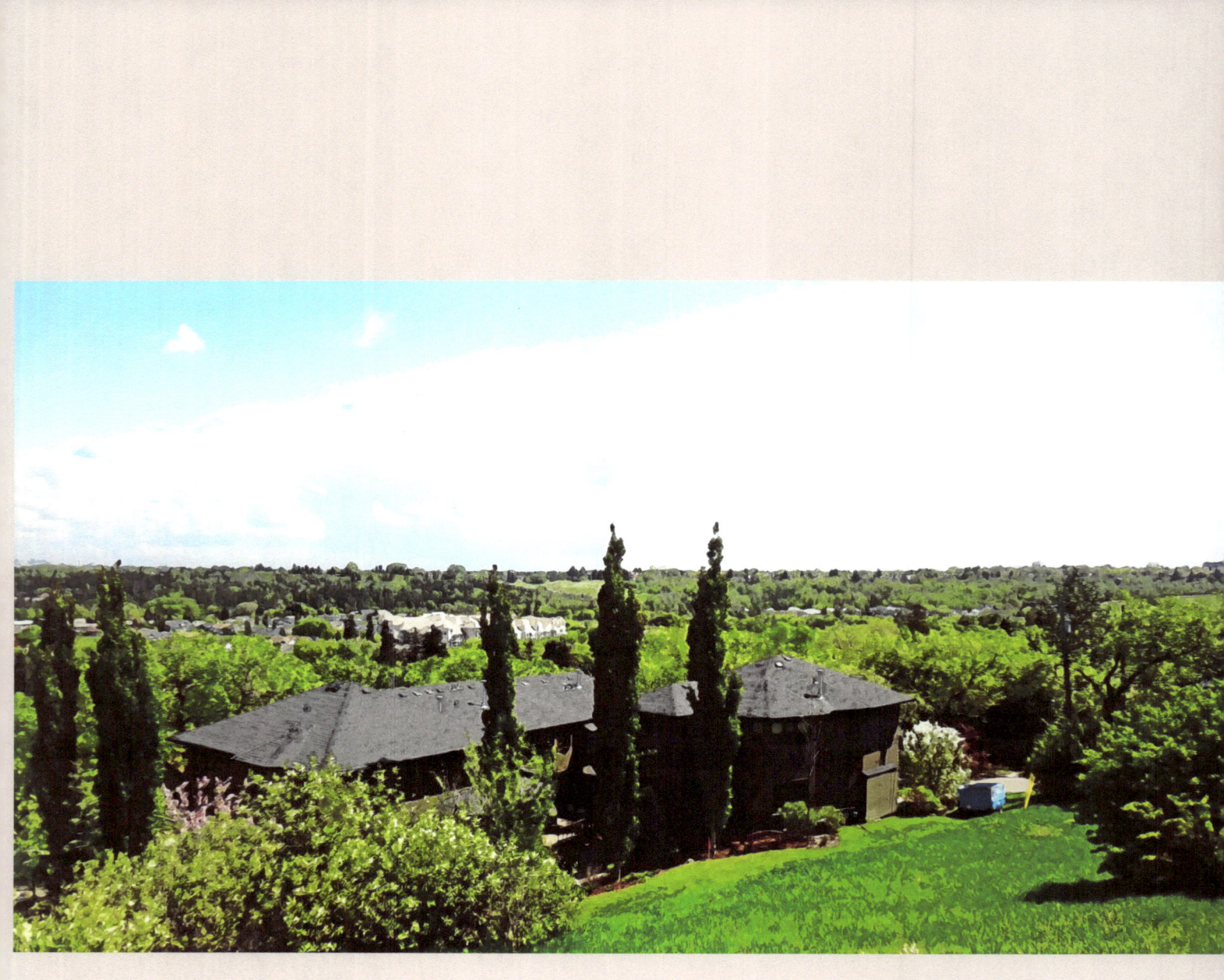

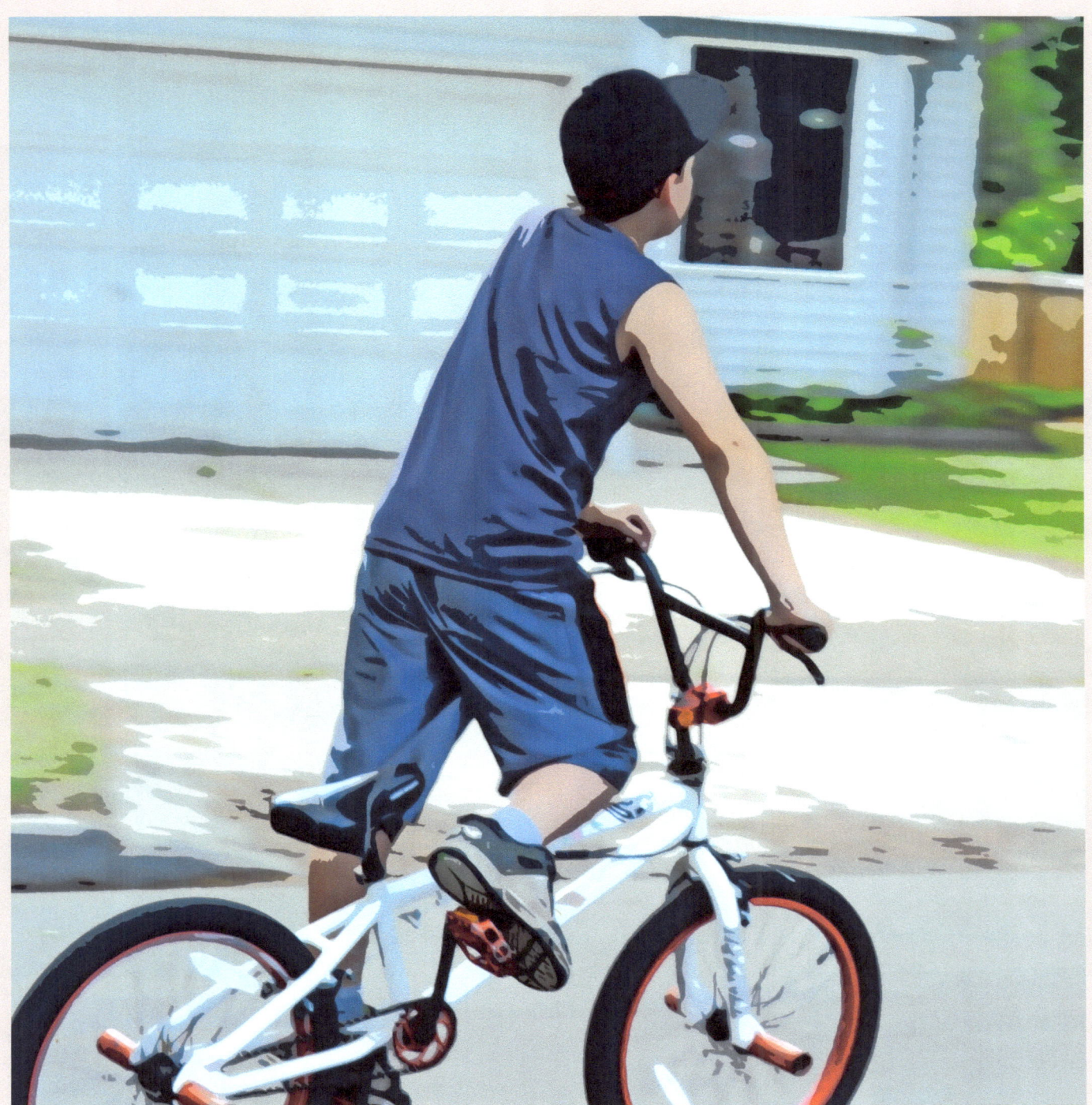

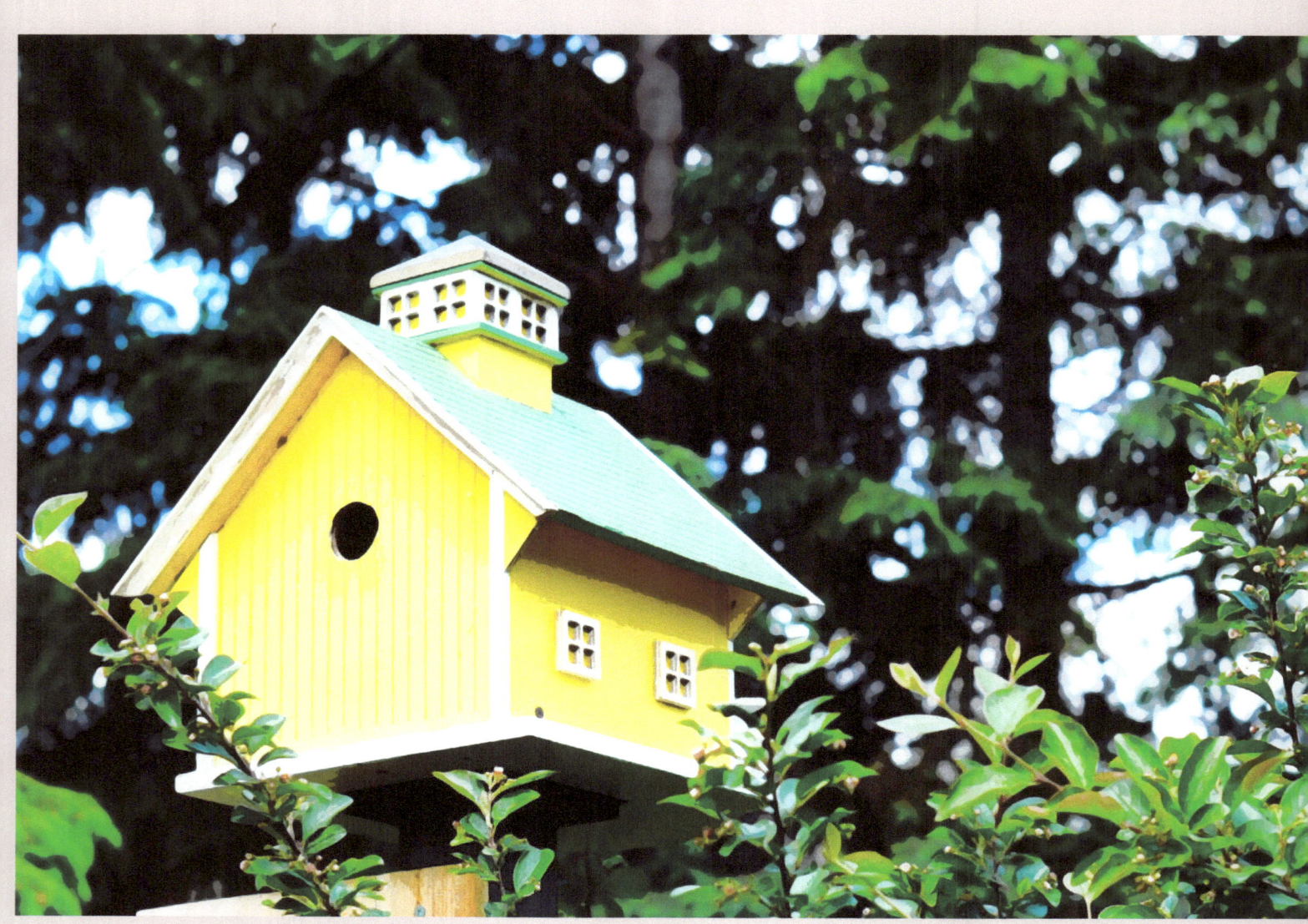

Room with a View

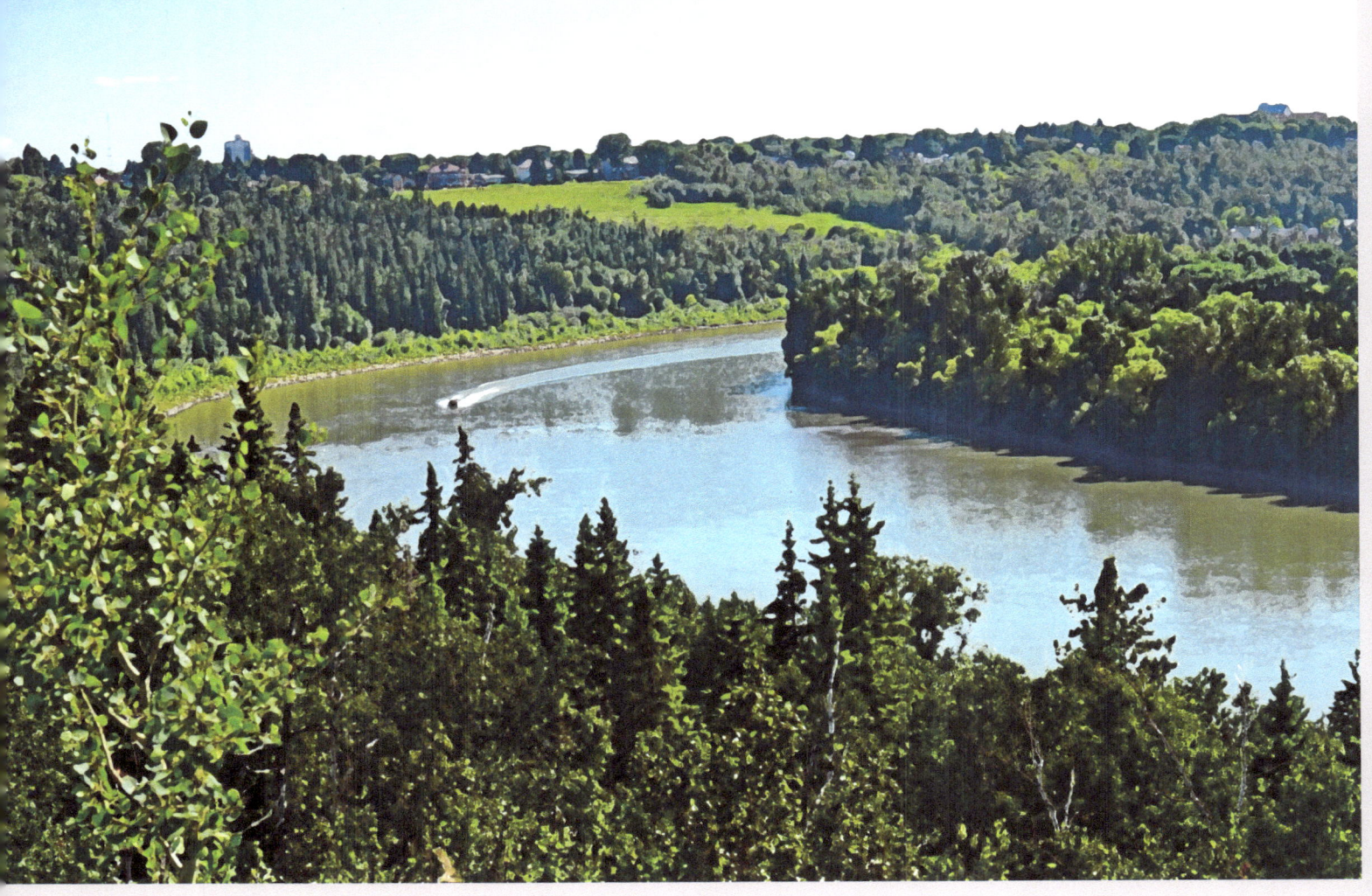

Autumn

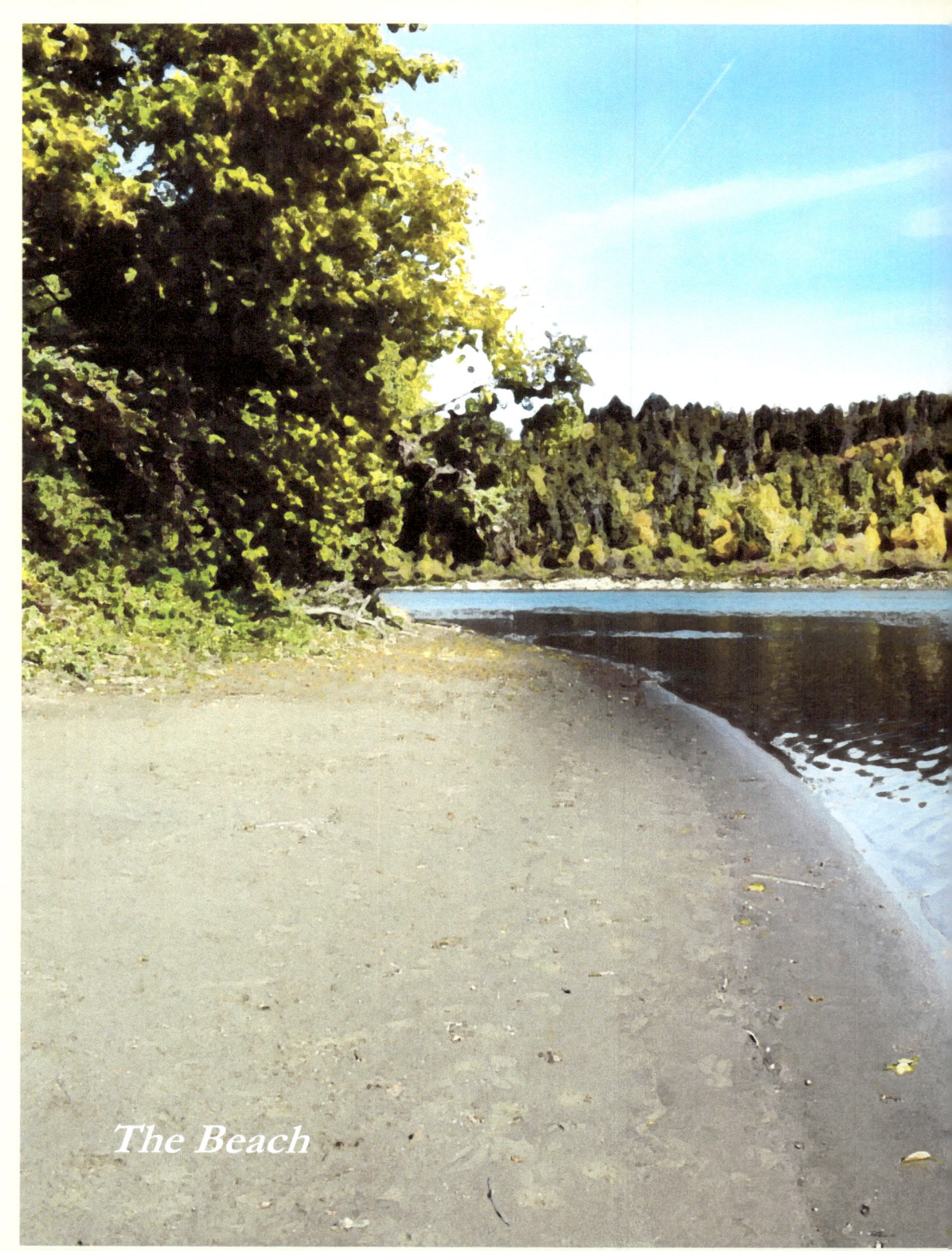

The Beach

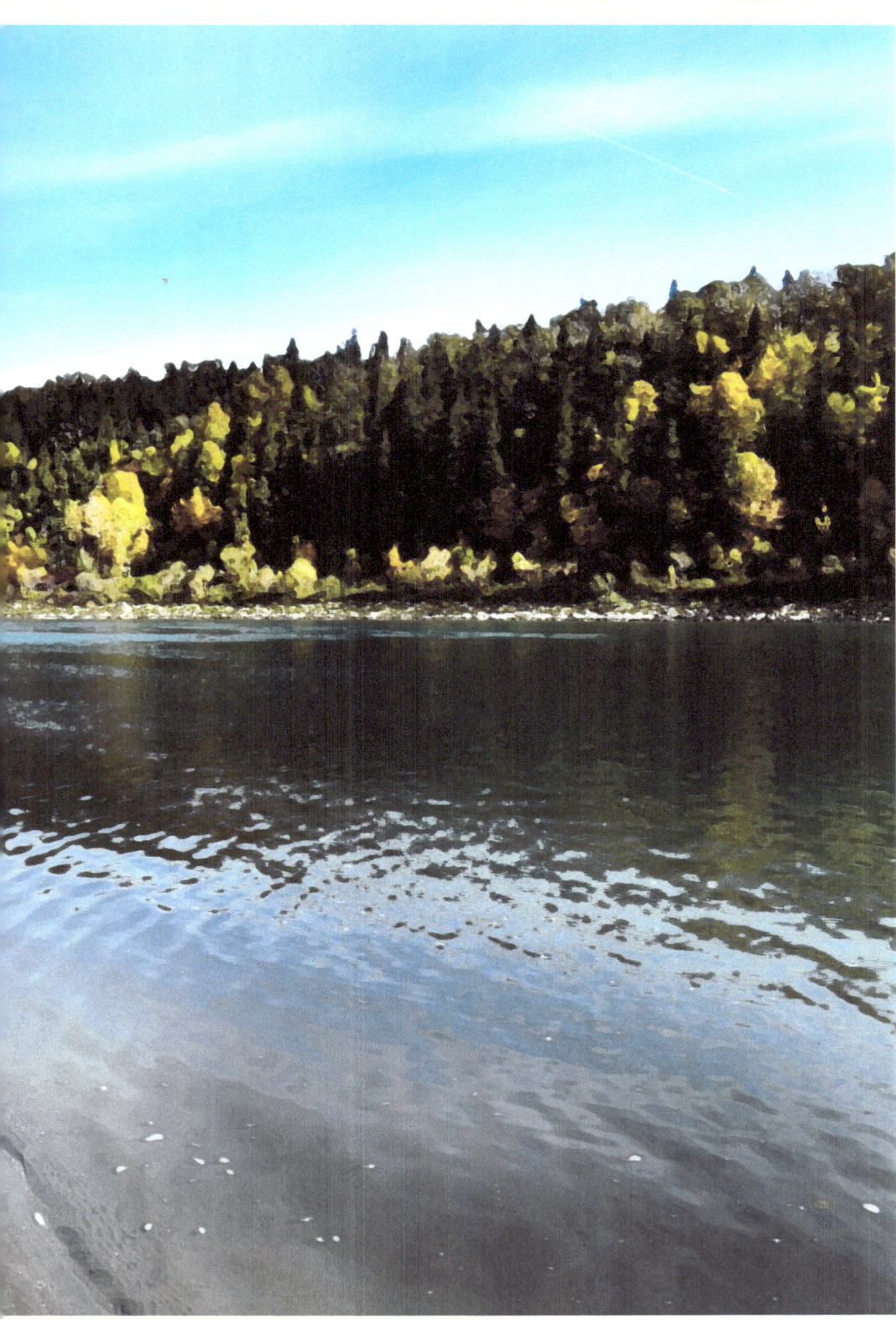

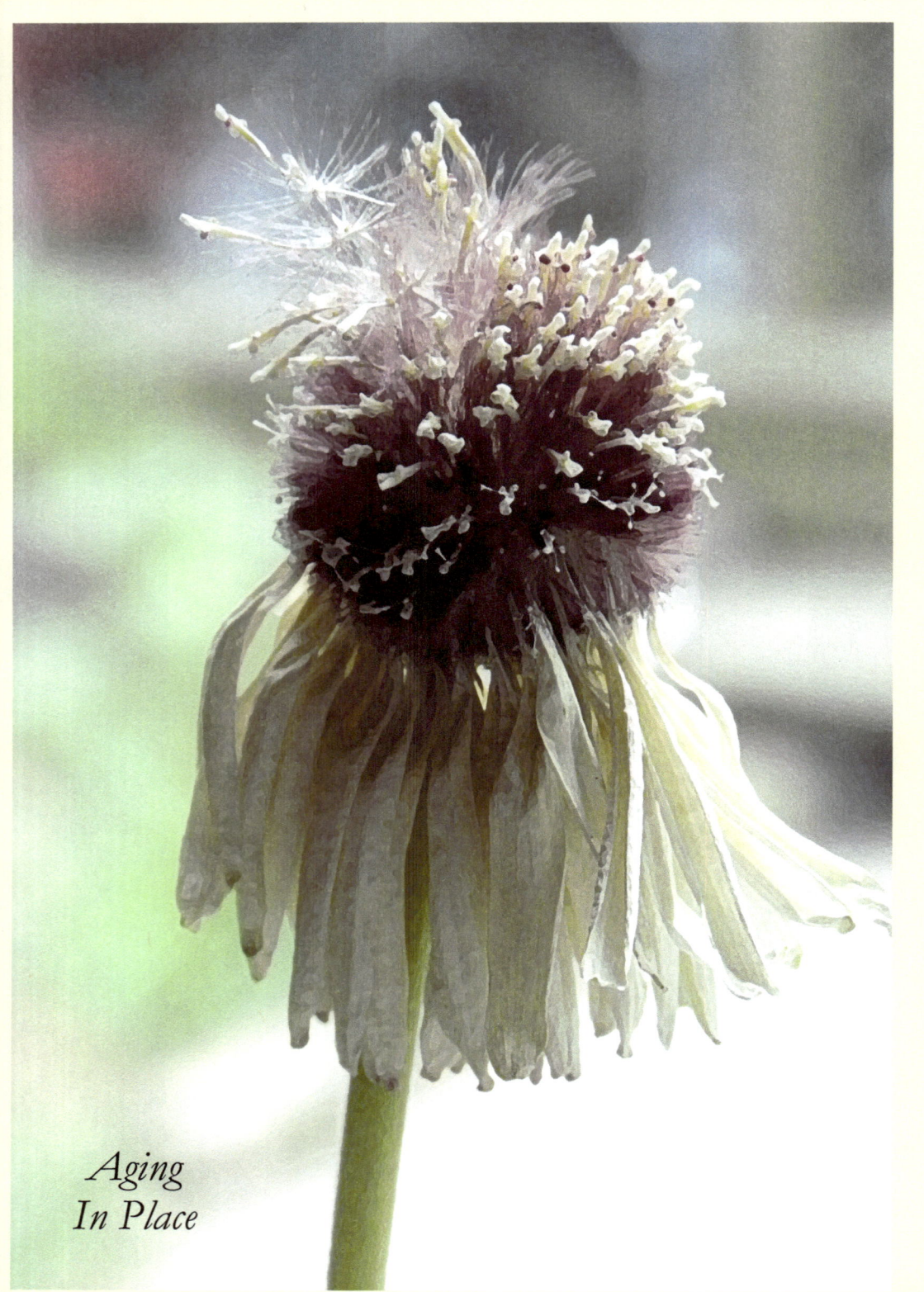

Aging
In Place

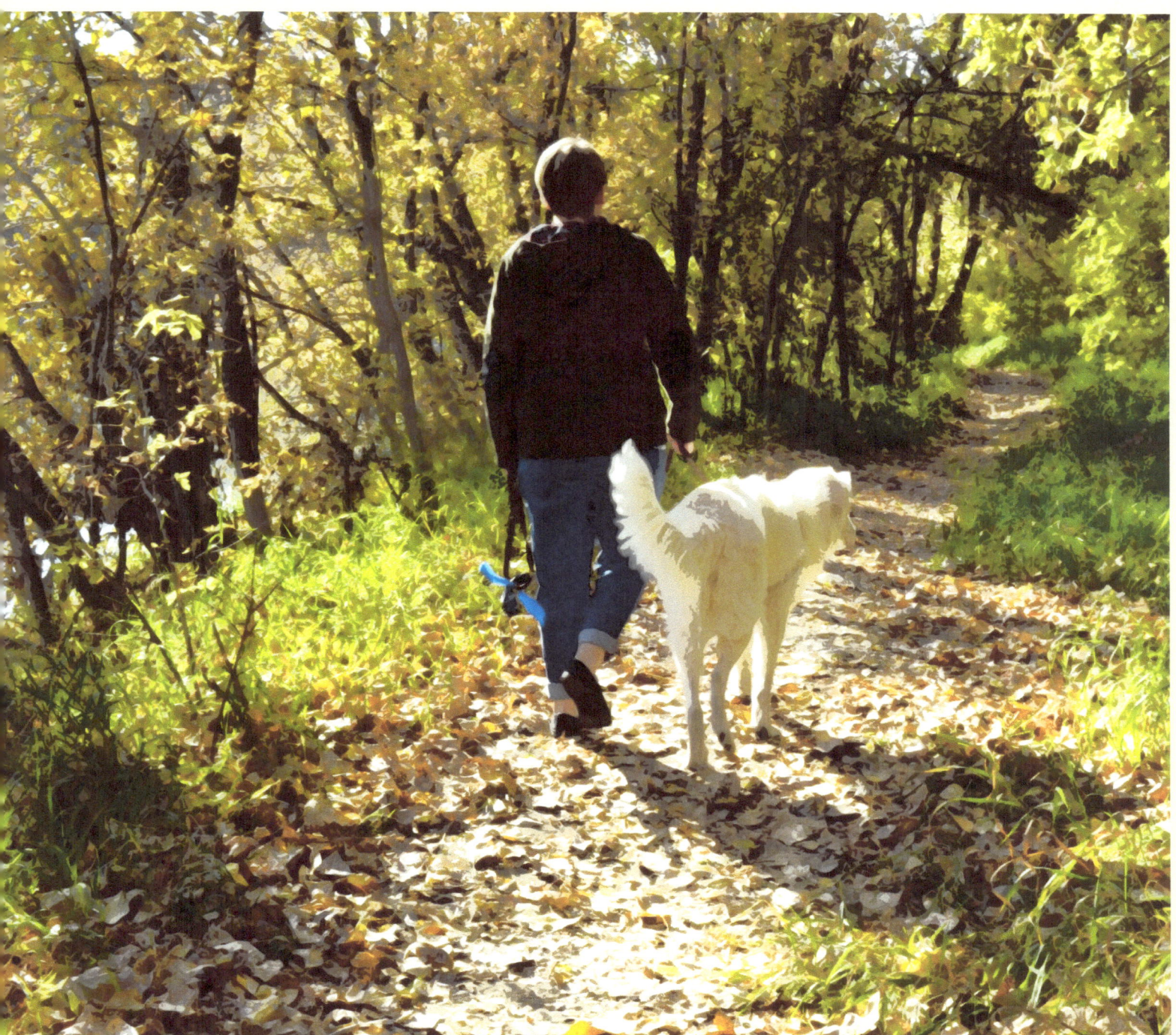

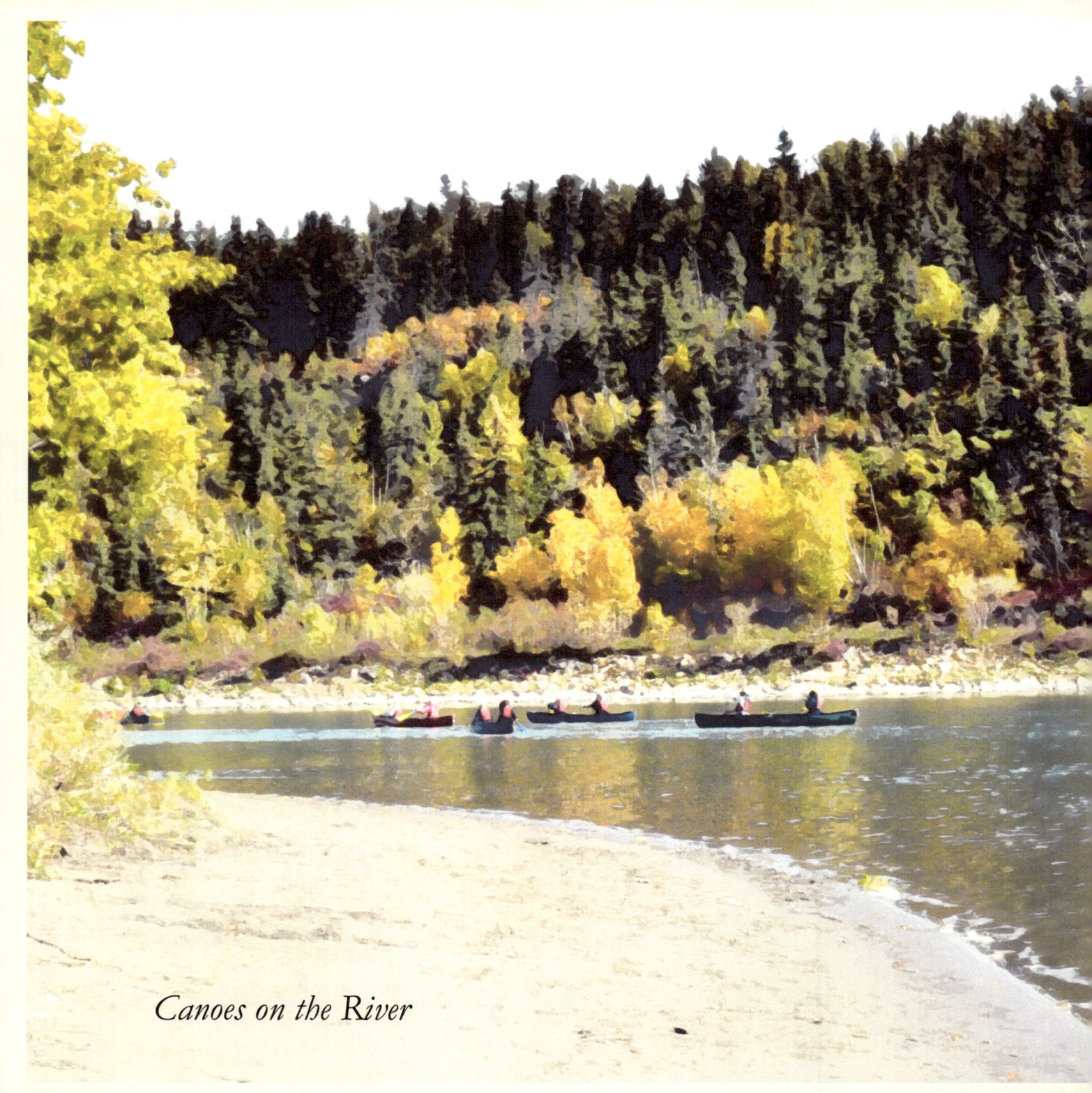

Canoes on the River

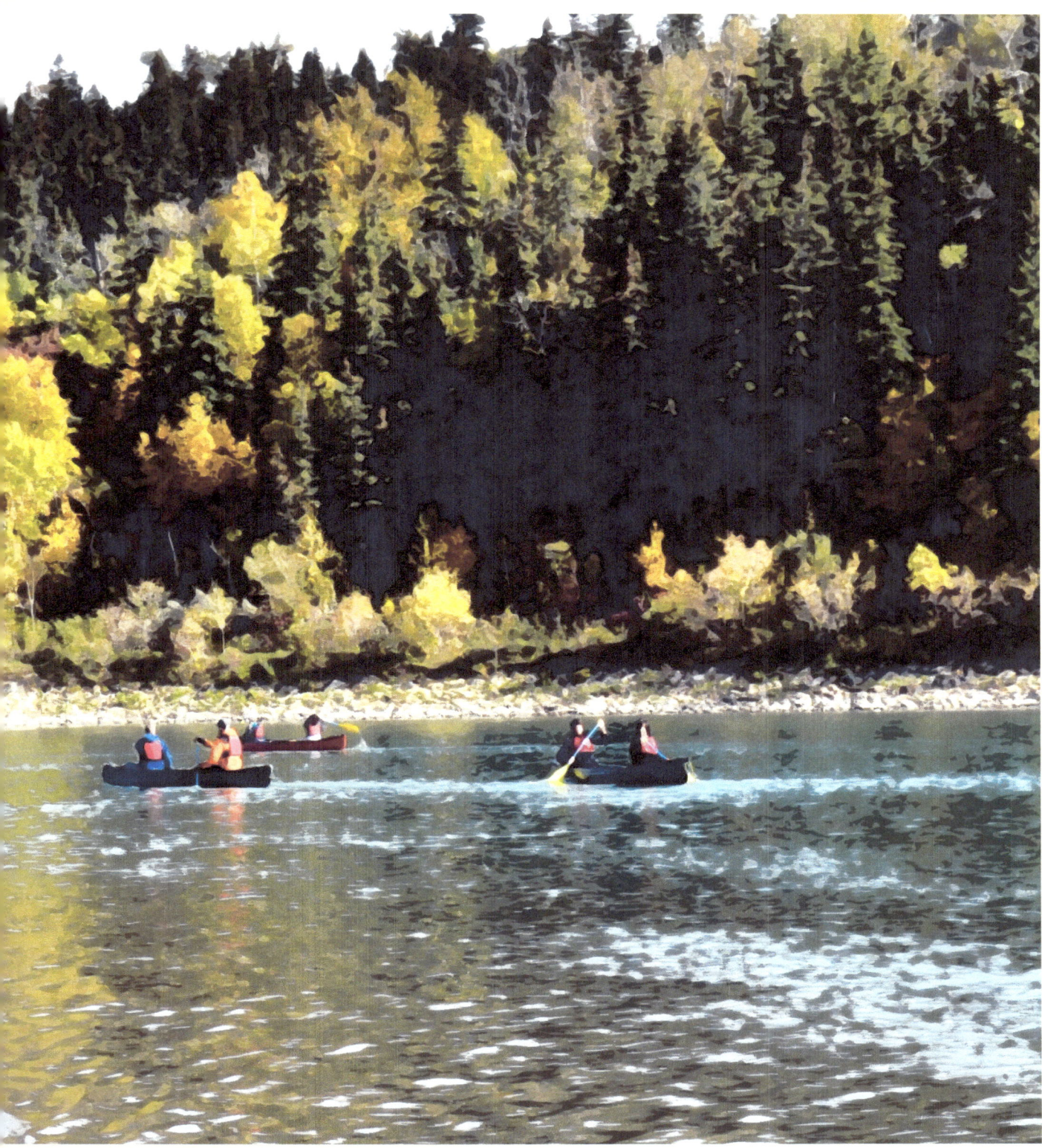

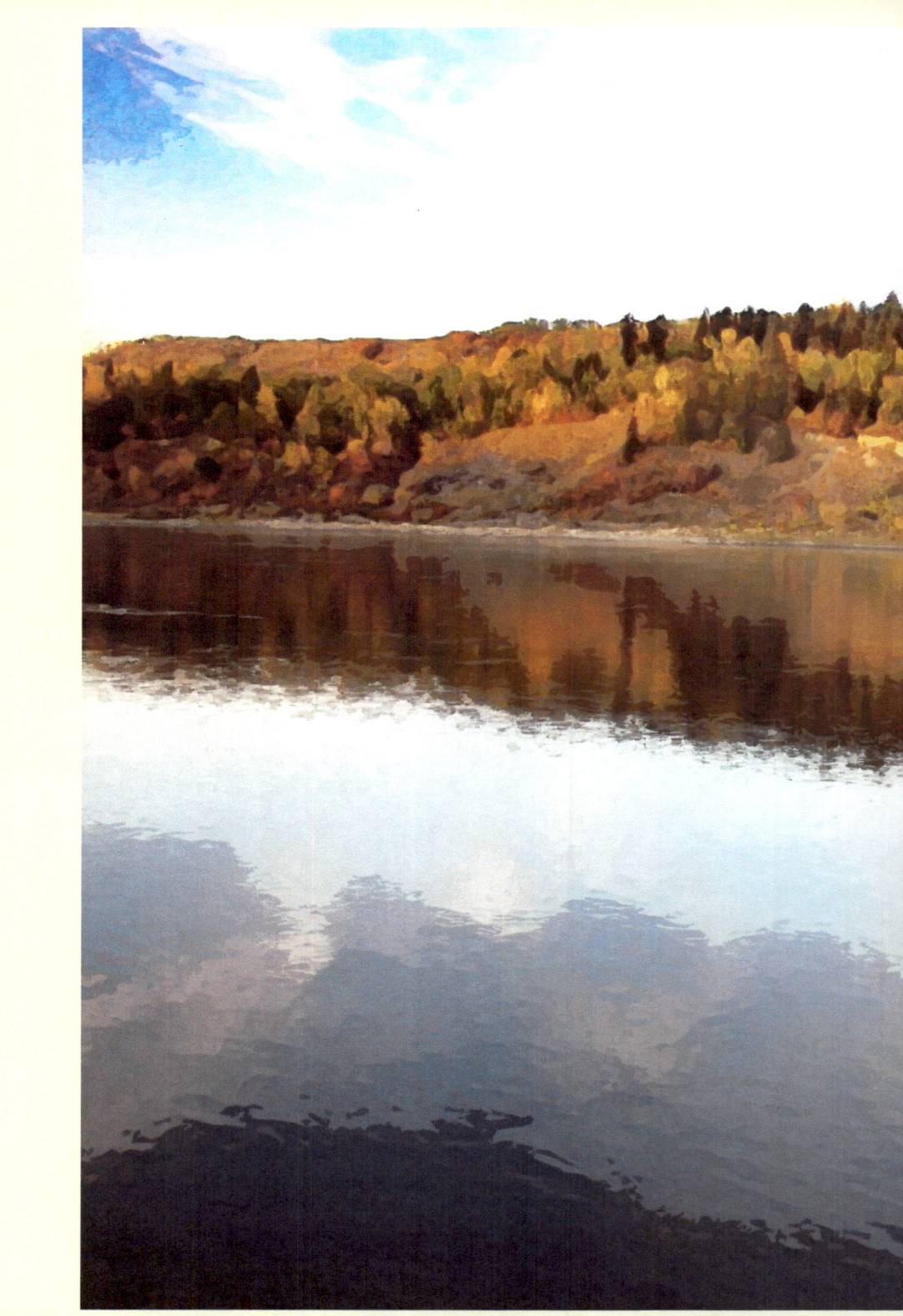

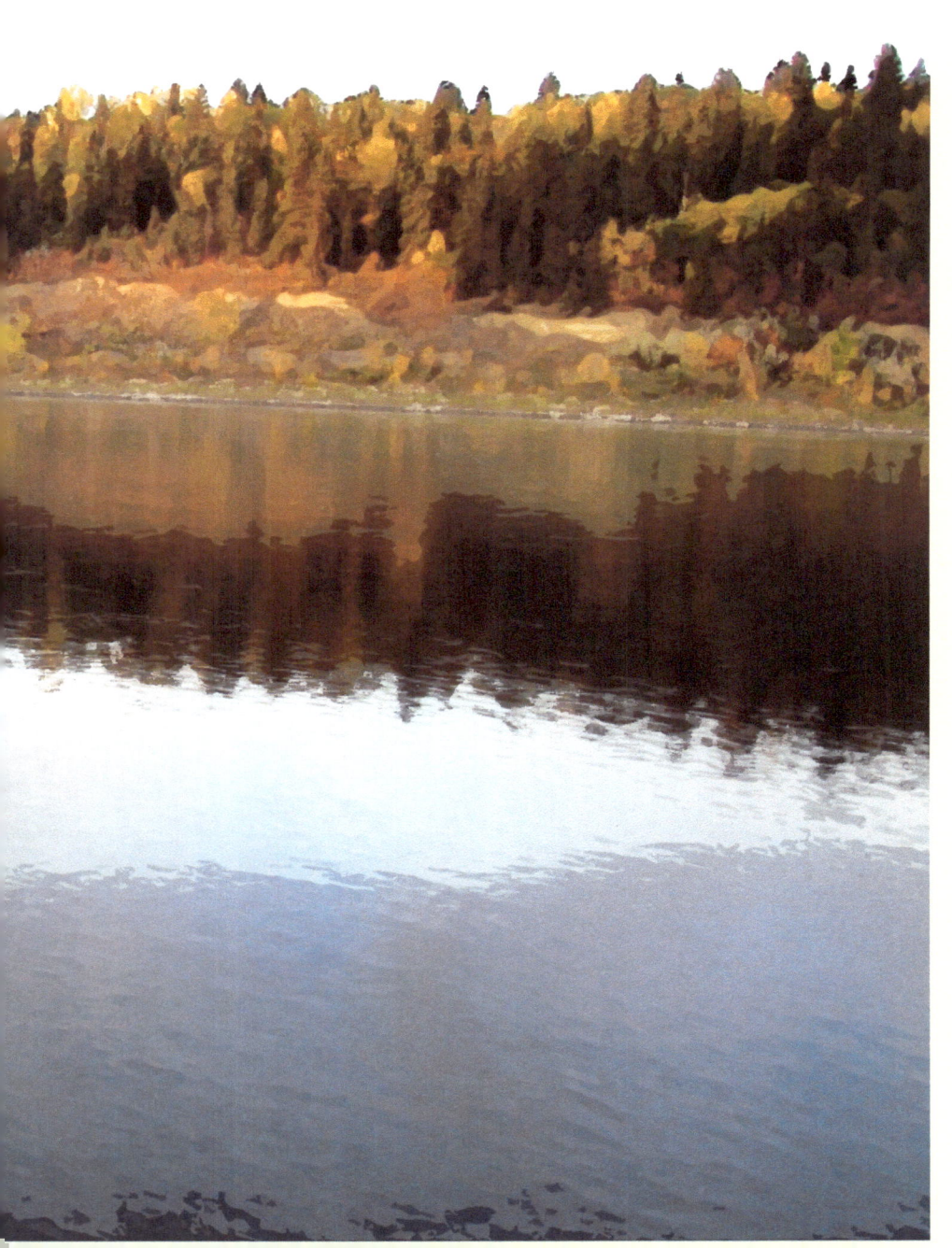

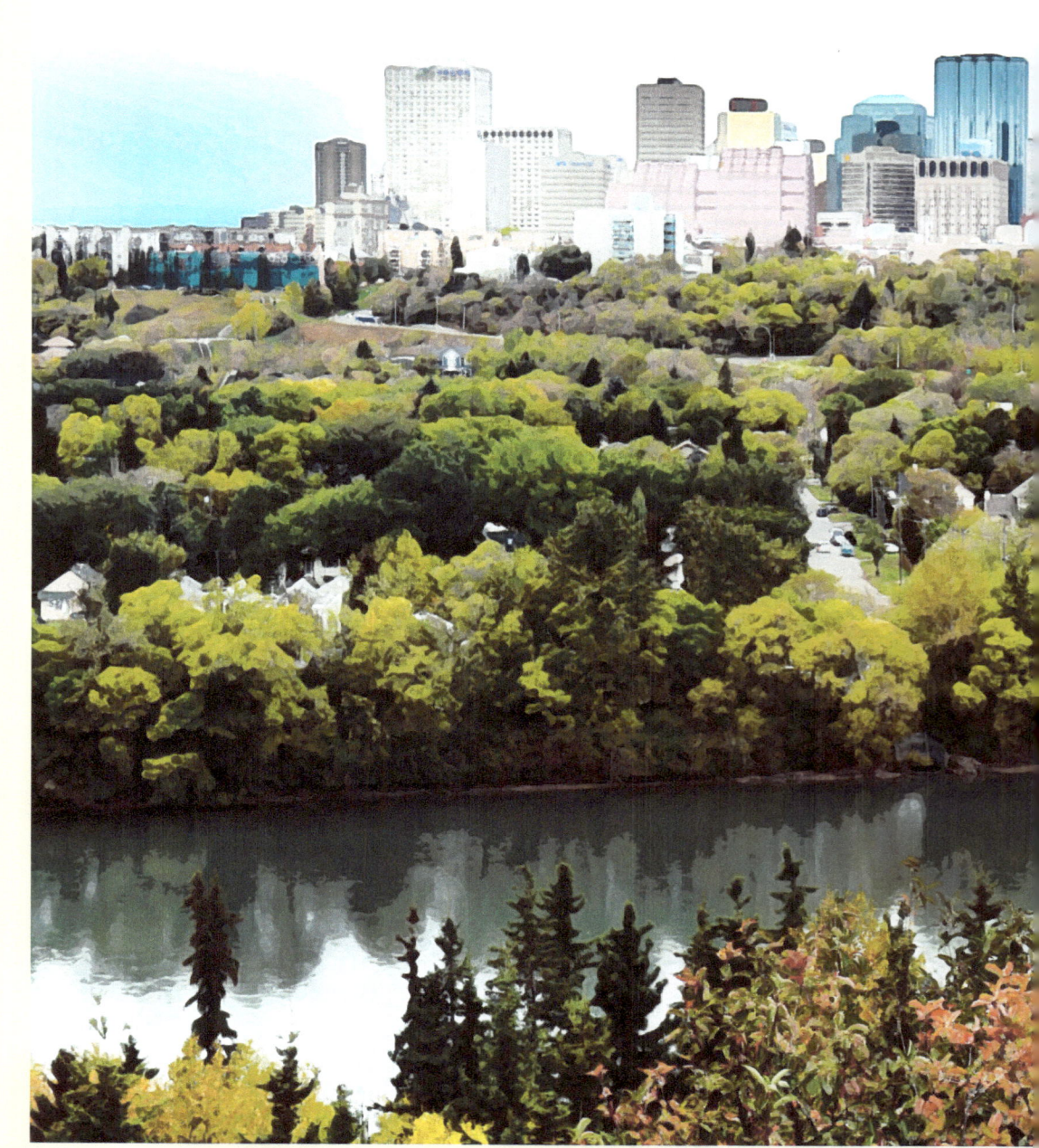

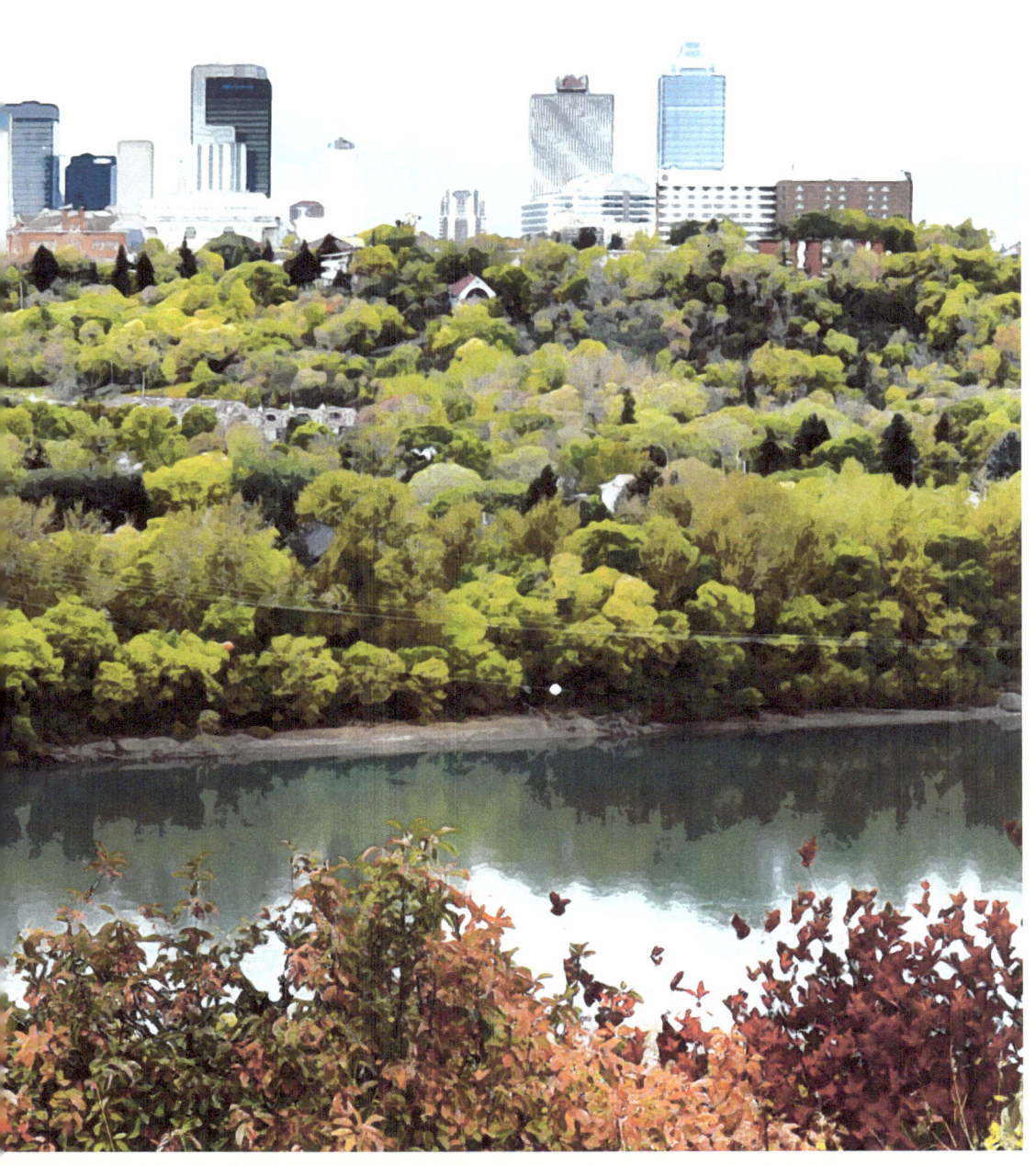

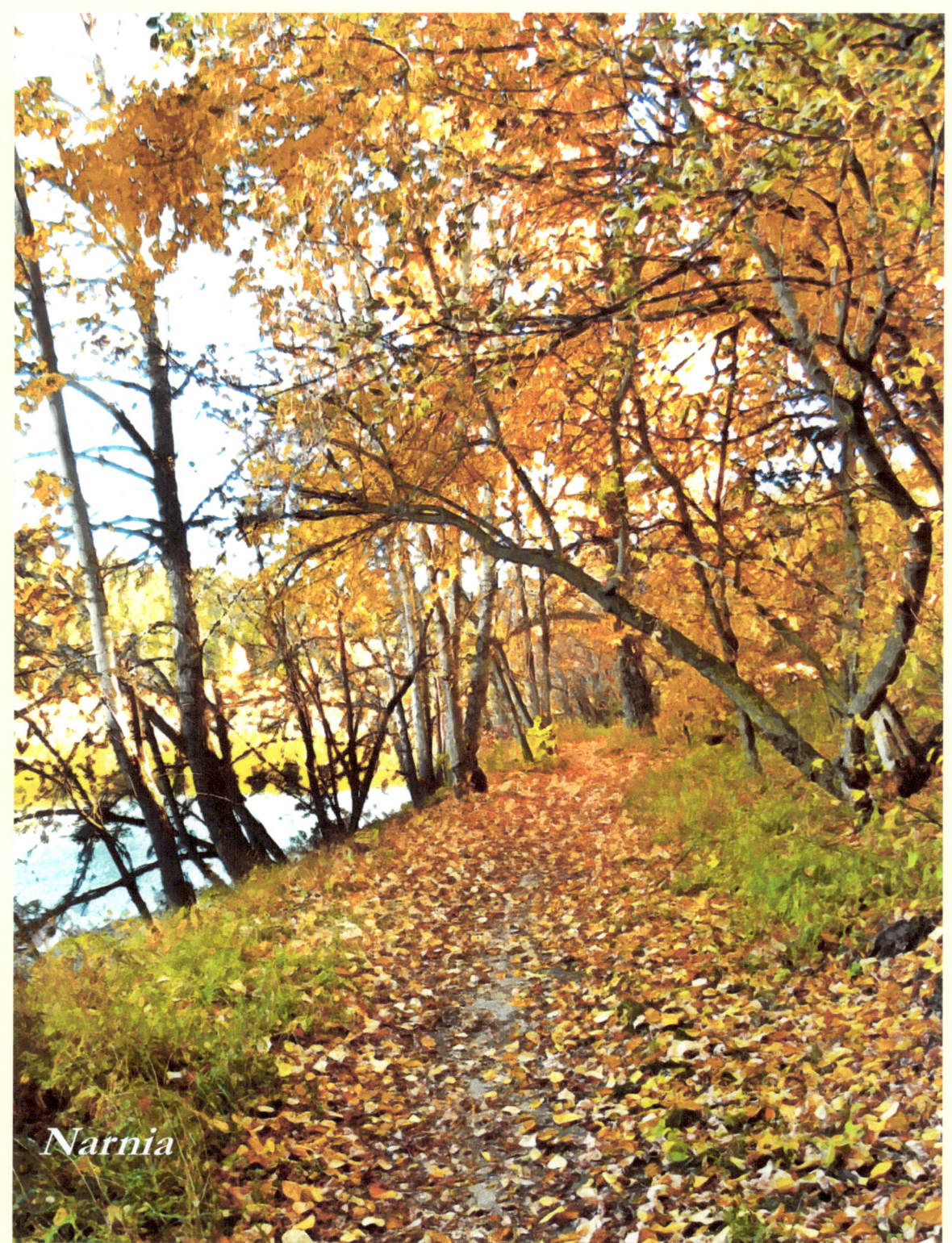

Narnia

Reflecting on Fall

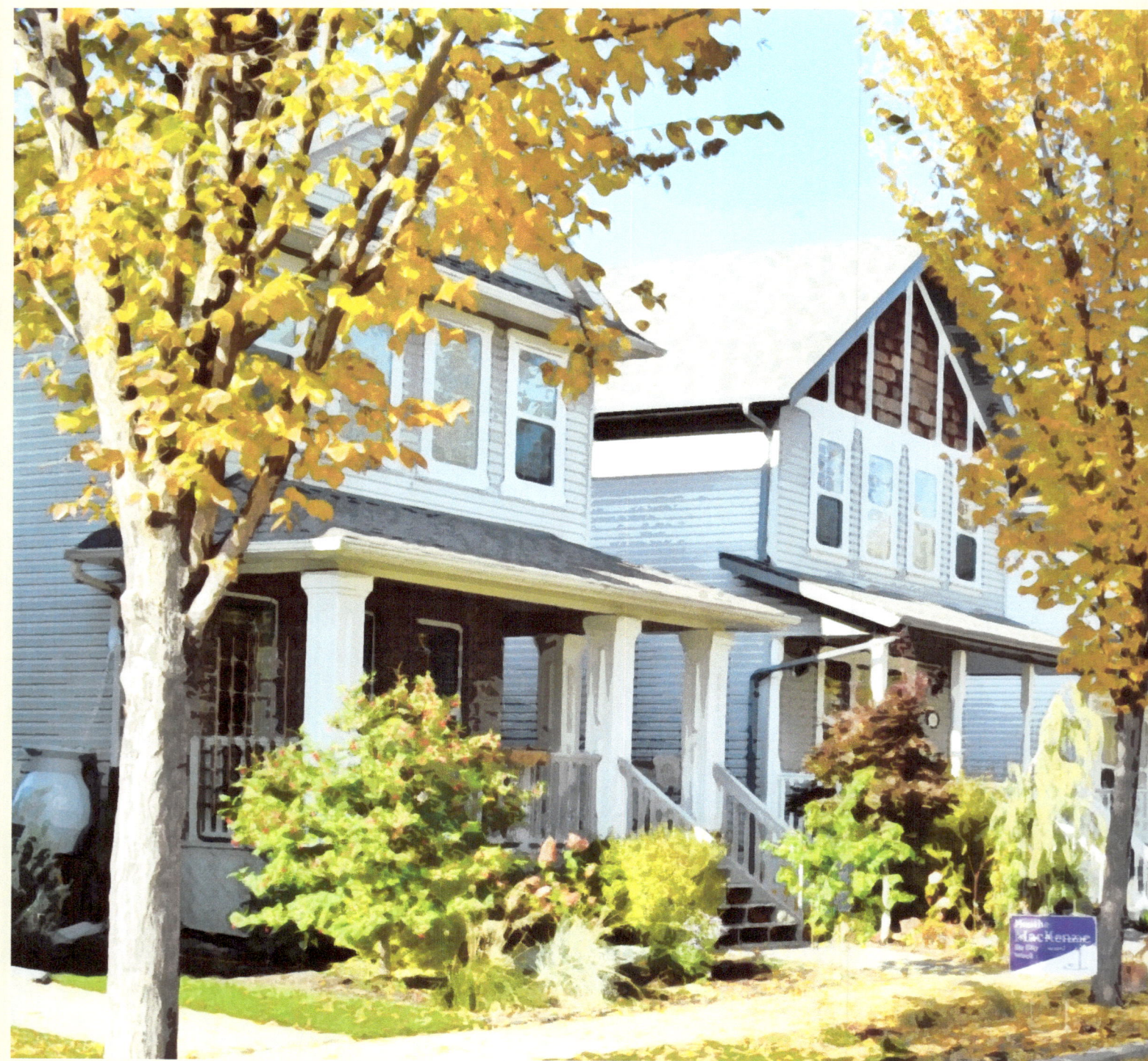

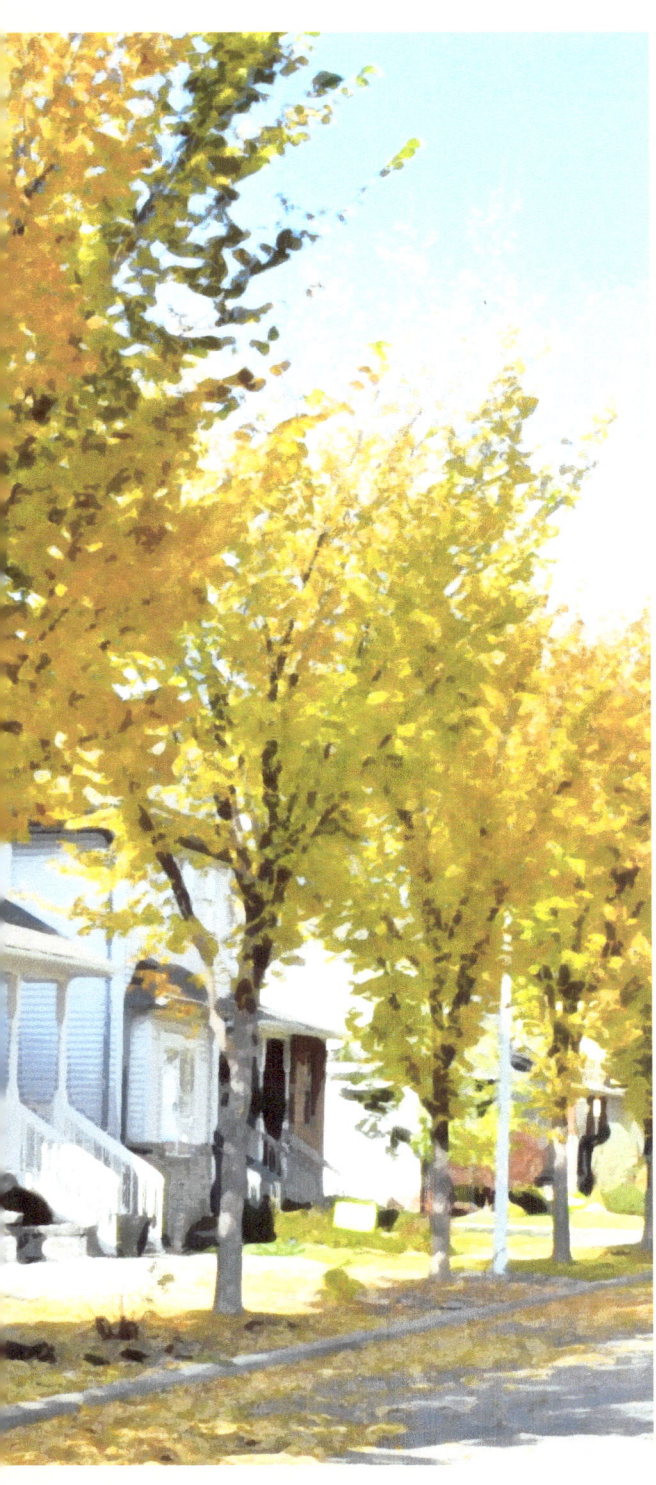

Brickyard in the Fall

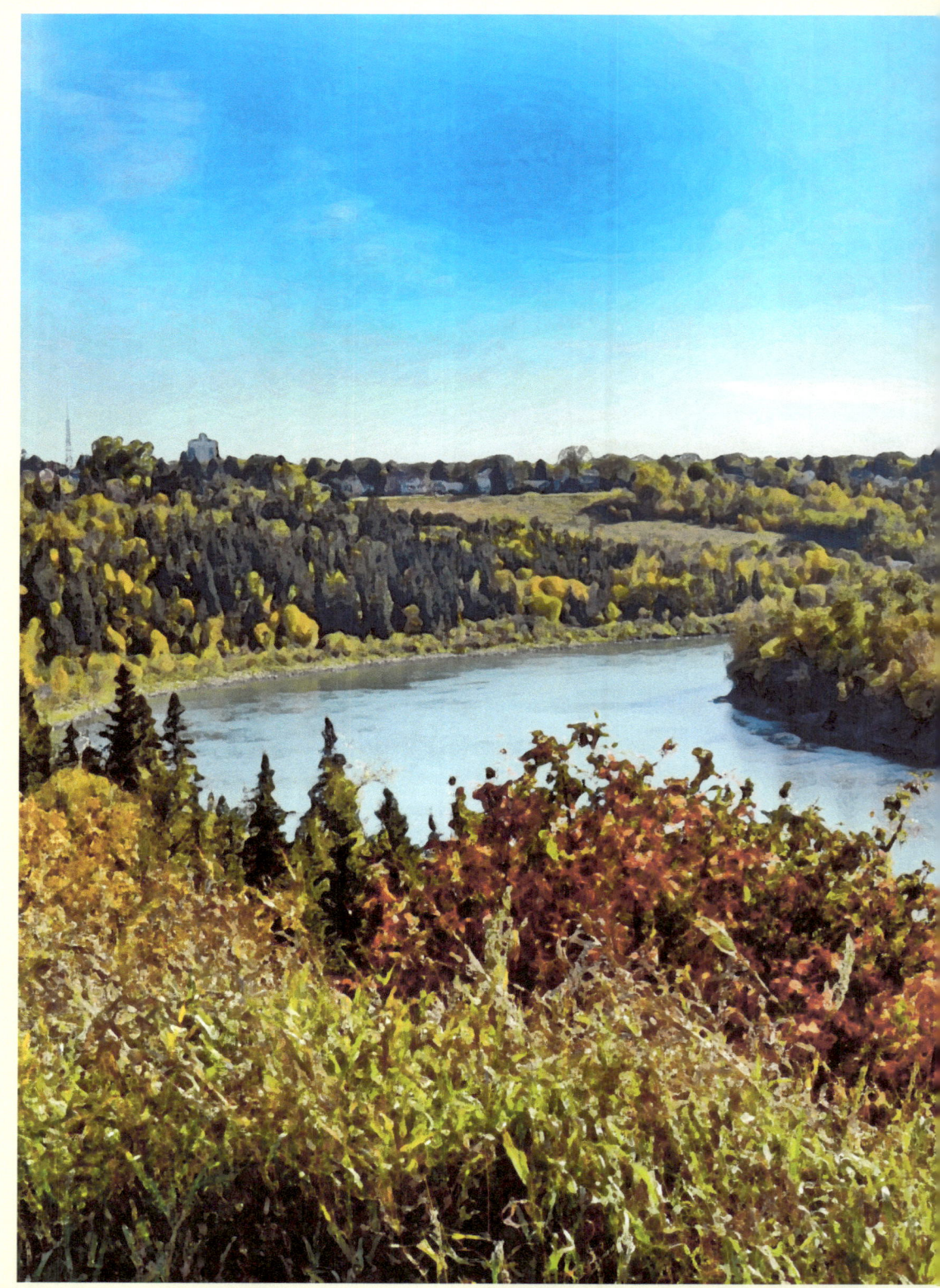

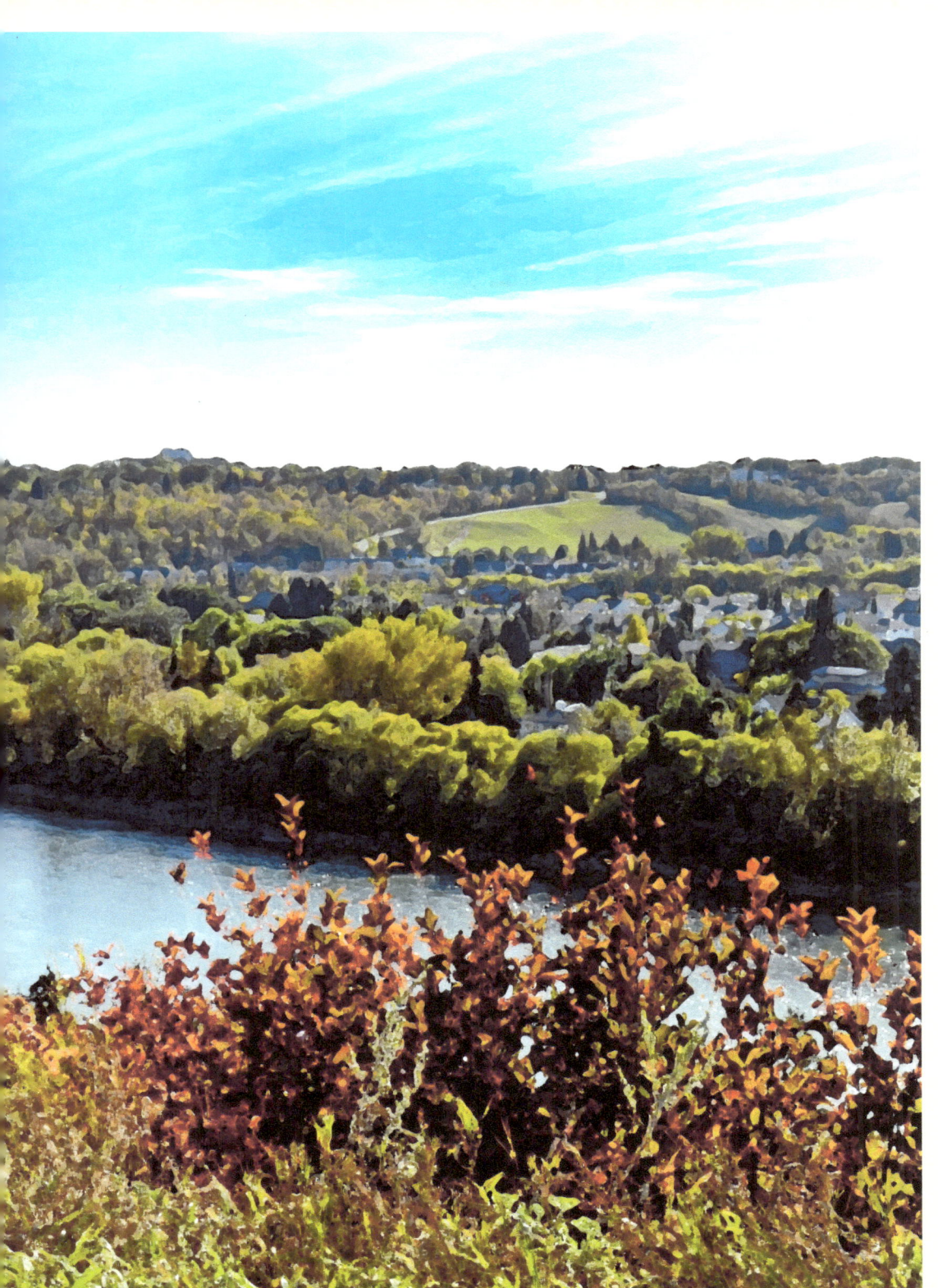

Winter

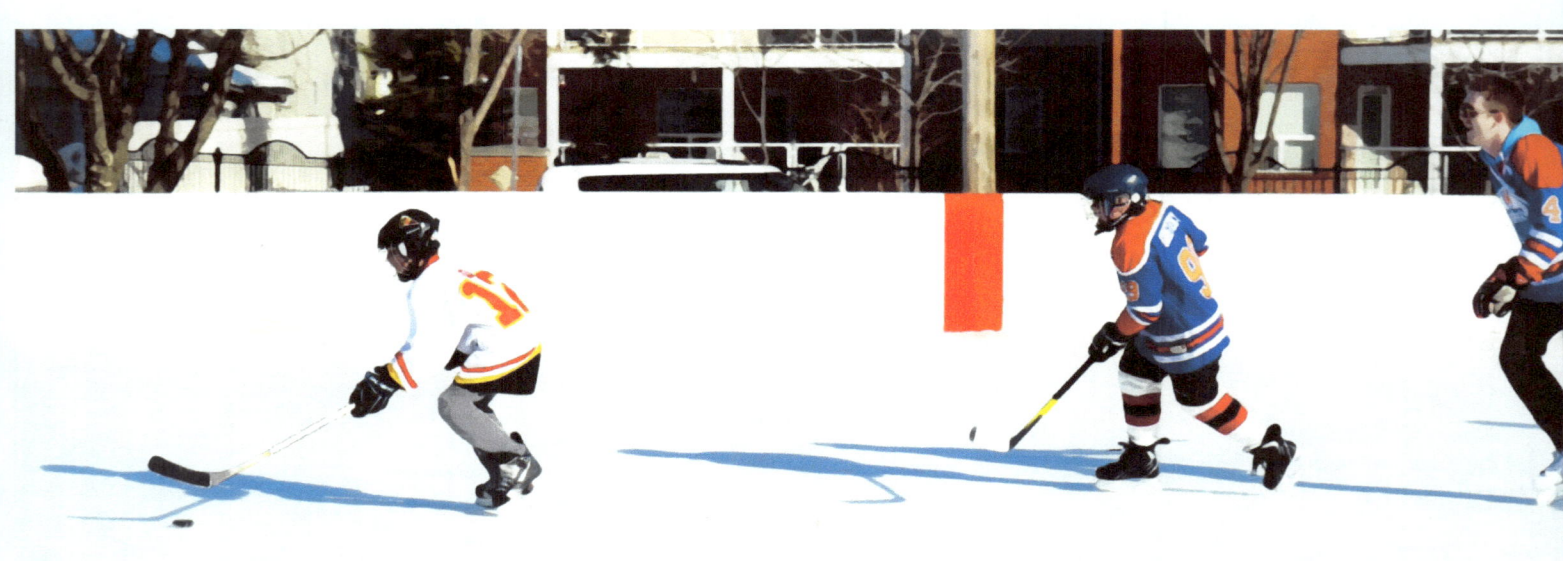

Going for the Goal

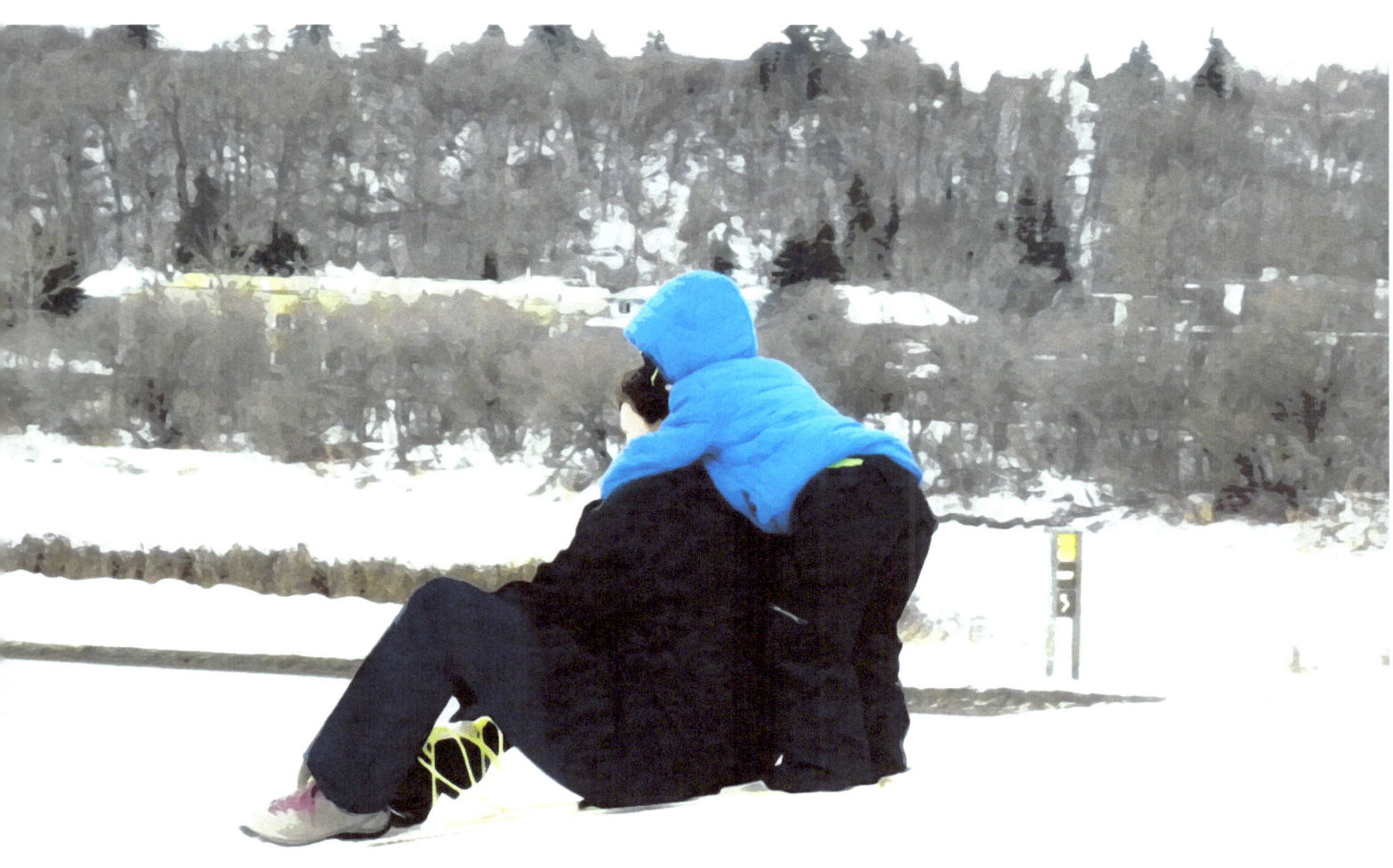

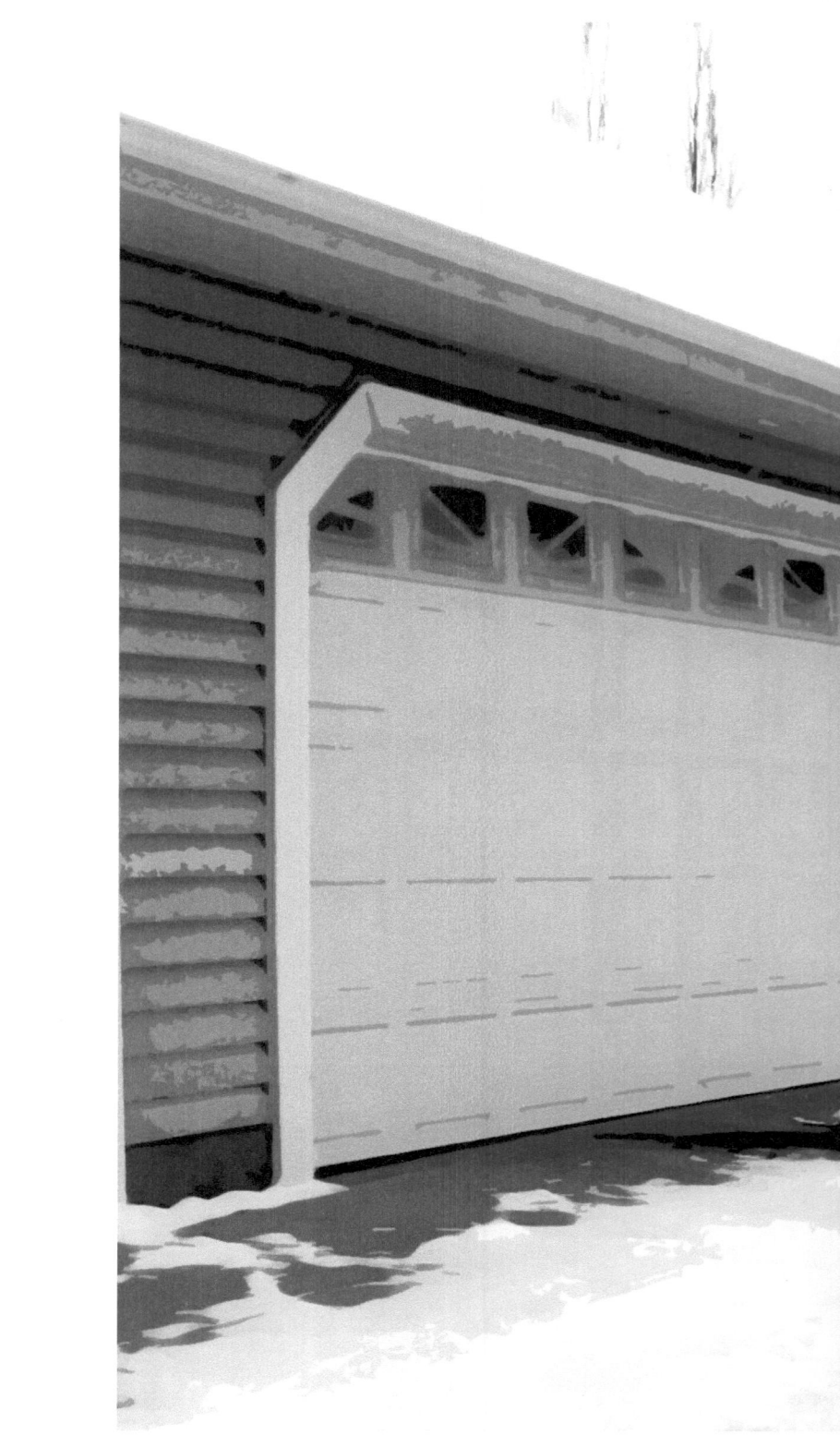

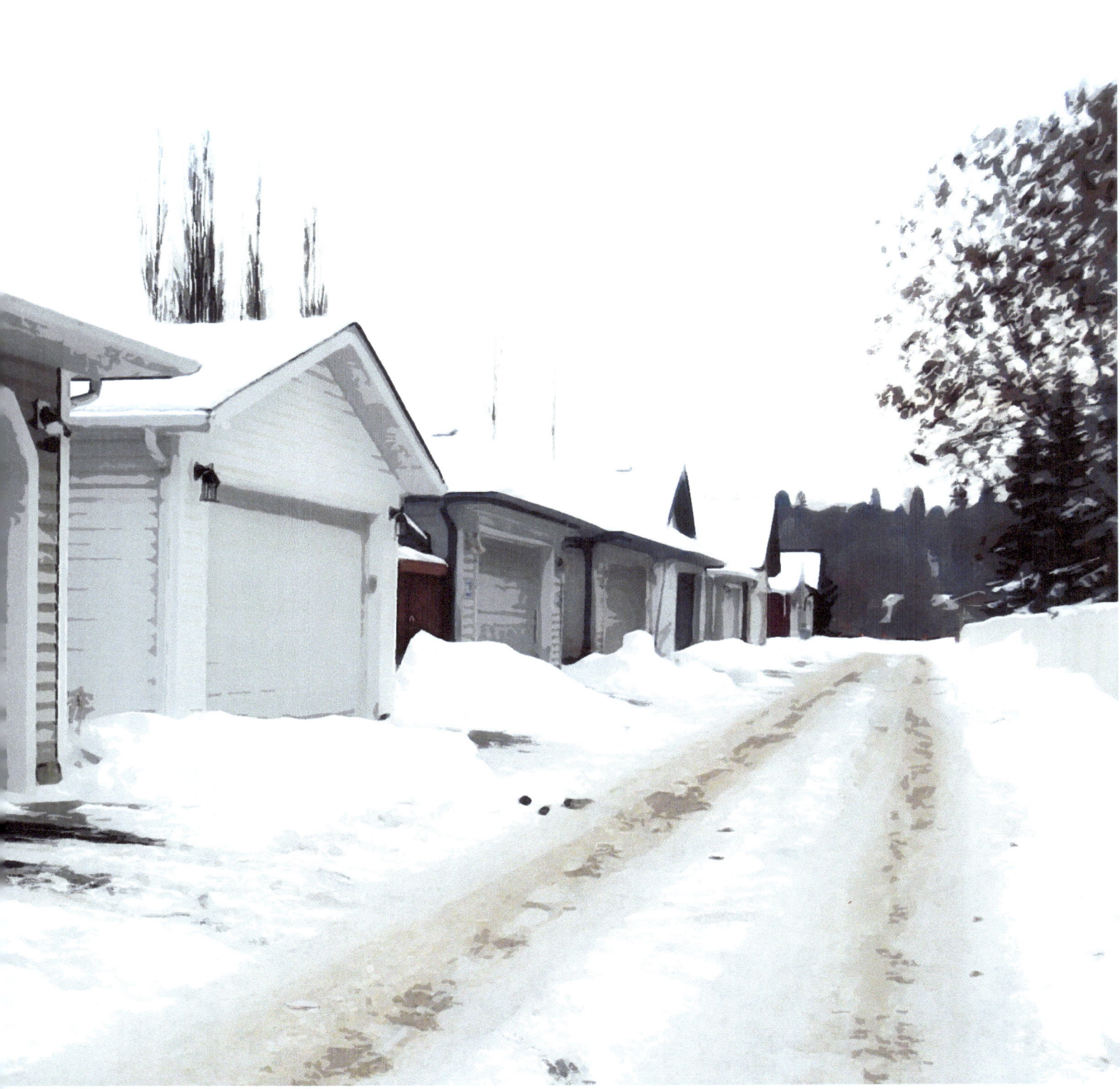

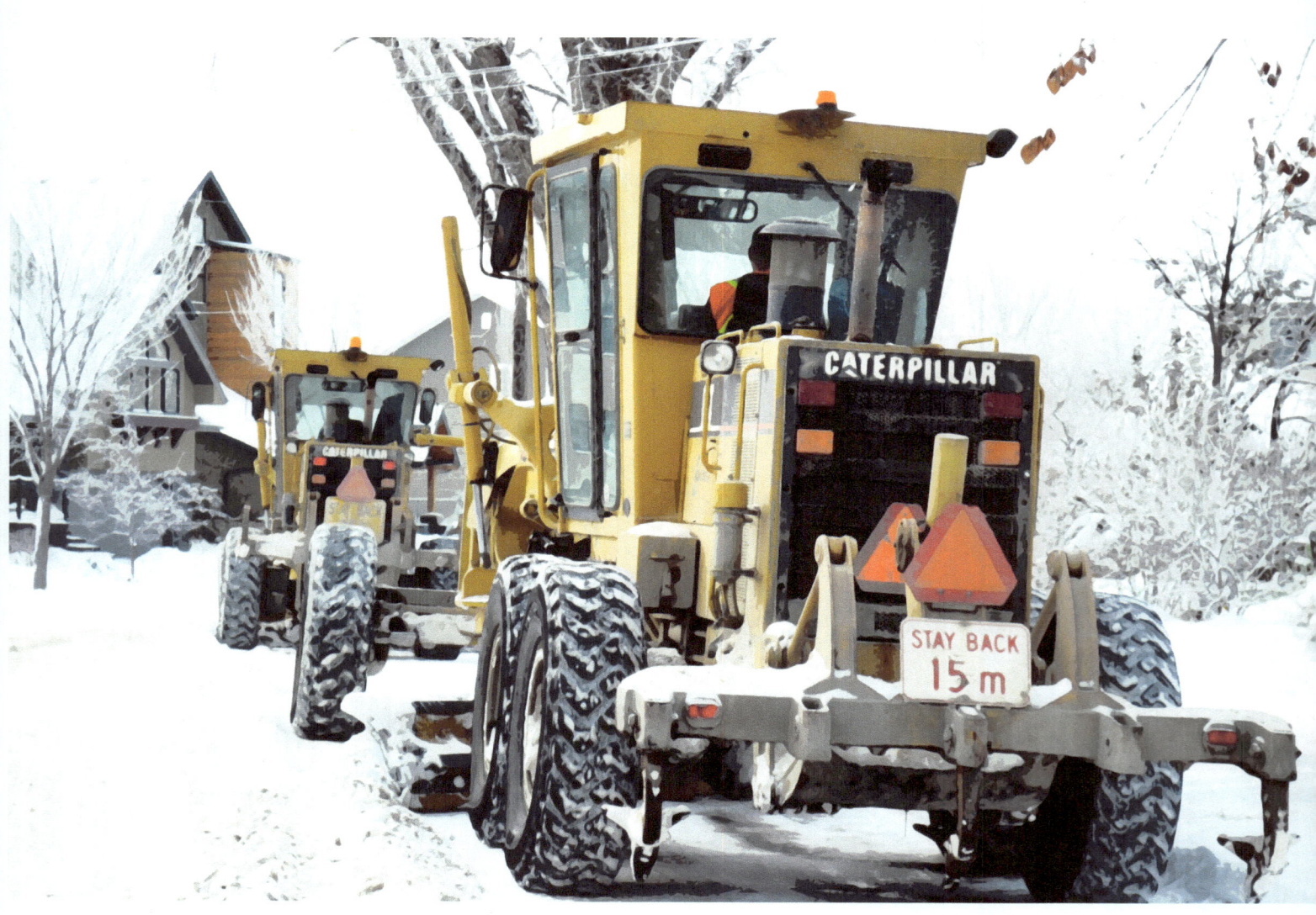

Clearing the Way

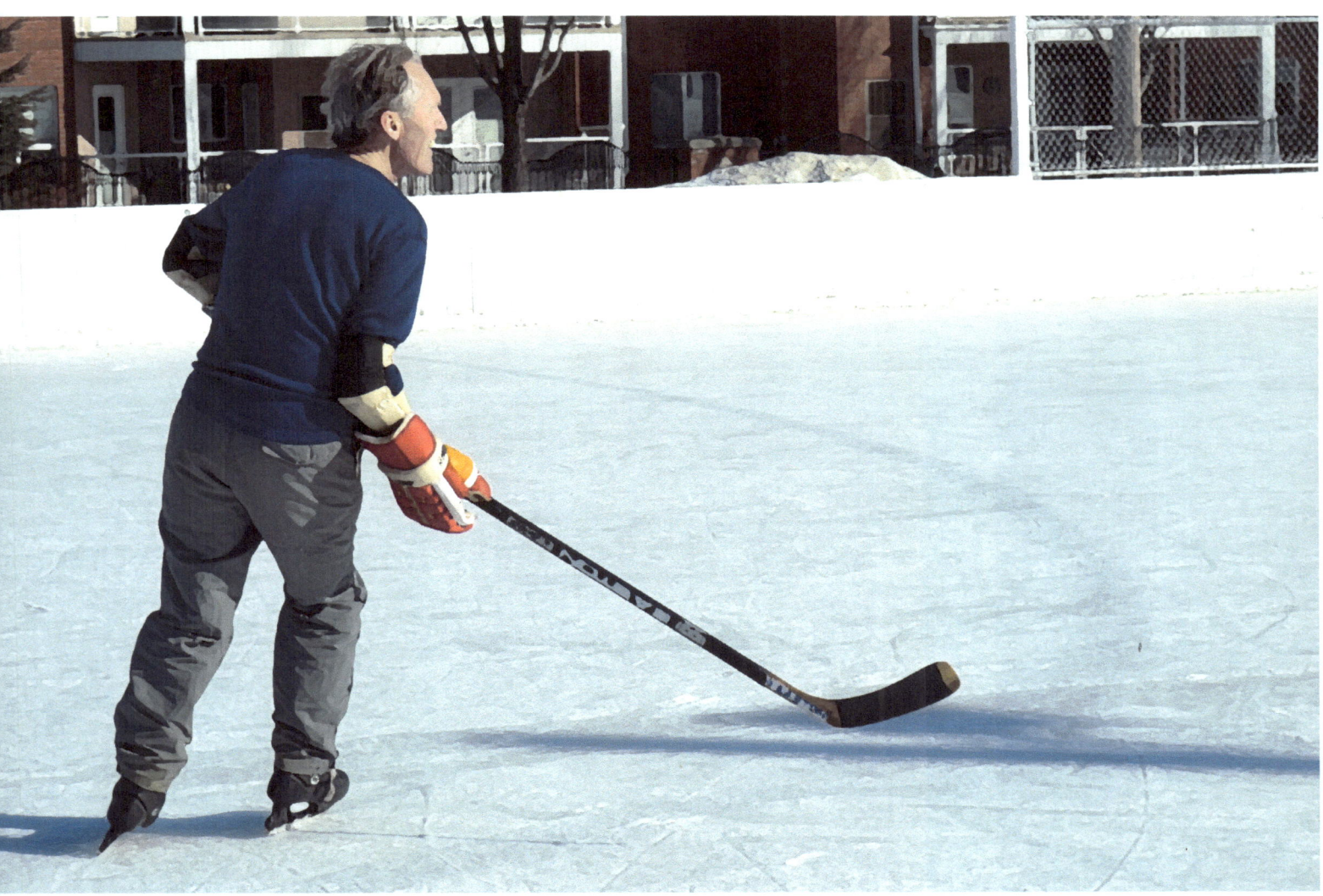

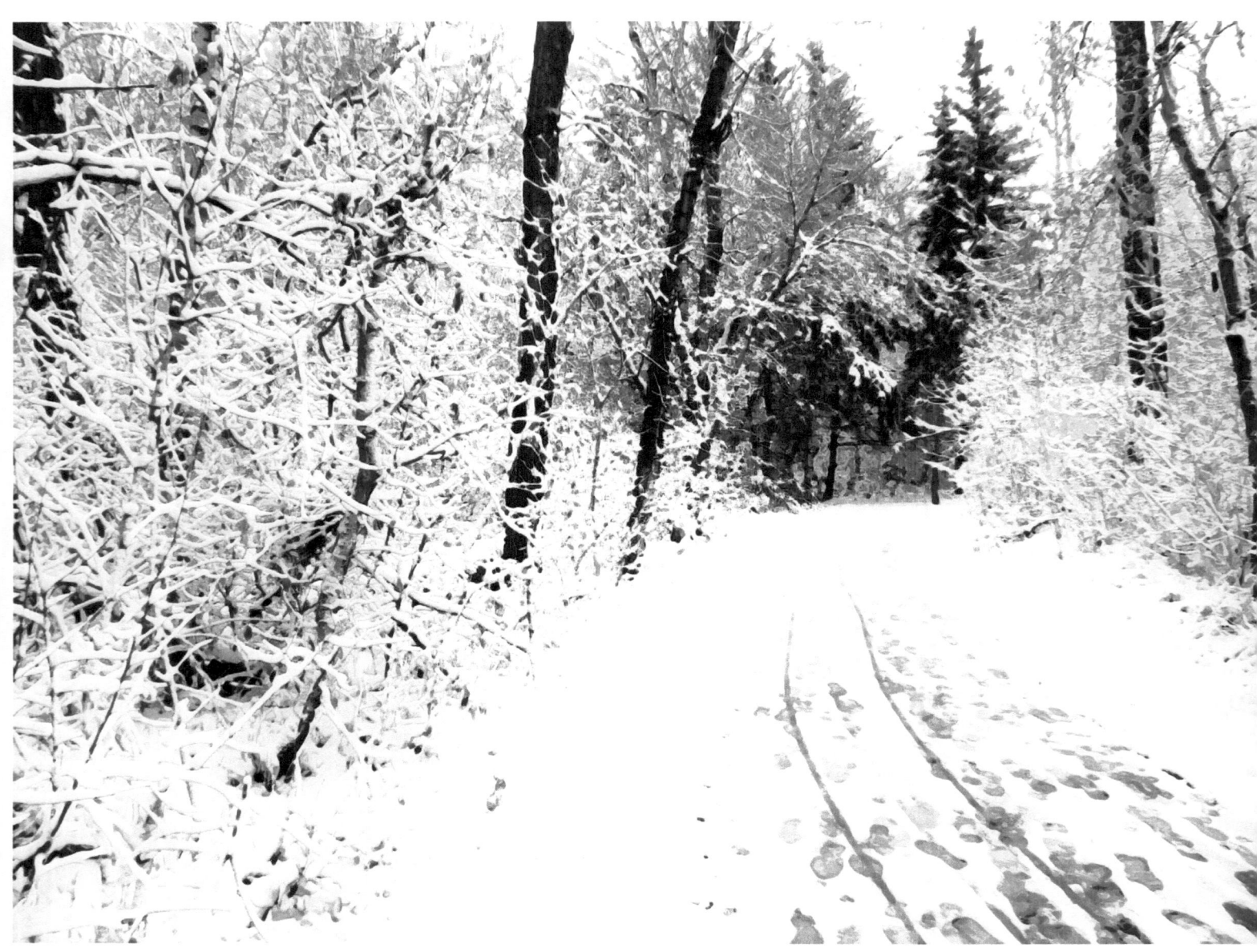

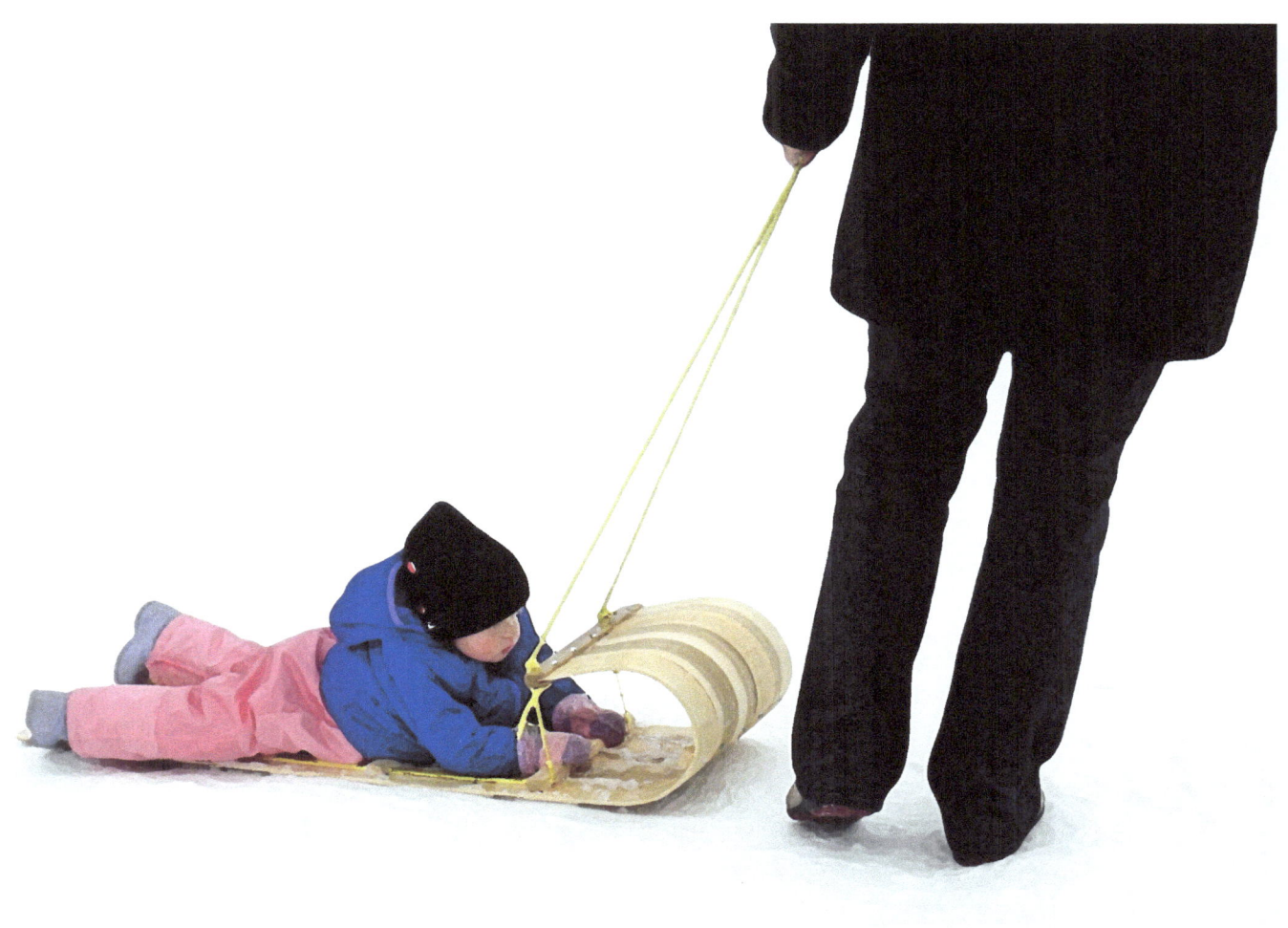

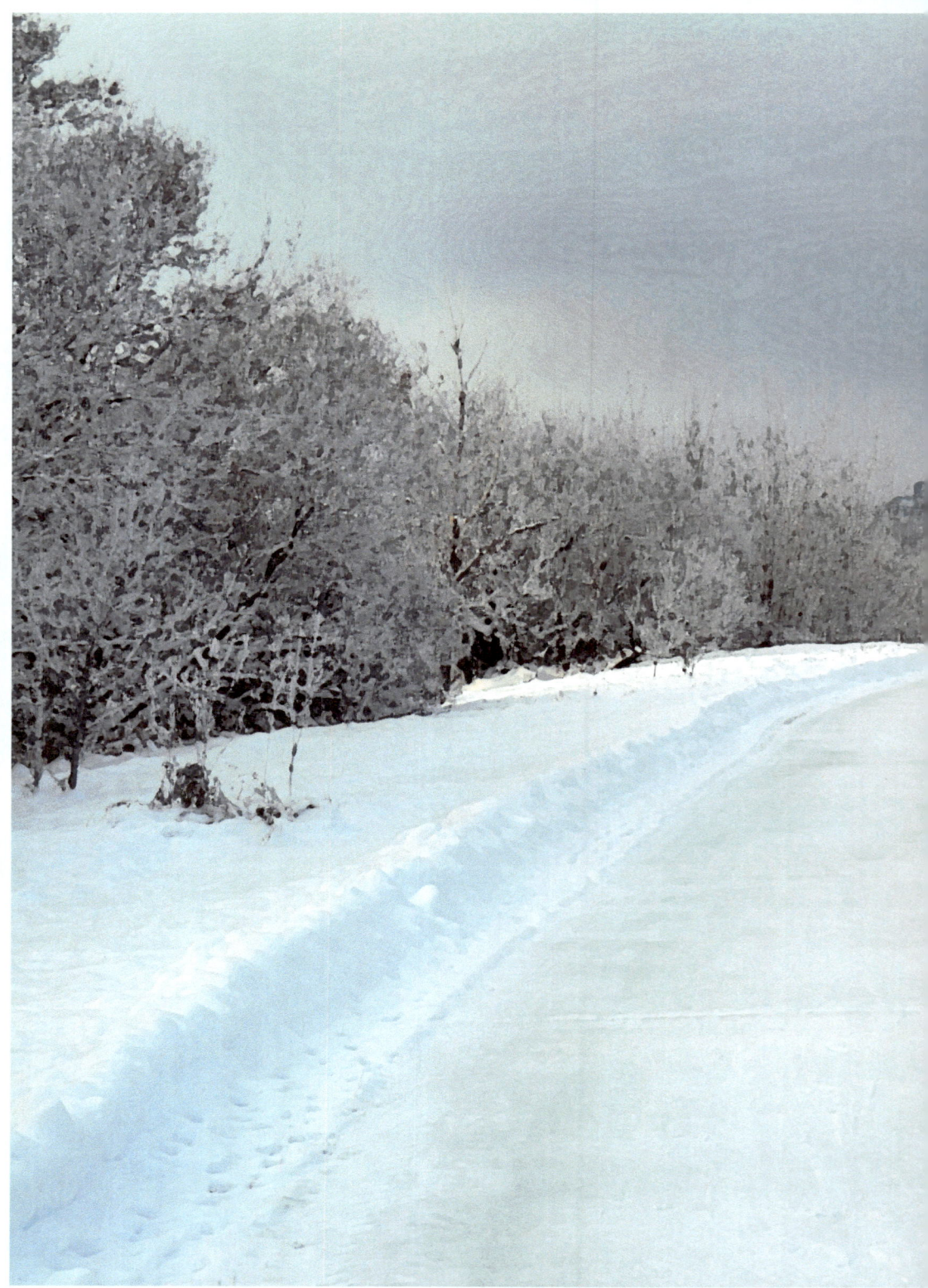

*Downtown on
the Horizon*

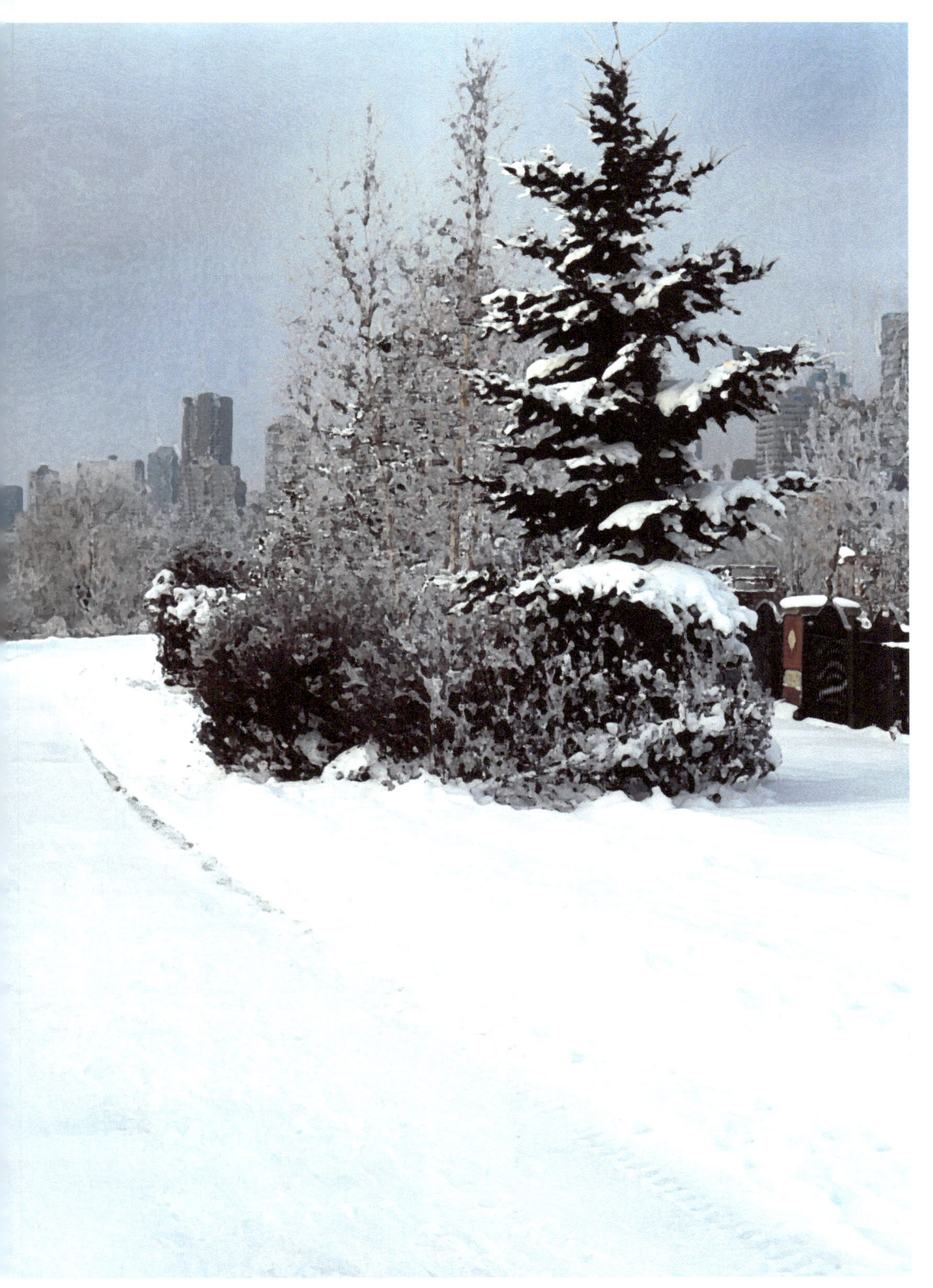

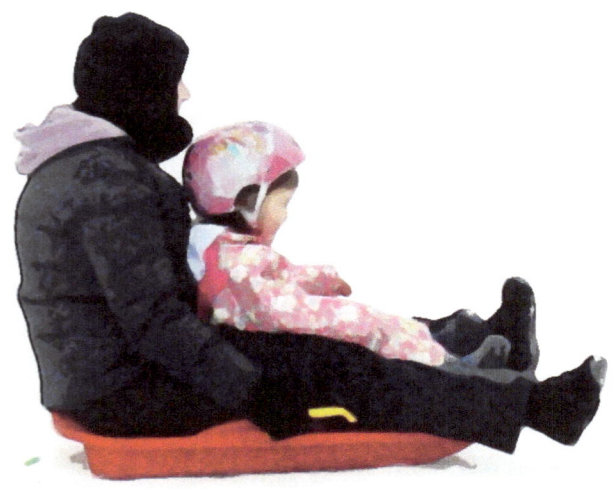

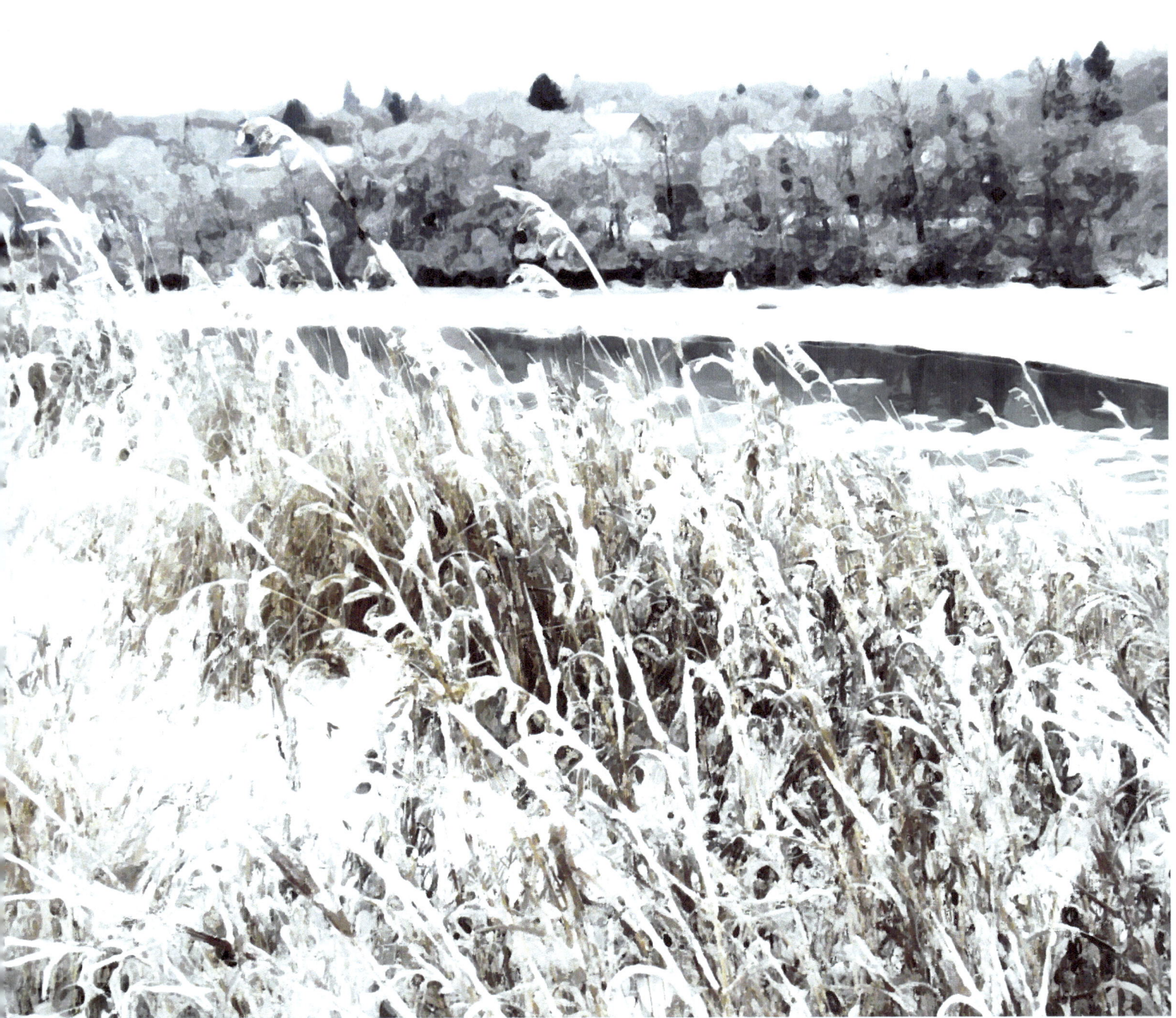

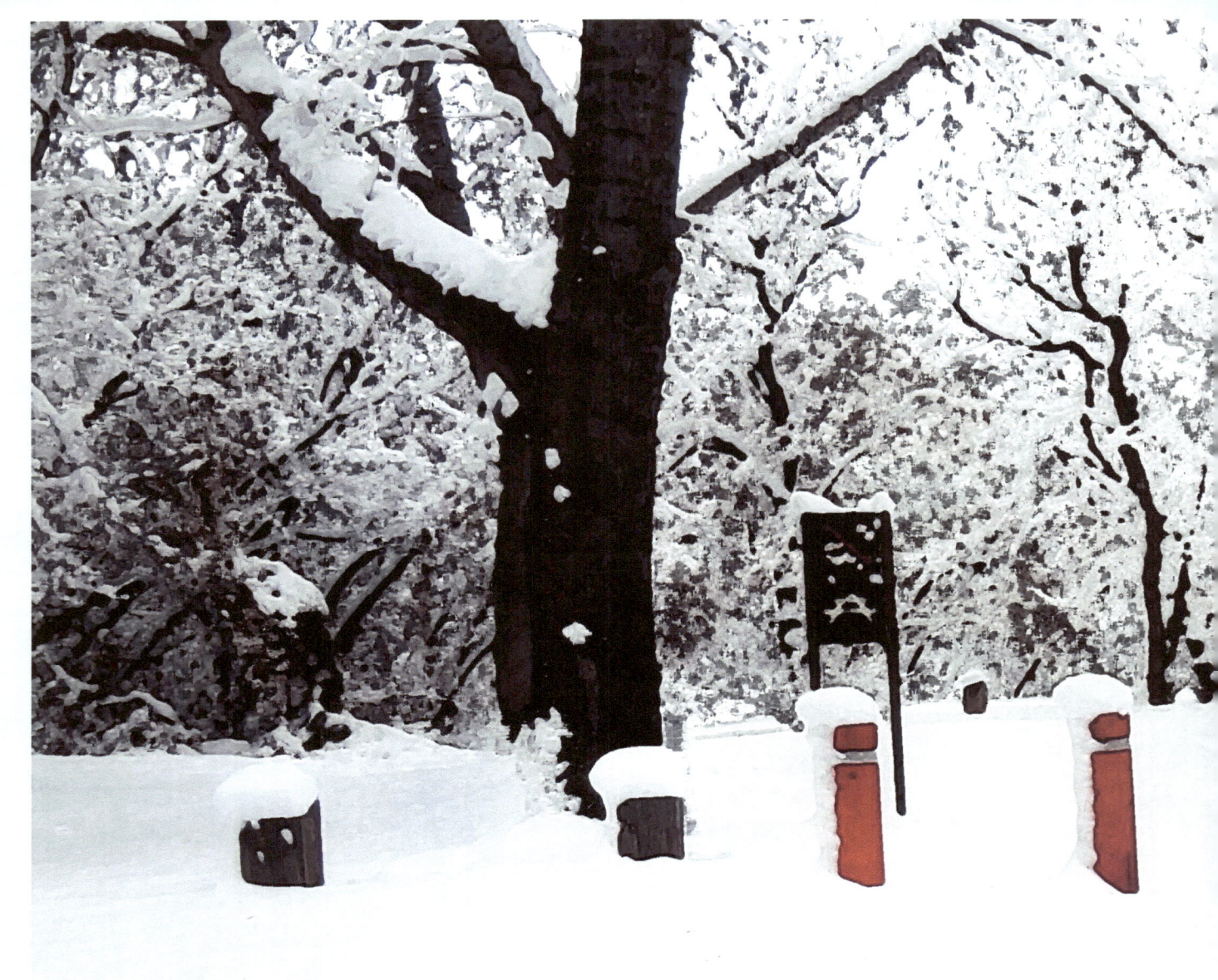

Allan Stein Park

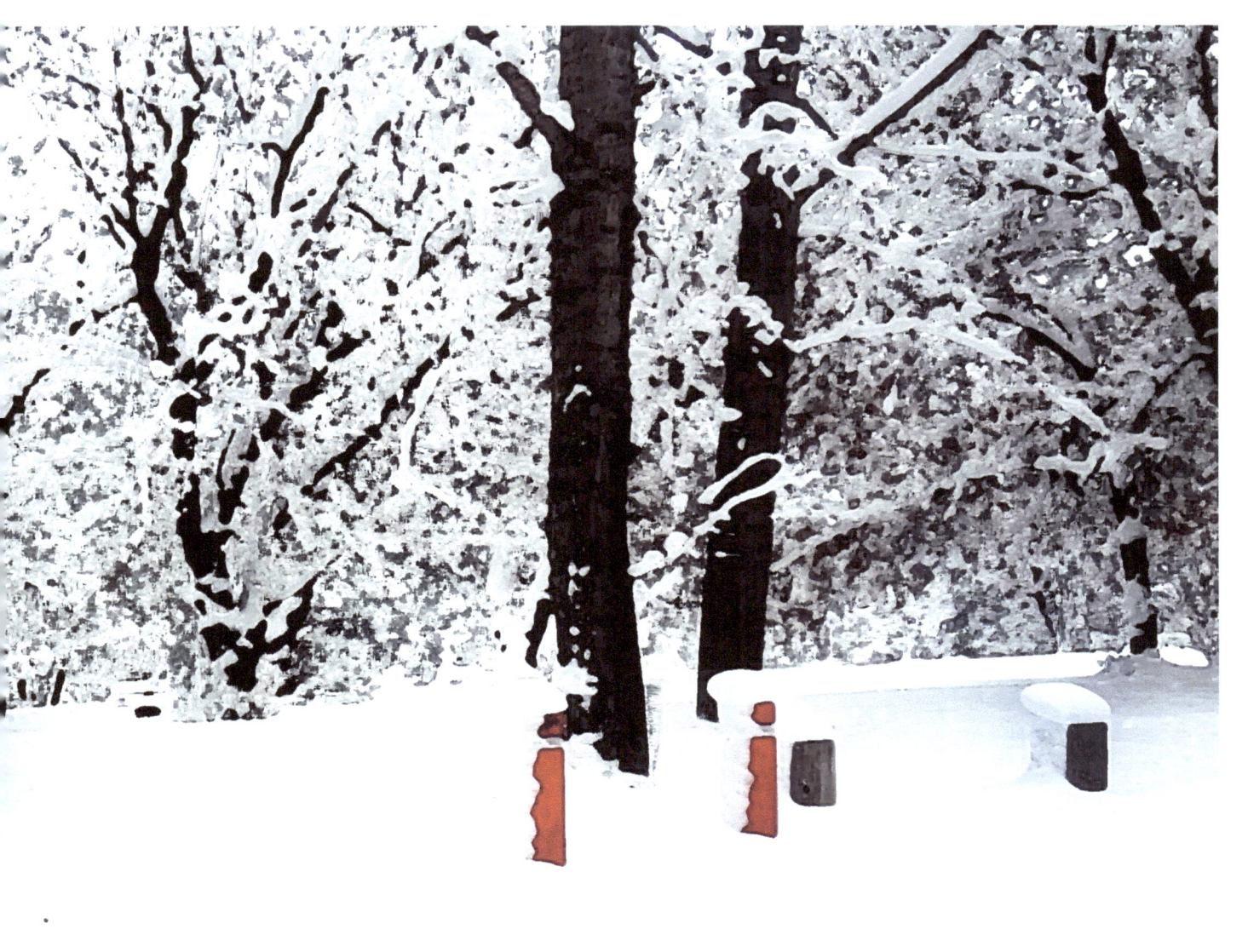

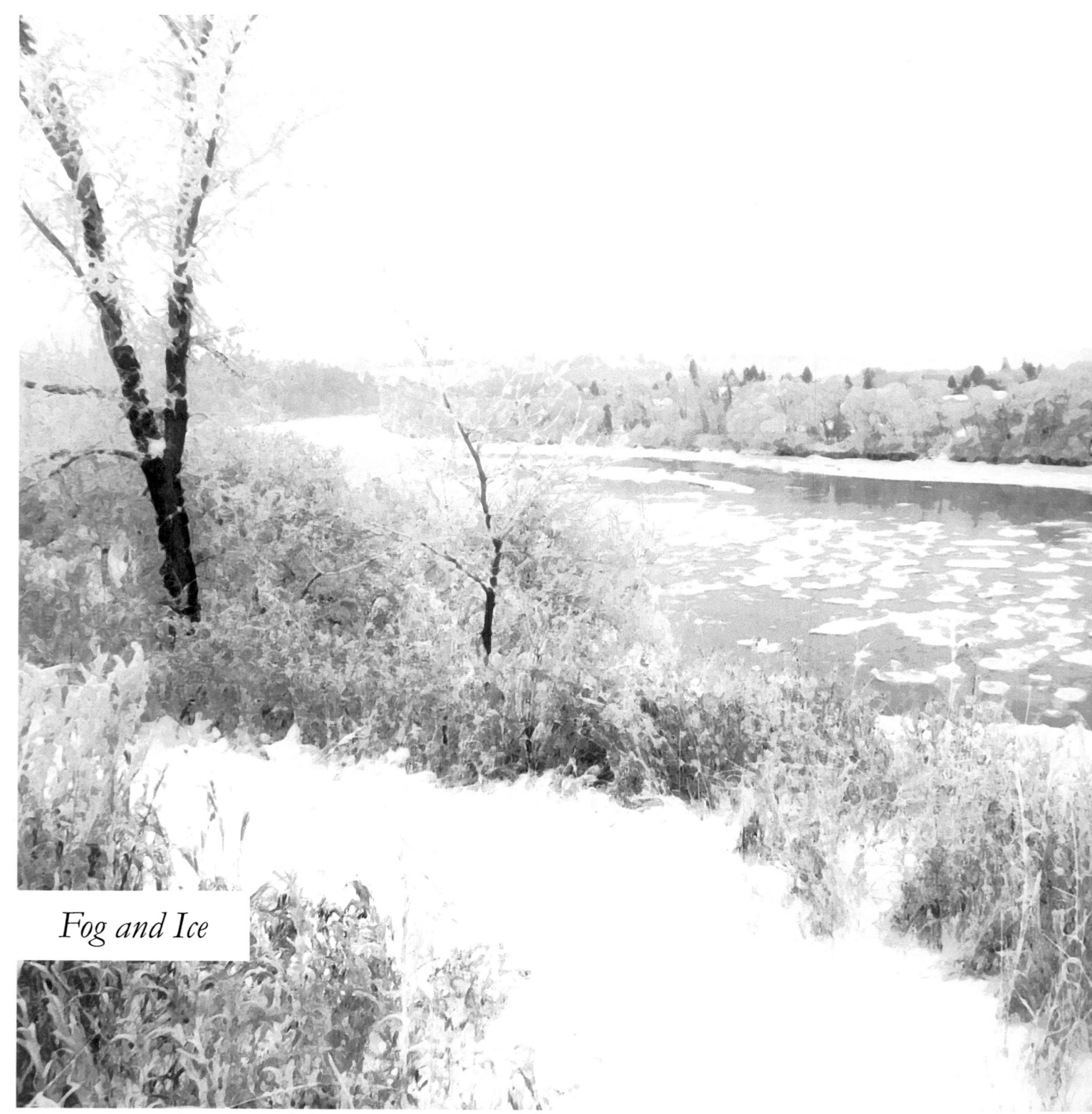

Fog and Ice

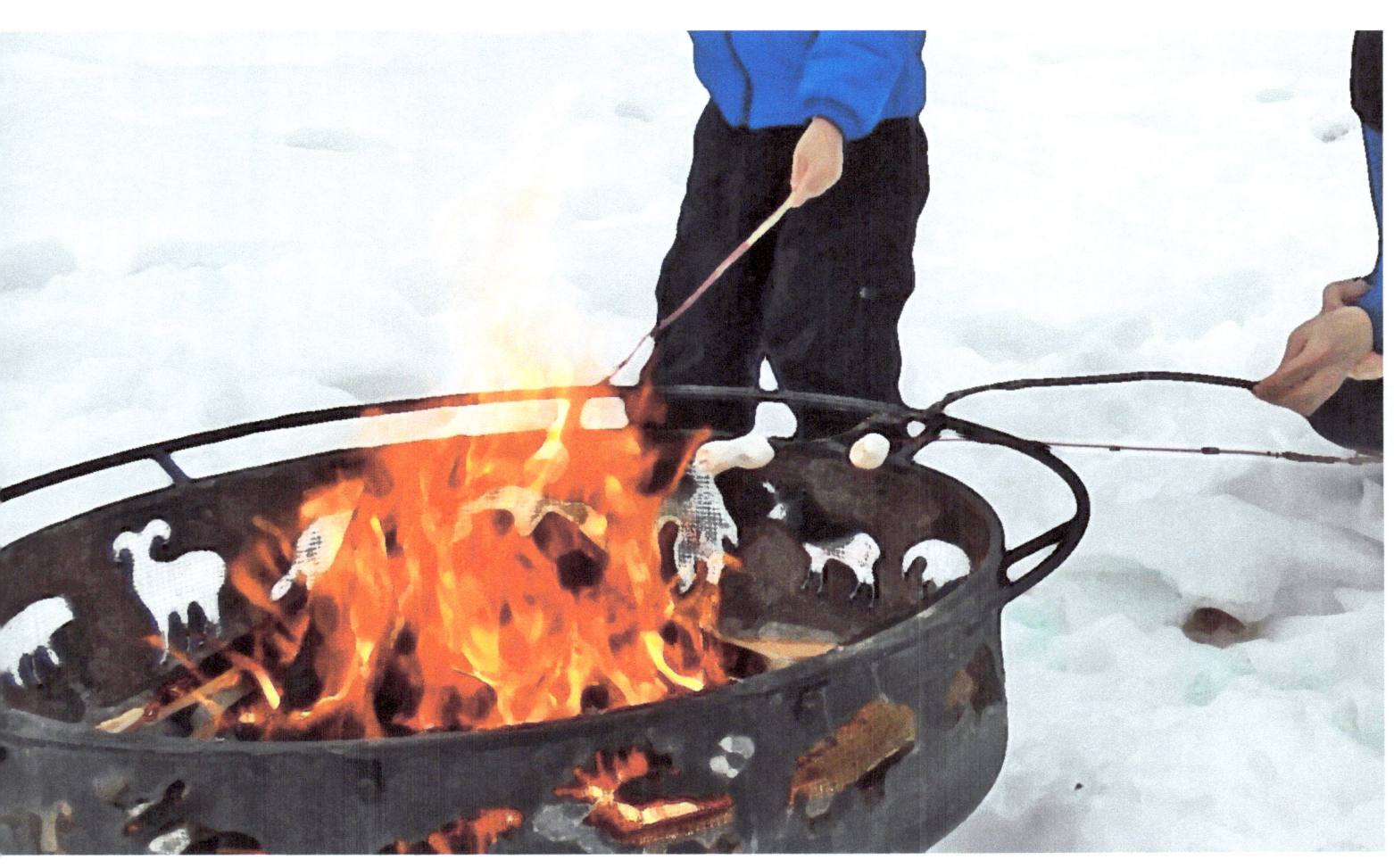

Roasting Marshmallows

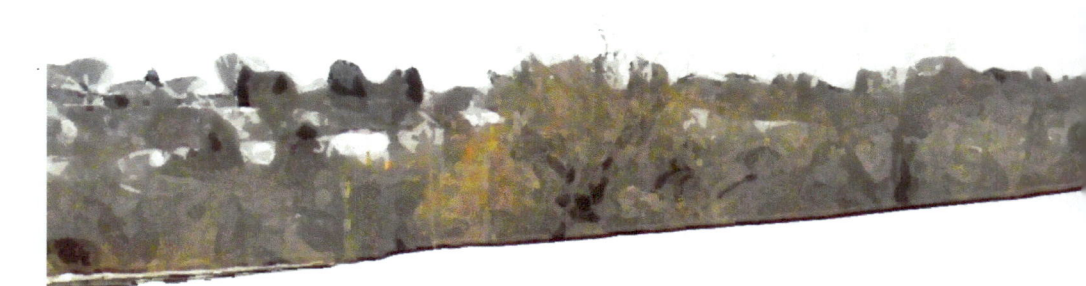
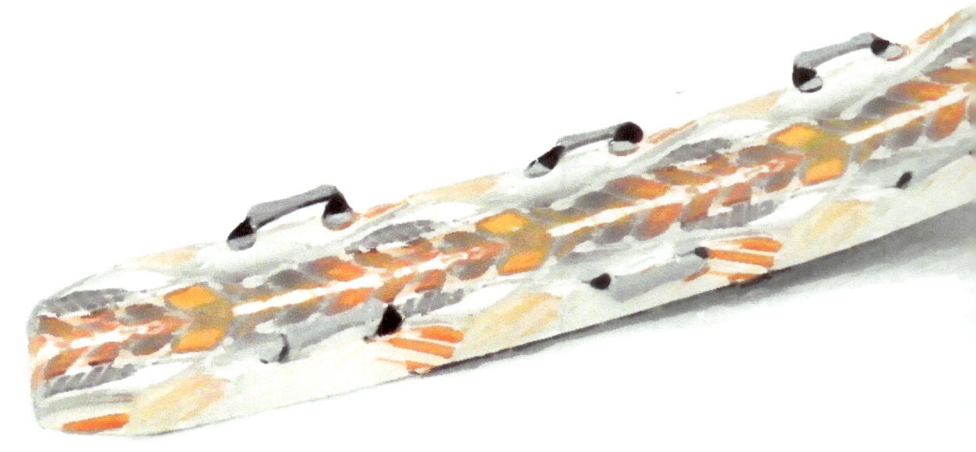

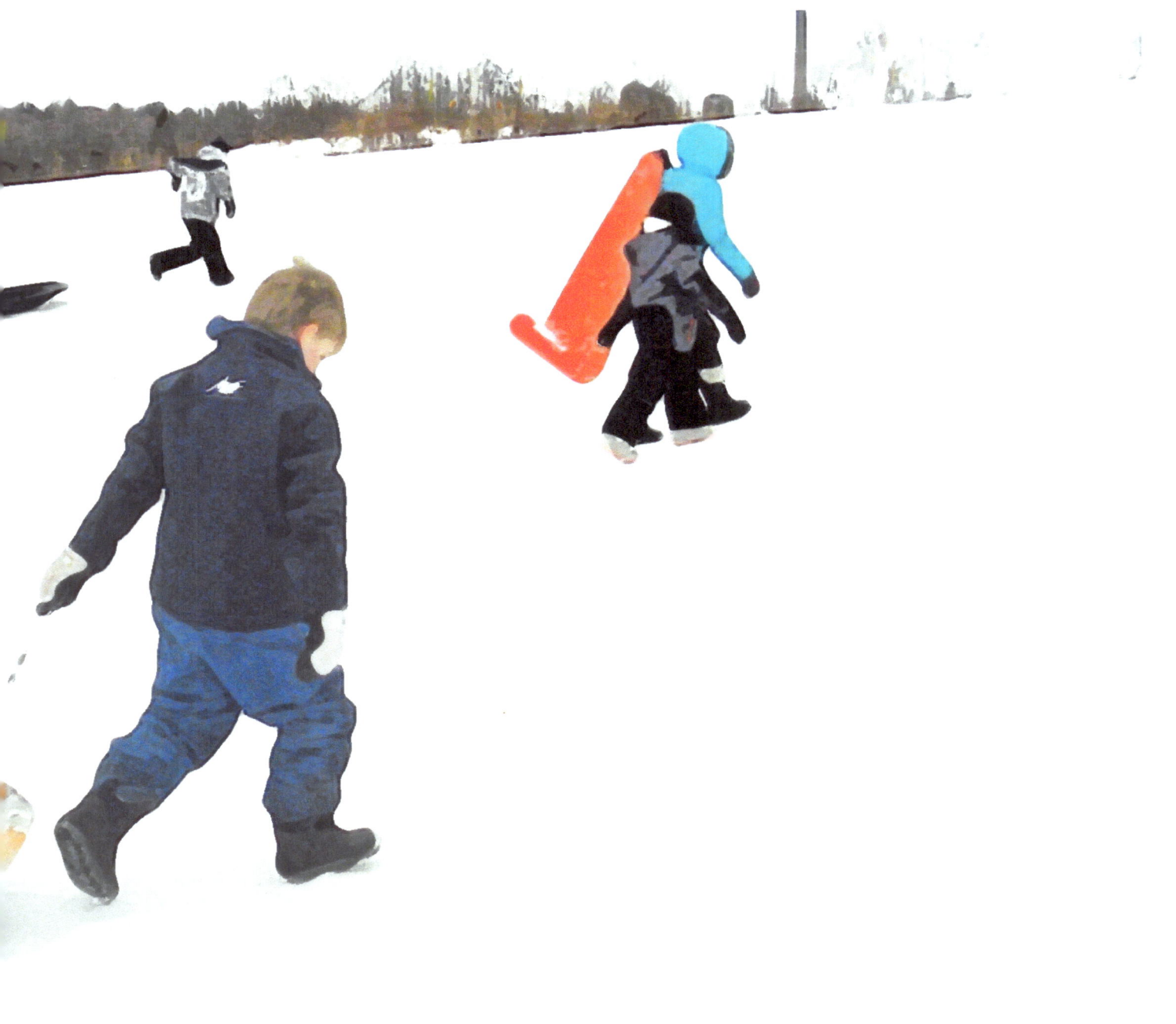

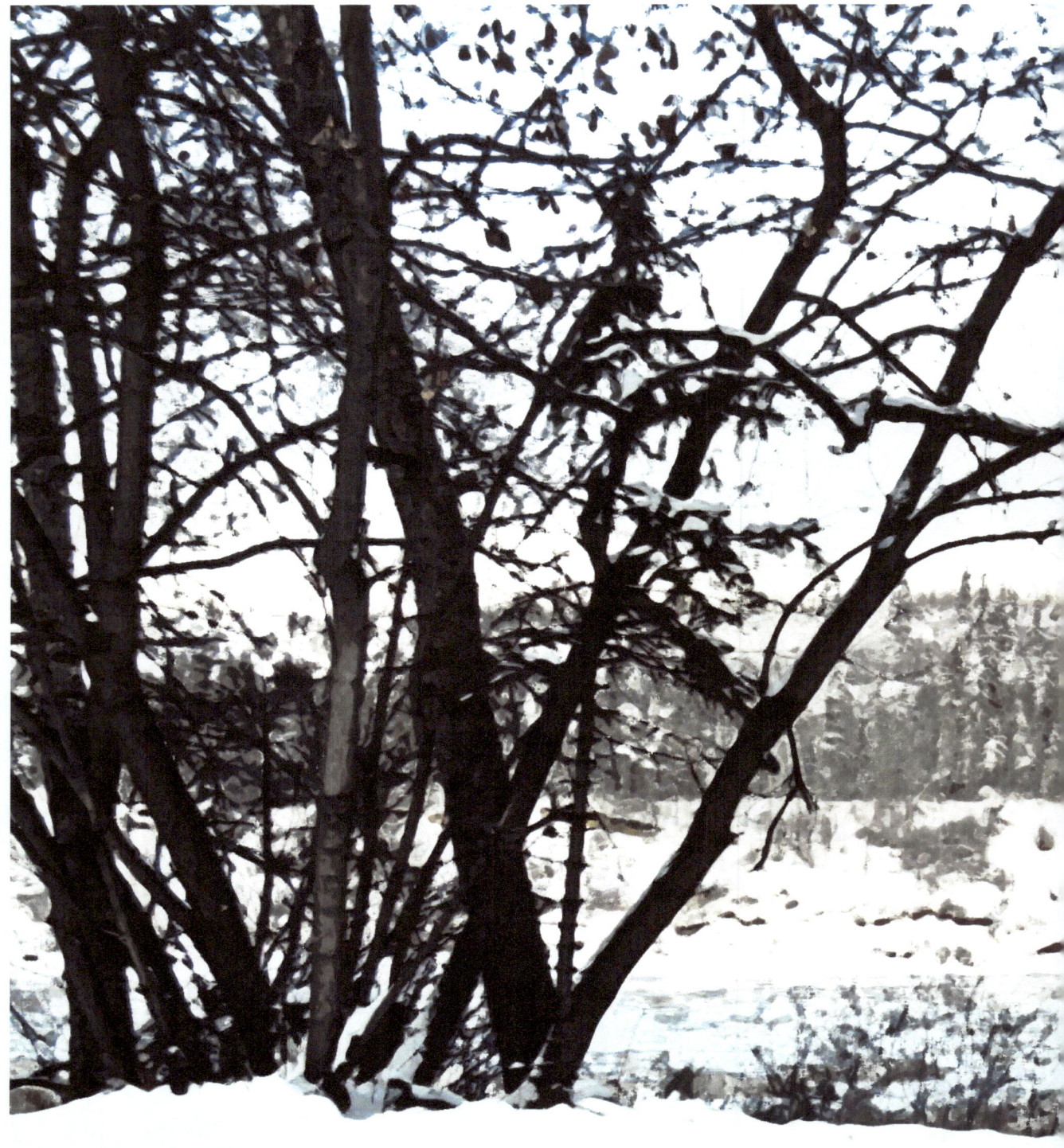

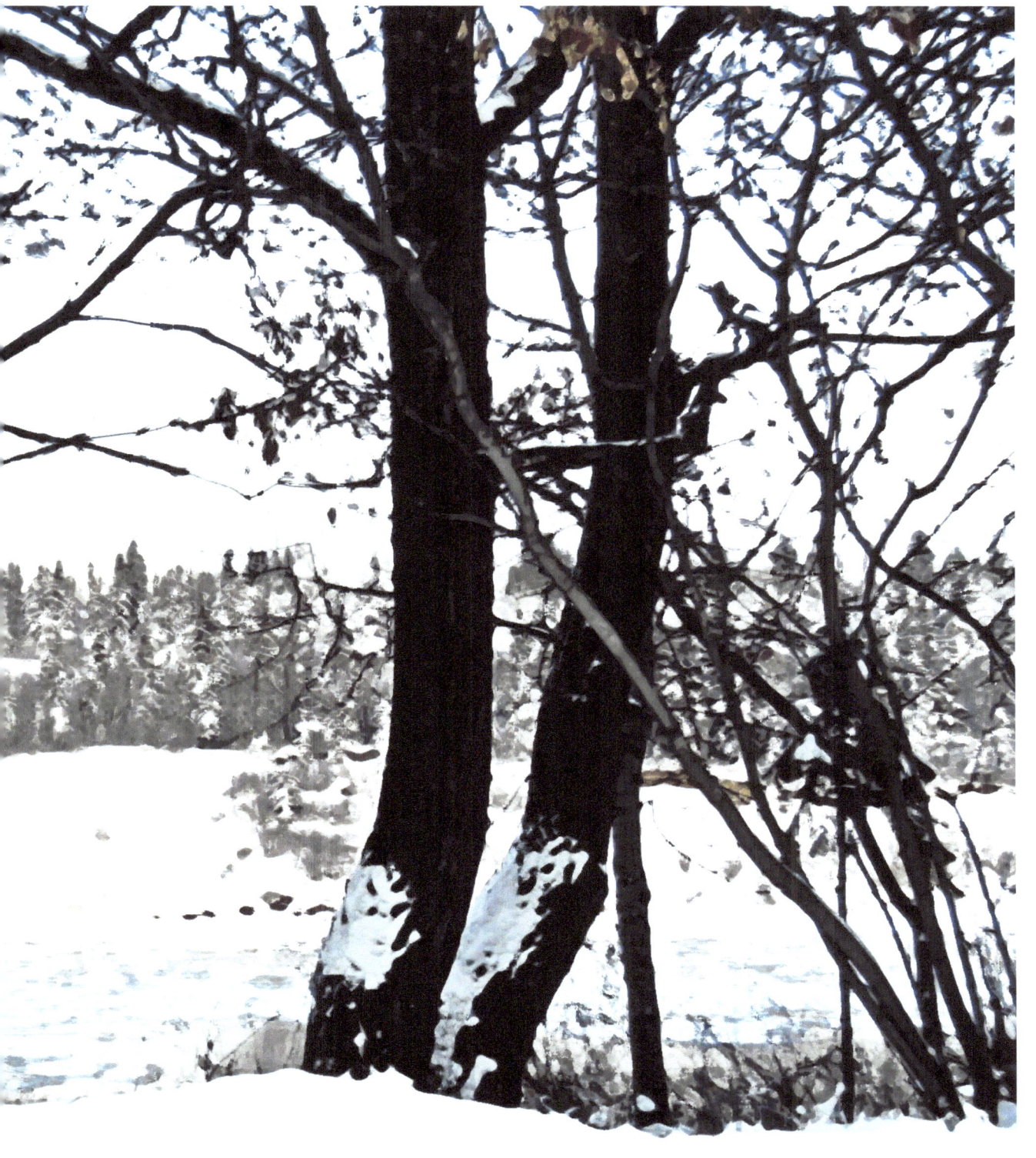

Afterword

I have been asked why I decided to manipulate the original photographs to create these digital paintings.

By using technology I have been able to take everyday images and enhance them to produce vivid digital paintings. I feel I have been able to create paintings that possess a more whimsical look that clearly illustrates Riverdale's uniqueness and magic. I would not have been as successful with my project using standard photographs.

I wanted my paintings to capture the spirit of the community in a more creative way and I wanted these images to represent a moment as well as possibly awaken a longing of something from the past; evoking a memory.

An individual's life experiences will cause a different reaction to the images included in this book. As a result these paintings will mean different things to different people. My hope is that those who view this book will look at something ordinary and discover something extraordinary.

Finally, my objective is that *Stand Right There* will suggest an idea or a longing for familiar places, to the reader, while still leaving room for imaginative interpretation.

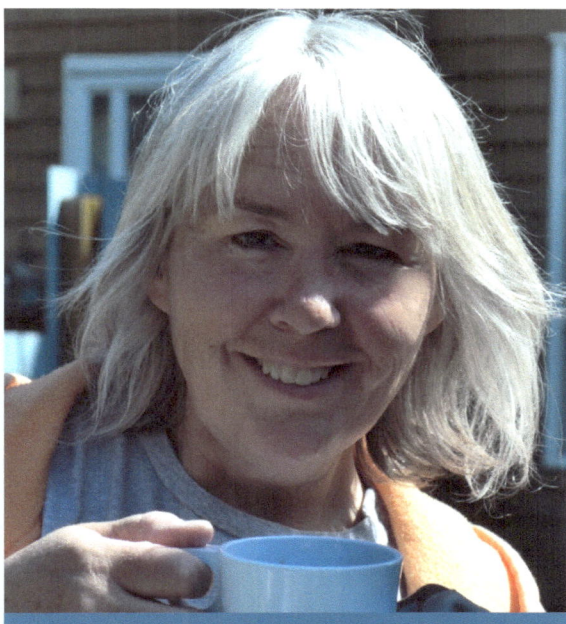

GILLIAN AUSTIN is a freelance graphic designer and photographer who lives in the community of Riverdale. Gillian has always been interested in photography. Her career began with her parents' Kodak Instamatic camera, evolved through the Polaroid years and finally to her first 35 mm camera in the early 1980s. Gillian has had many opportunities to hone her skill through formal training or during her jobs in camera and photo shops on Vancouver Island or in Edmonton.

Gillian feels that everyone should enjoy photography and picture taking regardless if they are a photographer or an audience. They are invaluable tools for celebrating "a mark in time" whether it be at an organized event or simply a "selfie"... these images should be treasured.

Thank you to my dad, Len, who taught me the joy of "being outside", the value of long Sunday afternoon walks and to appreciate the sound and songs of the Chickadee.

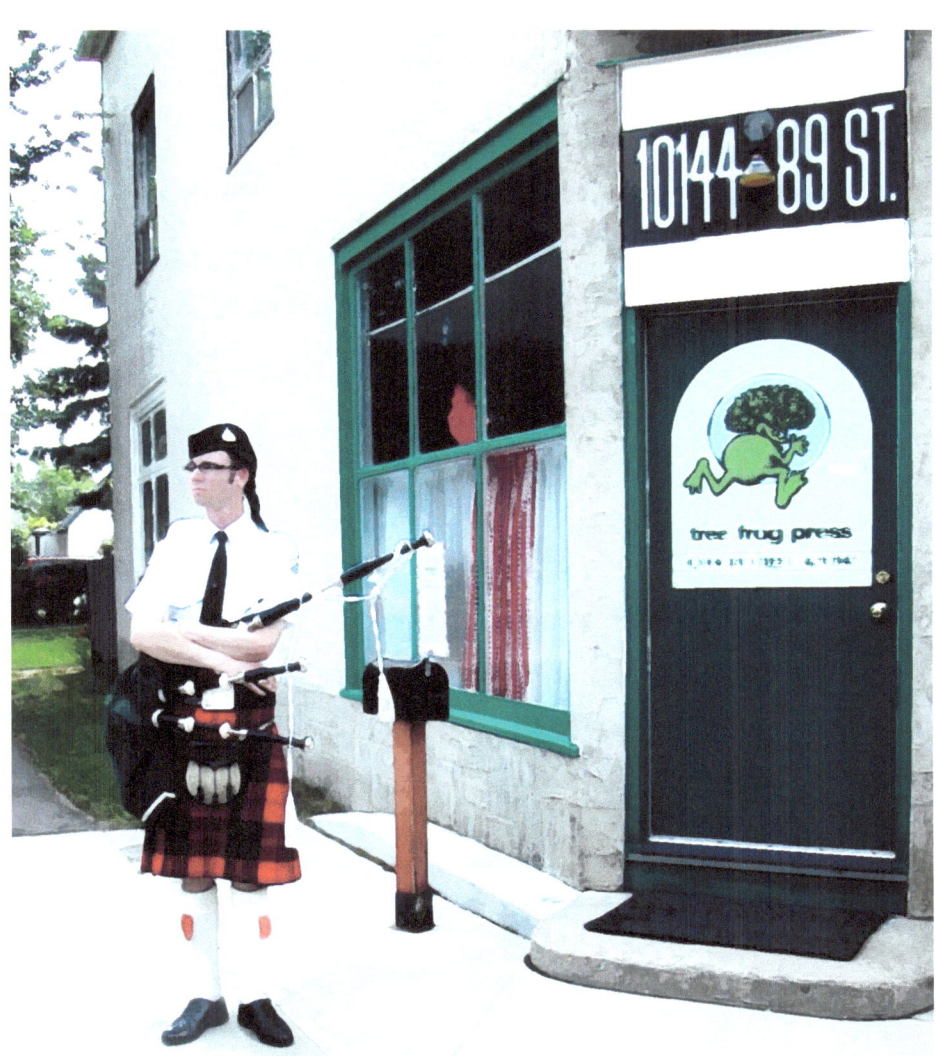

www.ingramcontent.com/pod-product-compliance
Lightning Source LLC
Chambersburg PA
CBHW050719180526
45159CB00003B/1078